Macroeconomics

With Some Empirical Evidence

Amit Kundu

KALPAZ

First Published, 2020

Published by

Kalpaz Publications
C-30, Satyawati Nagar,
Delhi – 110052
Ph.: 011-47034999, 9811692060
www.kalpazpublications.com
E-mail: kalpaz@hotmail.com

Printed at: Gyan Press, Delhi

Cataloging in Publication Data—DK
Courtesy: D.K. Agencies (P) Ltd. <docinfo@dkagencies.com>

Kundu, Amit, author.
Macroeconomics : with some empirical evidence / Amit Kundu.
pages cm
ISBN 9789353242565

1. Macroeconomics. I. Title.

LCC HB172.5.K86 2020 | DDC 339 23

Contents

Preface

According to Samuelson, "Economics is the study of how people and society choose, with or without the use of money, to employ scarce productive resources which could have alternative uses, to produce various commodities over time and distribute them for consumption now and in the future among various persons and groups of society."

The study of economics is conventionally divided into a micro ground and macro ground. Microeconomics deals with the behavior of disaggregated individual decision-makers such as single consumer. On the other hand Macroeconomics is in aggregative in nature. Macroeconomic variables are

1. National Income
2. National Investment
3. Changes in the purchasing power of money
4. The overall state of employment in the economy
5. Budgetary policy of the government
6. The condition of the nation's balance of international payments

Macroeconomists try to understand how an actual economy operates and, on the basis of that understanding, suggest polices that may be adopted to improve the performance of the economy. Thus, understanding and policy prescription are two critically interlinked aspects of the economist's role in society.

In this book I try to represent some objectives. These objectives are as follows.

- Try to simplify some thoughts of macroeconomics. Such as
  Quantity Theory Of Money & Simple Keynesian Models,
  Money, Inflation And Interest Rate
  The ISLM Model
  The Mundell –Fleming Model: Money, Capita Flows And The Open Economy

Phillips Curve Analysis

Theories of Business Cycle

Consumption

Investment

- Representation of Keynesian and neoclassical understandings
- On the basis of some macroeconomic thoughts there are some case studies in this book. These case studies would be helpful for research on macroeconomic thoughts. The case studies are as follows.
  - Determinants of Inflation: Evidence from Bangladesh
  - Economic Growth & Government Expenditure in Pakistan – A Time Series Analysis
  - An Econometric analysis of Effect of Changes in Money Supply on Interest Rate in Bangladesh
  - An Econometric Enquiry to the Relationship Between Export And Economic Growth in Bangladesh
  - Export and Economic Growth in the Economy of Indonesia – An Econometric Study (1971-2007)
- Some multiple choice type questions are included in this book to make the book user friendly.
- Some numerical examples are there in this book.
- To learn the language of macroeconomics a glossary is given at the back of the book.

I hope that this edition will find favour with professors and students and get reasonable success.

Acknowledgements

In writing this book I obtained valuable help and guidance from many. Without them, it would have been an insurmountable task for me. I am very much indebted and grateful to all of them. In reference I have mentioned all those authors whose writing inspired me in completion of this book. This book is nothing but the simplification of some macroeconomic thoughts that had been presented in some macroeconomics books (mentioned in reference). In this book special focus has been given to the simplification of macroeconomic thoughts and on some case studies.

My greatest debts are to Professor Chandan Kumar Mukhopadhyay. Actually, words are few to express my gratitude to him. My gratitude remains for him forever. Everything cannot be expressed in terms of words yet words are the only coin I have to offer in repayment. However, I offer my sincere most gratitude to him and acknowledge that his memory will remain vivid in my life.

I thank my parents. I stand also thankful to my life partner Satabdi Kundu for her altruistic support to fulfill my research work. After all, I got peach in my mind seeing the innocent face of my son at the time of my research work.

I offer my wholehearted pranam to all mighty God for giving me the opportunity to fulfill my research work. Without His invisible support, nothing can get a materialistic form.

It is now up to the students and researchers to assess its usefulness and indicate the deficiencies that remain.

In the end, I accept all the responsibility of errors and omissions and other drawbacks in my work.

Amit Kundu

Chapter - 1

Introduction

Macroeconomics

Macroeconomics studies the behavior of the entire economy. It determines output, inflation, unemployment, balance of payment in the economy. In an economy where individuals won factors of production and use them to produce output, macroeconomics mostly is used there. In simple, in the capitalist economy macroeconomics has a profound role to play. In the capitalist economy firms play independently and on the basis of the output and prices are determined.

In recent time economics mostly depends on Keynesian thought [John Maynard Keynes's *The General Theory of Employment, Interest and money,* published in 1936]. *The General Theory* is complex book and not particularly easy to understand. In order to make simpler and circulate its ideas, a number of Keynes's followers developed a relatively simple hypothetical structure to present the main arguments. According to Keynes if an economy diverts from the equilibrium path and increases high unemployment, the price mechanism would not be able to bring a situation where high full employment persists. Here government plays an important role. By using fiscal policy government increases the aggregate demand and following the increased demand firms increase output and employment. In this way the performance of capitalist economy can be improved and this is the political implication of Keynesian thought.

The chief principle of neoclassical economics is that the markets have an important role to do work and price movements will produce the necessary adjustments in the economy in response to economic adjustment. Neoclassical theory was used by Keynes himself regarding investment functions and labor demand functions. According to neoclassical economists government involvement to control the economy was needless and created distortions in the economy.

Most macroeconomic models are highly aggregated in order to make them simpler. There are number of households and firms who are buying and selling huge quantities of various goods and services at their own price and it is useful to suppress all the information to get a association which seems to be important.

In an economy there are number of heterogeneous goods and services. Here measurement is problem. If a monetary unit is considered to measure those goods and services then this type of problem can be overcome. But here is another problem. If money is used then volume of goods and services would increase keeping physical quantity intact. National output in real term or in physical unit indicates standard of living of the people of the economy. So nominal value of a variable and real value of a variable is matter of concern. Nominal value of a variable is its value in current prices and real value of a variable is its value in its constant prices.

Equilibrium is an elementary concept in economic analysis. It is nothing but a state of rest where no forces can change the situation. There is a difference between short run equilibrium and long run equilibrium. In short run equilibrium all variables will not consider. It is purely temporary. On the other hand in the long run equilibrium system gets total rest. Only disturbances from outside can affect the system.

Now we distinguish between stationary equilibrium and dynamic equilibrium. In a stationary equilibrium all variables remain at a constant level but in dynamic equilibrium ratios between variables are constant but variables grow steadily.

Market-clearing in traditional neoclassical economic analysis market clears when trade occurs at a price at which demand equals supply. It is a necessary condition from neoclassical point of view. But Keynesian models got equilibrium without much stress on market-clearing.

In microeconomics theory we consider savings behavior of a household in relation to rate of interest. But macroeconomics deals with the household's behavior of savings and firm's behavior of investment to determine the rate of interest in the economy. The post-war work of both Keynesian and neoclassical economists were affected by microeconomics foundation of macroeconomics.

Chapter - 2

Quantity Theory of Money & Simple Keynesian Models

The quantity theory of money

A vital inquiry in macroeconomics is that if any changes of supply of money do have any effect on real variables like unemployment, GDP, Investment, consumption etc. The appropriate response given by this hypothesis of money is that adjustments in the money supply may have genuine impacts in the short run yet won't have over the long haul. Neoclassical approach mostly derived from the quantity theory of money.

According to quantity theory of money the demand for money equation can be written as

$$M^D = kY$$

$$Or,\ M^D = k(Y/P)P$$

$$Or,\ M^D = kyP$$

The amount of money which an economic manager desires to hold on average over a given period of time is called demand for money. The demand for money depends on the value of transactions being financed over a period and factors affecting payments habits. If the latter part is remained constant then demand for money depends on the value of transactions. The value of transactions is equal to the product of number of transaction over a period and the average price per transaction.

M^D is the demand for nominal money balances. ***k*** is the fraction of the real money income (Py) which people desire to hold in cash and demand deposits or the ratio of money stock to income, P is the index of aggregate price level, and y is the real national output over a time period. This equation tells us that other things being equal, the demand for money in normal terms would be proportional to the nominal level of income for each individual, and hence for the aggregate economy as well.

If we multiply both sides by 1/k of equation

$$M^D = kyP$$

We get,

$$\frac{1}{k}M = \frac{k}{k}yP$$

$$Or, VM = yP$$

$$Or, MV = yP$$

V (income velocity in circulation of money) is measured by dividing the value of national output in current prices (nominal national output) by the money supply in existence. This can be written as

$$V \equiv \frac{yP}{M}$$

It is an identity.

The condition for money market equilibrium is

$$M^D = M^S$$

Nominal demand for money = Nominal supply of money

$$M^S = kyP$$

$$\text{Or, } M^S = (I/V)yP$$

If money supply is increased then to restore equilibrium in money market can be found by increasing demand for money. In demand for money *k* and *y* are fixed. So equilibrium can be restored by increasing price level *P*. This type of equilibrium analysis is called comparative-static analysis. It compares the equilibrium positions depending on changes in the parameters. If money supply goes beyond the demand for money the surplus money will be spent on output. When people save more cutting their consumption demand for money will be more than supply of money. If demand for goods goes beyond the supply of goods, prices are raised to reduce the demand. So that demand is equal to supply. The opposite will happen if demand is less than supply. The fundamental policy implication of the model is that changing the money supply will affect the real variable in the short run and keep real variables unaffected in the long run.

Simple Keynesian Model

Simple Keynesian model is a one-sector model which includes goods market only. There is no role of monetary sector. Here price is fixed. In the quantity theory of money price is flexible. The basic of the Keynesian model is that here equilibrium output may be less than firms could produce. Firms' capacity is more. Equilibrium is restored at where aggregate demand is equal to aggregate supply. Depending on the aggregate demand equilibrium is found. It is a short run model. For example, real national output for a quarter or a year can be determined in this model. In simple Keynesian model there is a 45 degree line which represents the equalities between the supply of real national output (y) and the output (E) desired by the people. Therefore, the condition for static equilibrium is

The supply of real national output (y) = The quantity of national output which people desire to buy (E)

In this model the maximum amount of output firms would be able to produce is not equal to the equilibrium output at fixed prices. Here maximum amount of output is the full employment output. Keynesian cross is a cross of two lines. One is y=E and another is aggregate demand line (E= C+I).

In Keynesian model there are three structural equations.

$$y = E \quad \dots\dots\dots..(i)$$

$$E = C + I \dots\dots \quad \dots\dots\dots..(ii)$$

$$C = a + bY \quad \dots\dots\dots..(iii)$$

C = Autonomous Consumption+ Marginal propensity to Consume Y

Consumption and income are endogenous variables. Now we substitute equation (ii) and (iii) in (i) to find out static equilibrium value of consumption and income.

$$y = a + bY + I_0 \quad \dots\dots\dots..(iv)$$

$$y - bY = a + I_0$$

bY

$$y(1-b) = a + I_0$$

$$y = \frac{a + I_0}{1 - b} \dots\dots\dots\dots\dots\dots(v)$$

$$y = \frac{Autonomous\ Expenditure}{Multiplier}$$

This the static equilibrium value of income.

Now we substitute the value of static equilibrium income in equation (iii) and get

$$C = a + b\,\frac{a + I_0}{1 - b} \dots\dots\dots\dots\dots\dots(vi)$$

$$C = a + b\,\frac{Autonomous\ Expenditure}{Multiplier}$$

Equation (v) and equation (vi) are the reduced form equations. Here each endogenous variable is expressed in terms of independent variables only.

It is a model where equilibrium can be restored without clearing product market and labor market. Producers could supply more than the equilibrium national output because resources are still available in producers' hand. If aggregate demand or autonomous expenditure is increased the static equilibrium output will increase by multiplier method. $1/(1–b)$ is the Keynesian multiplier.

In a Keynesian model in which prices as well as money wages are assumed fixed, the quantity of national product supplied depends entirely on the level of aggregate demand, up to the full-employment level of output.

Up to the full-employment level output aggregate demand plays an important role to determine the supply of national product. But beyond the full employment level if aggregate demand exceeds aggregate supply prices will go up and persistence increase in prices will bring inflation. Inflation can be controlled by reducing aggregate demand. The point from where aggregate demand exceeds full-employment level the model gets discontinuity. i.e., before full-employment prices are fixed but after full-employment prices are flexible.

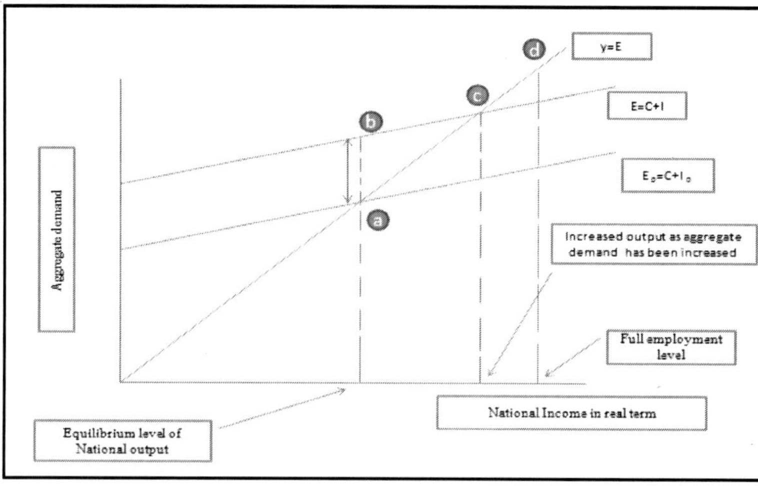

Source: Rosalind, L., & Alexander, R.1982.

Figure 1.1

The above figure depicts Keynesian one-sector model. Distance from point ***a*** to ***b*** shows change in investment. Point ***a*** is the initial static equilibrium. Point ***c*** is new equilibrium as because of increase in investment. Point ***d*** represents full-employment level of output. Aggregate demand beyond point ***d*** shows the discontinuity. Prices are fixed up to point ***d*** and are flexible beyond point ***d***. Increase in output from ***a*** to ***c*** has happened through Keynesian multiplier.

In static model a variable moves from one position of equilibrium to another position of equilibrium and the variable takes only one value. Values that a variable takes on between two equilibrium positions cannot be forecasted by the static model. In our figure points ***a*** and ***c*** are two points of equilibrium. Values of the variable between the two points cannot be forecasted in static model. If we like to find out values of output between two equilibrium positions ***dynamic model*** is needed. In dynamic model time path of output can be found.

If investment increases time path of income can be determined. After one period income increases as a result of increase in investment. At the initial period consumption does not increase (since $C_t = \alpha + \beta y_{t-1}$). Consumption will increase in the next period. Income in the next period will be mpc (marginal propensity to consume) times the previous period's rise in income. Each time output increases as a fraction of *mpc* and is injected back into aggregate expenditure via an increase in consumption and become next period's increase in output. This process is the expenditure multiplier at work. The final increase in income is obtained by summing the increase for each period, i.e.

$$\Delta y = \Delta I(1 + b + b^2 + \cdots . b^{N-1}) \qquad ...(1)$$

[b implies marginal propensity to consume]

Multiplying both sides by b we get,

$$b\Delta y = b\Delta I(1 + b + b^2 + \cdots . b^{N-1}) \qquad ...(2)$$

Subtracting equation (2) from (1) we get,

$$\Delta y - b\Delta y = \Delta I(1 + b + b^2 + \cdots . b^{N-1})$$
$$-b\Delta I(1 + b + b^2 + \cdots . b^{N-1})$$
$$Or, (1 - b)\Delta y = \Delta I\ (1 + b + b^2 + \cdots . b^{N-1}$$
$$-1 - b^2 - b^3 - \cdots b^{-1} - b^N)$$
$$Or, (1 - b)\Delta y = \Delta I(1 - b^N)$$
$$Or, \Delta y = \Delta I \frac{(1 - b^N)}{1 - b}$$
$$\Delta y = \Delta I \frac{(1)}{1 - b}$$

In dynamic model income moves toward equilibrium gradually. As long as b lies between plus and minus one, the model is a stable equilibrium model and it will be convergent. On the contrary, if b is greater than one the model will be unstable and it will be divergent.

Chapter - 3

Money, Inflation and Interest Rate

Money

Money is not a wealth. It is nothing but stock of assets that can be used for transaction. Money functions as a medium of exchange, a unit of account and as a store of value. If you like to understand the importance of money then try to understand the economy without money. For example, I earn money as salary. I purchase product-A. Therefore, my salary goes to the producer as her income. Producer uses his earning for raw materials. Owner of raw materials uses their income for her child education. Educational institution uses its income for the payment of its employee as salary. Therefore, in the modern system has need of money.

Fiat money turned out to be the standard after U.S. President Richard Nixon decided to throw out the gold standard in 1971. By doing so, He declared that the dollar was no longer convertible into gold. Fiat money has an inflationary risk as because it can no longer be converted into gold and is not directly attached to the amount of gold that a government stores. It means that it can lose its value in economic crisis. If too much money is printed by a government, the importance of its currency will go down.

Fiat money is one that is stated legal tender. This comprises any form of currency in circulation such as paper money or coins. Fiat money is backed by a country's government instead of a physical commodity.

The quantity of money available in an economy is called the money supply and through which this money supply is controlled is called monetary policy. Through open market operations i.e., the purchase and sale of government bonds a government controls the supply of money.

Money is measured by C, M_1, M_2 and M_3. C implies currency, M_1 implies currency plus demand deposits and checkable deposit, M_2 implies M_1 plus retail money market mutual fund balances, saving deposits and small time deposits and M_3 implies M_2 plus large time deposits, repurchase agreements.

Now we examine the four variables equation.

$$M.V = P.T$$

or, Money x Transactions Velocity of Money = Price x Transactions

This equation is an identity. It is always true. If one of the four variables changes one or more variables also change to maintain the equilibrium. For example, V is constant and money supply increases then price will increase alone or T will increase alone or both price and T will increase.

It is difficult to measure the value of T. So T is replaced by Y i.e., total output of the economy. Transaction and output are same because more the economy produces, more there is transactions.

Therefore, modified version of the quantity equation is as follows.

$$M.V = P.Y$$

Or, Money x Income Velocity of Money = Price x Output

Income velocity of money implies in a given period of time is the number of times a dollar bill enters someone's income.

The quantity of money should be considered in terms of real money balances as real money balances are useful for buying the quantity of goods and services. Purchasing power of the stock of money is measured by real money balances. Determinants of quantity of real money balances are called money demand function. The function can be written as

$$(M/P)^d = kY$$

Here k is constant and it implies how much money people want to hold for every dollar of income.

To maintain equilibrium demand for real money is equal to supply of real money.

Therefore,

$$M/P=kY$$

$$\text{Or, } M.(1/k)=PY$$

$$\text{Or, } M.V = PY$$

It is clear from the above mathematical transformation that

$$V=1/k$$

It means that income velocity of money is inversely related to holding of money for each dollar income. When people hold money in huge amount money does not change hand frequently and vice versa. So this is the fundamental relation between V and k.

Now we are going to see how money supply relates with inflation. We consider the modified version of the quantity equation.

$$M.V=P.Y$$

Now we multiply the four variables by 'percentage change in' and we get, Percentage change in M x Percentage change in V= Percentage change in P x Percentage change in Y

Now we consider that V is constant as percentage change in V replicates change in money demand. Percentage change in Y is only possible by increasing factors of production or introducing new technology and it is assumed that it is given for a given period. Percentage change in P is nothing but inflation. So change in money supply determines inflation. Therefore, it can be conclude that inflation could be controlled by monetary authority as far as the quantity theory of money is concerned.

Nominal and Real Interest rate

Nominal interest rate is nothing but the interest rate that banks pay to their customers. Suppose the banks pay 7% interest rate then nominal interest rate is nominal interest rate. Nominal interest rate is not adjusted to inflation. On the contrary real interest rate is adjusted to inflation. It increases the purchasing capacity of the consumers. There is a simple linear relationship between nominal interest rate real interest rate.

Real interest rate = Nominal interest rate – Inflation

$$\text{Or, } r = i - \pi$$

$$\text{Or, } r = i + \pi \qquad \text{...............(1)}$$

Nominal interest rate is the sum of real interest rate and inflation. This relationship is called *Fisher equation*. Irving Fisher (1867-1947) was the pioneer of *Fisher equation.*

The relationship among money growth, inflation and nominal interest rate can be shown by the two concepts. One is quantity theory and another is Fisher equation. Quantity theory of money shows the relationship between money growth and inflation. Fisher equation shows the relationship between nominal interest rate and inflation. So among the three variables there is an economic link.

As borrowers are unable to predict inflation with certainty equation (1) can be written as

$$\text{Or, } r = i + \pi^e$$

where π^e is the expected inflation.

It is known to us that demand for money $(M/P)^d$ is functionally related with nominal interest rate (*i*) and level of income (*y*). Money demand is inversely related with nominal interest rate and proportionally related with level of income. Holding money has a cost. If you hold money you will lose nominal interest rate. This is the opportunity cost of holding money.

In equilibrium demand for money $(M/P)^d$ is equal to supply of money (M/P).

Therefore, in equilibrium

$$M/P = L(i, Y)$$

$$M/P = L(r + \pi^e, Y) \qquad \text{...............(2)}$$

So, real money balances is functionally related with expected inflation.

Equation (2) is partially different from quantity theory equation. In quantity theory equation present money supply determines present price level keeping other things constant. In quantity theory level of income and nominal interest rate is constant. But nominal interest rate is not constant. It depends on expected inflation and expected inflation depends on the increase in the money supply. So there is an additional channel through which money supply affects price level. Suppose monetary authority will increase money supply. This future increase money supply will increase expected inflation. So high expected inflation increases present nominal interest rate. As holding money has a cost and due to high nominal interest rate now holding money bears more cost. Naturally people will demand less real money. As money supply is constant today price level will increase. Therefore, higher anticipated future money supply leads to a higher price level. Here the Cagan model exists. The Cagan model depicts the dependency of price level on present money supply as well as on future money supply.

Now we develop the Cagan model.

Some assumptions are as follows.

(i) Level of output that is a determinant of money demand function is excluded,

(ii) Real interest rate is constant,

(iii) Inflation is considered in place of nominal interest rate and

(iv) Actual inflation is considered in place of expected inflation.

Therefore, money demand function can be written as

$$\frac{M}{P} = \gamma \frac{P_t - P_{t+1}}{P_{t+1}}$$

Taking of log of both sides we get,

$$Or, LogM_t - LogP_t = \gamma Log\frac{P_t - P_{t+1}}{P_{t+1}}$$
$$Or, LogM_t - LogP_t = \gamma Log(\frac{P_t}{P_{t+1}} - 1)$$
$$Or, LogM_t - LogP_t = \gamma[Log(\frac{P_{t+1}}{P_t}) - Log1]$$
$$Or, LogM_t - LogP_t = \gamma[Log(\frac{P_{t+1}}{P_t}) - Log1]$$

Since $Log1 = 0$

$$Or, LogM_t - LogP_t = \gamma Log(\frac{P_{t+1}}{P_t})$$
$$Or, LogM_t - LogP_t = \gamma(LogP_{t+1} - LogP_t)$$

Now replacing $LogM_t$ as m_t , $LogP_t$ as p_t and $LogP_{t+1}$ as p_{t+1} we get,

$$m_t - p_t = \gamma(p_t - p_{t+1})$$
$$Or, m_t - p_t = -\gamma(p_{t+1} - p_t)$$

Therefore, the money demand function is

$$m_t - p_t = -\gamma(p_{t+1} - p_t) \qquad \text{...............} (3)$$

where, m_t is the log of quantity of money at time t, p_t is the log of price level at time t , p_t+1 is the log of price level at time t+1 and γ is the sensitivity of money demand to inflation. $(m_t - p_t)$ is the log of real money balances and $(p_{t+1} - p_t)$ is the inflation rate.

Now, equation (3) can be rearranged as

$$"p_t = (\frac{1}{1+\gamma})m_t + (\frac{\gamma}{1+\gamma})p_{t+1} \qquad \text{...............}(4)$$

Current price level depends on current money supply and one period ahead price level

In the same way,

$$p_{t+1} = (\frac{1}{1+\gamma})m_{t+1} + (\frac{\gamma}{1+\gamma})p_{t+2} \qquad \text{...............}(5)$$

$$p_{t+2} = (\frac{1}{1+\gamma})m_{t+2} + \frac{\gamma}{(1+\gamma)^2}m_{t+1} + \frac{\gamma}{1+\gamma}p_{t+3} \quad \text{..............} (6)$$

Now we substitute in equation (4)

$$p_t = \frac{1}{1+\gamma}m_t + \frac{\gamma}{(1+\gamma)^2}m_{t+1} + \frac{\gamma^2}{(1+\gamma)^2}p_{t+2} \quad \text{..............}(7)$$

Equation (6) shows that current period price level depends on current period money supply, one period ahead money supply and on the two period ahead price level.

Now we modify equation (7) by putting the value of p_{t+2}.

$$p_t = \frac{1}{1+\gamma}m_t + \frac{\gamma}{(1+\gamma)^2}m_{t+1} + \frac{\gamma^2}{(1+\gamma)^3}m_{t+2} + \frac{\gamma^3}{(1+\gamma)^3}p_{t+3}$$

$$\text{..............}(8)$$

For infinite number of times

$$p_t = \frac{1}{1+\gamma}[m_t + \frac{\gamma}{1+\gamma}m_{t+1} + \left(\frac{\gamma}{1+\gamma}\right)^2 m_{t+2} + \left(\frac{\gamma}{1+\gamma}\right)^3 m_{t+3} + \cdots.] \quad \text{..............} (9)$$

So it is proved that price level at current period is a function of current period money supply as well as future period money supplies.

As γ is the sensitivity of money demand to inflation the value of γ has an important role. If value of the γ is zero then $p_t = m_t$ i.e., current period price level is equal to current period money supply. It merely represents quantity theory of money. If the value of γ is small then $\frac{\gamma}{1+\gamma}$ is small and it values declines as time passes. Here the current money supply has an important role. On the contrary, if the value of γ is large then $\frac{\gamma}{1+\gamma}$ becomes one and the future periods money supplies play an important role in determining current period's price level.

If we consider expected inflation in place of actual inflation then

$$p_t = \frac{1}{1+\gamma}[m_t + \frac{\gamma}{1+\gamma}Em_{t+1} + \left(\frac{\gamma}{1+\gamma}\right)^2 Em_{t+2} + \left(\frac{\gamma}{1+\gamma}\right)^3 Em_{t+3} + \cdots.]"$$

(Mankiw N. Gregory. 2010, pp.112-113) .... (10)

Equation (10) represents price level at current period is a function of current period money supply as well as expected future period money supplies.

Chapter - 4

The ISLM Model

We have discussed one sector Keynesian model. This sector is goods market. The goods market equilibrium represents the equalities between the supply of real national output (y) and the output (E) desired by the people. Receipts of national output by factors of production and the expenditure of income by household are matter of concern here.

But the ISLM model is a two-sector model. One is goods market and another is money market. i.e. one is real sector and another is monetary sector. The model was originally developed by J.R. Hicks.[1] In the Keynesian version of ISLM model prices are assumed fixed and in the neoclassical version of ISLM model prices are flexible. Demand side (IS functions and LM functions) assumptions are quite similar in both the Keynesian and the neoclassical version of ISLM model. But they are different in supply side assumptions.

Before get involved in the analysis we should have a clear idea about *flow equilibrium* and stock equilibrium. Flow equilibrium needs that produced output should be used by enthusiastic customers. It means that saved resources are transferred to deficit household. Stock equilibrium is a concept of financial sector. In *stock equilibrium* demand for assets equals to supply of assets at their current prices. If this does not hold assets prices will be altering and it will have effect on consumption as well as investment. If flow equilibrium does not hold i.e. investment does not equal to saving then assets prices will be changing. As assets prices change stock equilibrium will not exist. So both the equilibriums are needed to have overall equilibrium of the economy.

Keynesian Version of ISLM Model

Here price level is assumed to be constant and determined exogenously. In Keynesian models there are two identities. One is related to aggregate demand and another is related to real output or income.

---

1. J.R. Hicks, "Mr Keynes and the Classics": A Suggested Interpretation', Econometrica, 5(April 1937) 147-59.

Aggregate demand identity is as follows:

$$E \equiv C + 1 \qquad \text{..............(3)}$$

Real output or income identity is as follows:

$$y \equiv C + S \qquad \text{.............. (4)}$$

Where ***y*** implies real national output, ***Y*** implies nominal national output and ***E*** implies desired aggregate demand or national expenditure, ***C*** implies planned or desired consumption, ***I*** implies planned investment or desired investment, ***S*** implies planned or desired saving and ***i*** represents the market rate of interest.

Identity (4) represents that household dispose of their income either by consuming or saving.

To maintain equilibrium (static and flow) real output must be equal to aggregate demand.

$$C + S = C + I \qquad \text{..............(5)}$$

$$S = I \qquad \text{..............(6)}$$

Therefore, in equilibrium planned saving should be equal to planned investment.

In equilibrium planned saving is equal to planned investment. But actual saving is always equal to actual investment without considering the equilibrium situation. Now if planned/desired saving is greater than planned investment i.e. real output is greater than aggregate demand then firms' inventories will increase because unsold output will be added to the stock. As it is known that actual saving is always equal to actual investment firm will increase unplanned inventory investment. When actual investment is greater than planned investment firms will change their production plan in the next period to find out the equilibrium situation. The values of variables that actualize after economic pronouncement are called *ex post* values. On the contrary planned values of variables are called *ex ante* values. When real output is greater than aggregate demand i.e. planned saving is greater than planned investment then planned investment i.e. *ex ant* values is smaller than *ex post* value of investment. In simple way we can say that if desired saving surpasses desired investment real output exceeds aggregate demand. As a result of that inventory blows up and to maintain an equilibrium between actual saving and actual investment firms will increase the actual investment. So in this case when planned saving is greater than planned investment *ex post* value is greater than *ex an* value. In equilibrium *ex post* value is equal to *ex ant* value.

By assuming investment is inversely related with the rate of interest rate the ISLM model connects IS with LM i.e. goods market with financial sector. At first we have to understand what investment is. Investment is nothing but demand for capital goods. Capital goods are required to produce additional goods in the future. So expectation about the future is needed and in this way investment is associated with expectations. To produce goods firms buy capital goods and bear the cost at present but the capital goods produce in future. So comparison is necessary between revenue earned in different periods of time in future and the cost of capital goods needed for that production. This can be done by putting all future costs and revenues in a value that is measure at present. This value is called present value.

The net present value of an investment project is the discounted value of all revenues minus the discounted value of all costs.

$$\text{Net Present Value} = \frac{R_1}{1+i} + \frac{R_2}{(1+i)^2} + \frac{R_3}{(1+i)^3} + \cdots + \frac{R_n}{(1+i)^n} - C_0 \quad ....(7)$$

Where C_0 is the initial cost of capital and R_n is net revenue expected in the *n*th year. In the net revenue, cost is operating cost.

[To have a clear understanding about present value we consider an example. Let market rate of interest is 10% and \$100 is the initial amount. After one year it will be \$100+\$10 = \$100(1+0.1) = \$110. After two years with interest it will be $\$100(1+0.1)^2 = \$121$. In the same way if \$P with *i* interest rate after *n* will be $\$P(1+i)^n$. Now the present value of \$110 is equal to $\frac{\$121}{(1+0.1)}$ = \$100, the present value of \$121 is equal to $\frac{\$121}{(1+0.1)^2}$ = \$100, the present value of \$110 is equal to $\frac{\$110}{(1+0.1)}$=\$100, the present value of \$Y is equal to $\frac{\$Y}{(1+i)^n}$. Present value calculation is nothing but the reverse of a compound-interest calculation.][1]

Firms' objective is to maximize net present value and this can be done by improving net revenue, declining price of capital goods, falling market rate of interest. In the ISLM model net revenue and the price of capital is constant and rate of interest is endogenously determined. Therefore, investment function which connects goods market and financial market goes into the model in the form of

$$I = I(i) \quad ....(8)$$

1. This example has been taken from book written by Rosalind, L., & Alexander, R. 1982, pp. 29.

where i is the market rate of interest.

$$S = -a + sy \qquad \text{...............(9)}$$

S represents amount of savings, *a* represents autonomous savings and *s* represents marginal propensity to save.

For goods market equilibrium planned investment should be equal to planned saving. So

$$y = \frac{a + 1(i)}{s} \qquad \text{...............(10)}$$

Equation (10) is a goods market equilibrium equation. IS curve is nothing but locus of various combinations of real output and rate of interest at which goods market gets equilibrium. High rate of interest reduces investment and to balance the equation (10) *y* should be reduced. So high rate of interest is associated with low real output t get equilibrium in goods market. The figure-4.1 represents the derivation of IS curve.

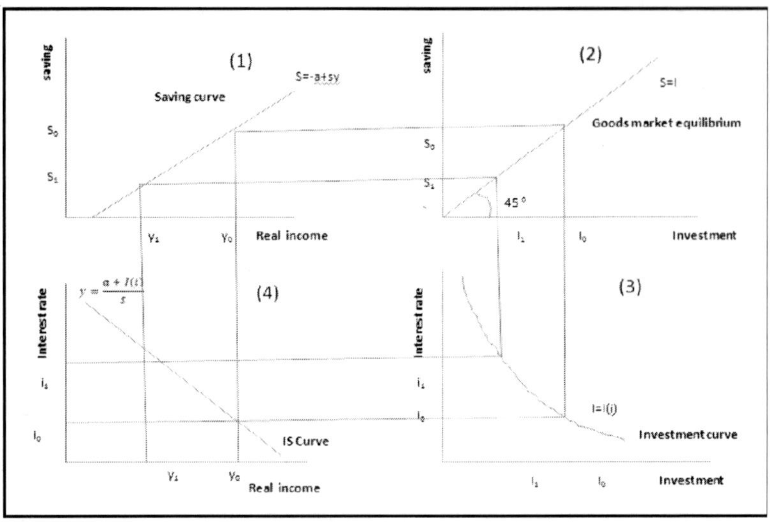

Source: Rosalind, L., & Alexander, R.1982, pp. 31.

Figure 4.1

In our figure-4.1, there are four sections. Section-1, depicts saving function, section-2 depicts goods market equilibrium i.e. S=I, section-3, depicts investment function and section-4 depicts investment- saving (IS) curve. At y_0 income saving is S_0. 45^0 line in section-2, investment and saving in equal part. At S_0 saving investment is I_0. At I_0 investment rate of interest is i_0. In section-4, points y_0 and i_0 are plotted. In the same way points y_1 and i_1 are plotted in section-4. In this way various points of y and i can be plotted in section-4. The locus of all combinations of all those points we get IS curve. Equation-10 has two variables such as y and i. One equation and two variables cannot be solved. So we need another equation and that equation can be brought from financial sector.

There are only two financial assets. One is money and another is bond. Money does not bear any interest rate. On the contrary bond bears interest rate. A bond is an imperfectly liquid asset. There is an inverse relationship between bond and the rate of interest rate.

$$\text{“Bond Price} = \mathrm{B_p} = \frac{A_n}{1+i} + \frac{A_n}{(1+i)^2} + \frac{A_n}{(1+i)^3} + \cdots + \frac{A_n}{(1+i)^n} \quad \ldots\ldots\ldots\ldots\ldots(8)$$

where A_n is the nominally fixed annual income. i is the rate of interest. Calculation is made by inversing the compound interest rate. Therefore, equation-8 represents the present value of bond price. Equation-8 can be simplified in the following ways.

$$\mathrm{B_p} = \frac{A_n}{1+i} + \frac{A_n}{(1+i)^2} + \frac{A_n}{(1+i)^3} + \cdots + \frac{A_n}{(1+i)^n}$$

$$\text{Or, } \mathrm{B_p} = \frac{A_n}{1+i}\sum_{t=0}^{\infty}\left(\frac{1}{1+i}\right)^t$$

$$\text{Or, } \mathrm{B_p} = \frac{A_n}{(1+i)}\left(\frac{1}{1-\frac{1}{(1+i)}}\right)$$

$$\text{Or, } \mathrm{B_p} = \frac{A_n}{(1+i)}\left(\frac{1+i}{i}\right)$$

$$\text{Or, } \mathrm{B_p} = \frac{A_n}{i} \quad \text{Rosalind, L., \& Alexander, R. 1982, pp. 32} \ldots\ldots\ldots\ldots\ldots(9)$$

Now we take an example to clarify the inverse relationship between bond price and rate of interest. Suppose the rate of interest is 5% on a bond issued at \$200. Therefore, nominally fixed annual income will be \$200 × 5 = \$1000. If the rate of interest rises to 10% then to keep the nominally fixed annual income at \$1000 bond price must be declined. Now the bond price would be \$1000/10 = \$100. So the bond price has fallen from \$200 to \$100. So it is clear from the above example that there is the inverse relationship between bond price and rate of interest.

Demand for money is the demand to clutch money in terms of quantity and in terms of assets. Demand for money depends on income level and on the rate of interest. If income increases demand for money increases proportionately. Demand for money is inversely related with the rate of interest. As at the higher rate of interest return on bonds will be larger money demand will be greater than interest bearing assets (bonds). Therefore, demand for money equation is as follows.

$$\left(\frac{M}{P}\right)^{D} = \frac{M}{P}(y,i) \qquad \text{...............(10)}$$

In stock equilibrium demand for money is equal to supply of money. Supply of money is exogenously determined i.e. money supply is determined out of the system of the model. Therefore, money market equilibrium condition is as follows.

$$\left(\frac{M}{P}\right)^{D} = \frac{M}{P}(y,i) = \frac{M_o^s}{P} \qquad \text{...............(11)}$$

Figure-4.2, represents equilibrium condition in the money market. Demand for money curve shifts because of transaction demand for money from D_0D_0 to D_1D_1 as real output increases from y_o to y_1. As a result of that equilibrium rate of interest will be i_o and i_1.

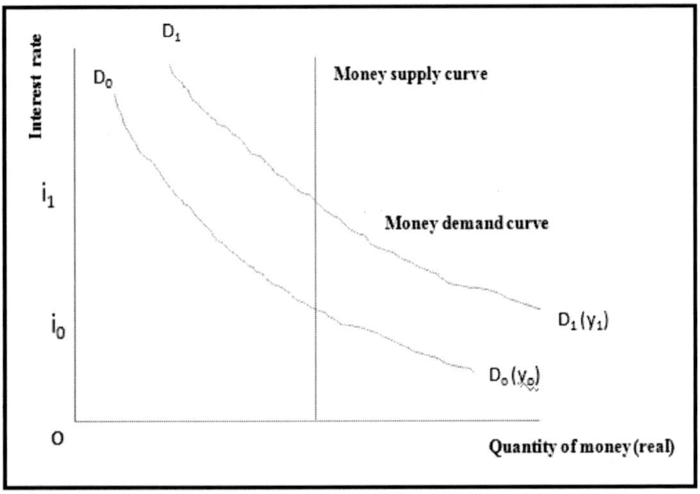

Source: Rosalind, L., & Alexander, R. 1982.

Figure - 4.2: Demand for money as a function of rate of interest.

In figure-4.3, we plot all the combinations of real output and rate of interest. These combinations are found from money market equilibrium. Locus of all those combinations is LM curve.

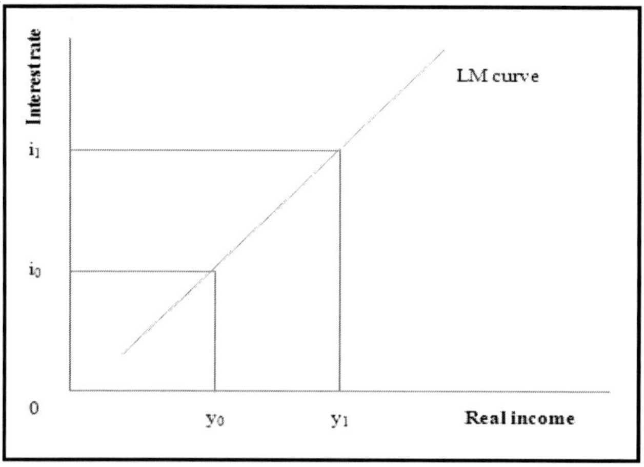

Source: Rosalind, L., & Alexander, R.1982.

Figure - 4.3: LM function.

By using IS and LM function which we have derived now we can find equilibrium real output and interest rate that equate both the goods market and the money market. Figure-4.4, clarifies this. This is the Keynesian ISLM model. Price is fixed here. This equilibrium happens before full employment. Before full employment there is no scope for increasing cost because resources are available. Firms will increase their production without affecting the cost of production. Hence average cost will be unchanged and price level also remains unchanged.

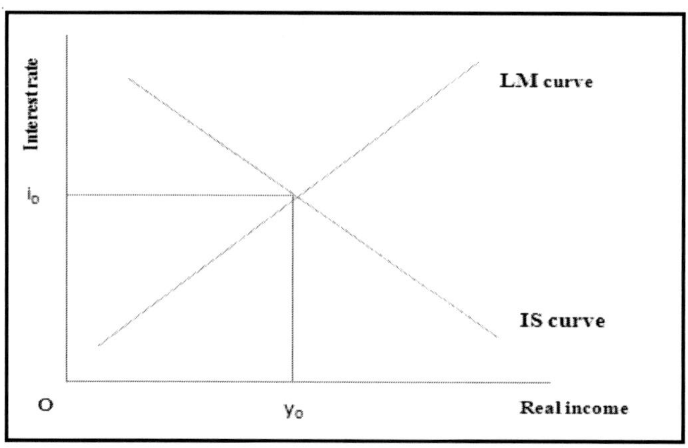

Source: Rosalind, L., & Alexander, R.1982.

Figure-4.4: ISLM Function.

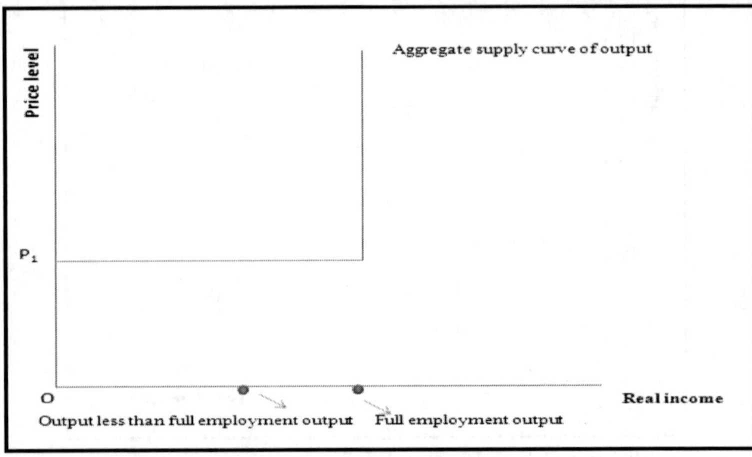

Source: Rosalind, L., & Alexander, R. 1982.

Figure-4.5: Aggregate supply function.

Figure-4.5, depicts the aggregate supply curve of real output. As price is unchanged in the Keynesian ISLM model aggregate supply curve is perfectly elastic. Before full employment this type of situation happens. But at full employment Aggregate supply curve is perfectly inelastic. As in the Keynesian model real output is determined by the demand Keynesian ISLM model is demand determined. If real output goes beyond the full employment output then output will not increase rather price level will increase. Now the role of labor market gets entry here.

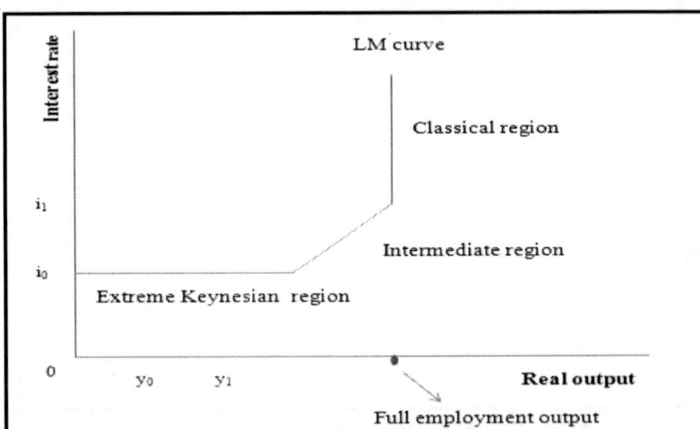

Source: Richerd T. F. 2005.

Figure-4.6: LM function representing Classical and Keynesian region.

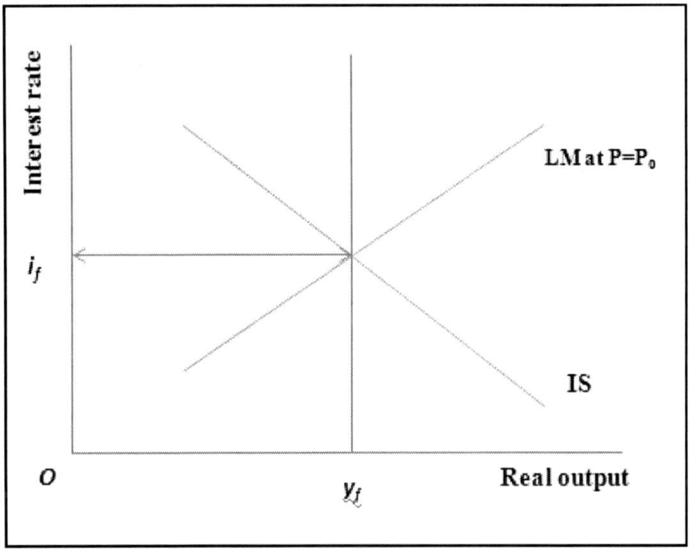

Source: Rosalind, L., & Alexander, R.1982

Figure-4.7: Neoclassical version of ISLM model

Figure-4.7, shows neoclassical version of ISLM model. i_f and y_f are equilibrium full employment interest rate and output respectively. Here, whatever is the place of LM curve equilibrium level of output and interest rate will be same because in goods market at full employment output equilibrium rate of interest is determined and this equilibrium interest rate equates investment with savings in goods market. As prices are flexible at full employment output equilibrium interest rate is determined independently in the goods market.

The fundamental differences between Keynesian and neoclassical version of ISLM model are as follows.

(a) In the Keynesian model prices are not flexible and in the neoclassical model prices are flexible,

(b) Output and interest rate are exogenously determined in the neoclassical model where both the variables are endogenously determined in the Keynesian model,

(c) Supply side assumptions are different in both the model and it is the basic difference between the two.

(d) Without making equilibrium in the money market equilibrium full employment output and interest rate are determined in the neoclassical model,

(e) Quite independently of money market goods market equilibrium determines equilibrium interest rate and this is because of flexible prices in the neoclassical ISLM model,

(f) Once the equilibrium full employment interest rate and output are determined money demand is determined on the basis of that. To make equilibrium in the money market money supply is determined. So money market equilibrium does not have any role to determine equilibrium rate of interest. But on the contrary in the Keynesian ISLM model do have an important role in determining equilibrium interest rate,

(g) Any shift of LM curve to the left or right does not have any impact in determining equilibrium full employment output and interest rate in the goods market. But in the Keynesian ISLM model money market equilibrium and goods market equilibrium jointly determine equilibrium output and interest rate.

Shifting of IS curve:

The IS equation is

$$y = \frac{a + I(i)}{s}$$

where a is the autonomous saving and s is the marginal propensity to save. Shifting of IS curve depends on parameters of the IS equation. IS curve will shift upward if new investment is found profitable at every rate of interest. The opposite (IS curve shift will shift downward) will happen if expected return from new investment declines.

(i) If autonomous saving increases IS curve shifts upward,

(ii) If autonomous saving decreases IS curve shifts downward,

(iii) If marginal propensity to save (s) falls IS curve shifts upward,

(iv) If marginal propensity to save (s) raises IS curve shifts downward,

(v) If marginal propensity to consume raises IS curve shifts upward,

(vi) If marginal propensity to consume falls IS curve shifts downward.

Change of any exogenous variables that affects investment actually shifts IS schedule.

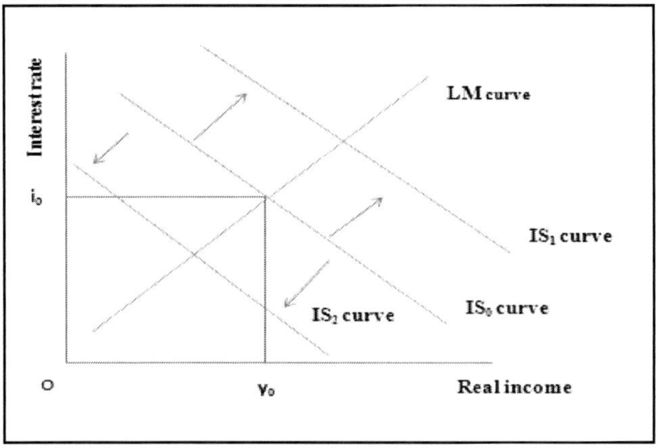

Source: Rosalind, L., & Alexander, R.1982.

Figure-4.8: Shifting of IS Curve.

Shifting of LM curve

A change of parameters that affects demand for money and supply of money function shifts the LM curve.

(i) Increase in nominal stock of money shifts the LM curve rightward,

(ii) Decrease in nominal stock of money shifts LM curve leftward,

(iii) Increase in price level (given nominal stock of money) shifts LM curve leftward,

(iv) Decrease in price level (given nominal stock of money) shifts LM curve rightward.

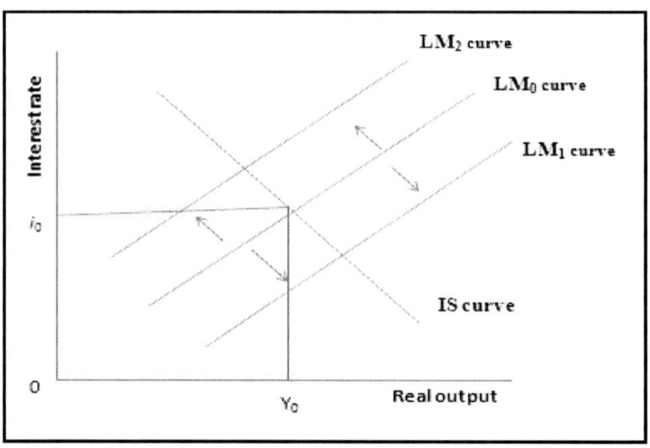

Source: Rosalind, L., & Alexander, R.1982.

Figure-4.9: Shifting of LM Curve.

Shifting of IS curve in two sectors model (The Keynesian Model)

If investment increases IS curve shifts to the upward. Equilibrium point shifts from initial equilibrium point (y_o, i_o) to new equilibrium point (y_1, i_1). Output and interest rate both have increased. As investment increases aggregate demand will increase. This increase in aggregate demand actually increases output in the Keynesian model (one sector). We have found disturbance in the goods market. Output has increased and this increased output should be financed. So there is a greater demand for money. As money supply is constant to bring equilibrium in money market rate of interest should be high. In our figure new rate of interest is i_1. This high rate of interest reduces investment. The rate of interest will be at i_o again if money supply increases. If money supply increases LM curve shifts rightward and new equilibrium output will be at y_2. Output has increased from y_1 to y_2 just because of disincentive effects of higher interest rate on investment.

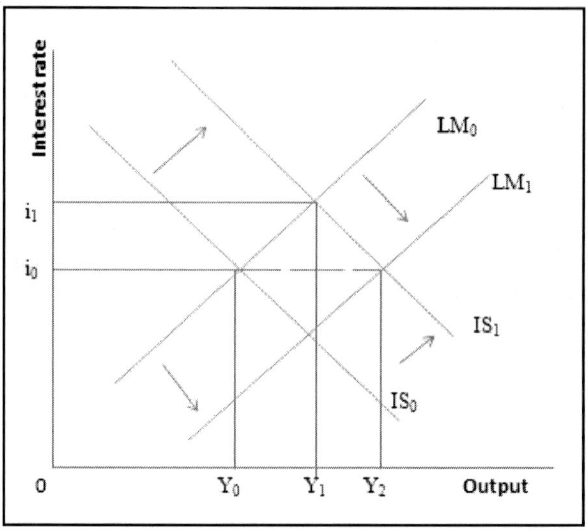

Source: Rosalind, L., & Alexander, R.1982.

Figure-4.10: Shifting of IS Curve and two sector model (Keynesian case).

Shifting of IS curve in neoclassical model

In the neoclassical model prices are flexible to clear the market. But real variables are totally invariant in changing of prices. As investment or consumption increases IS curve shifts upward. Since aggregate demand increases price will increase. As price increases money stock declines.

To get equilibrium in money market demand for money falls and LM curve shifts leftward. As there is full employment there is no scope of increasing output. New equilibrium interest rate is i_1. This high interest rate has a negative effect on investment and investment declines. As a result of that aggregate demand falls and price level declines. Money stock will increase as result of price fall. To get equilibrium in money market demand for money will decrease and LM curve will shift rightward. Our figure depicts the whole mechanism. So in the neoclassical model prices play an important role to maintain equilibrium at full employment.

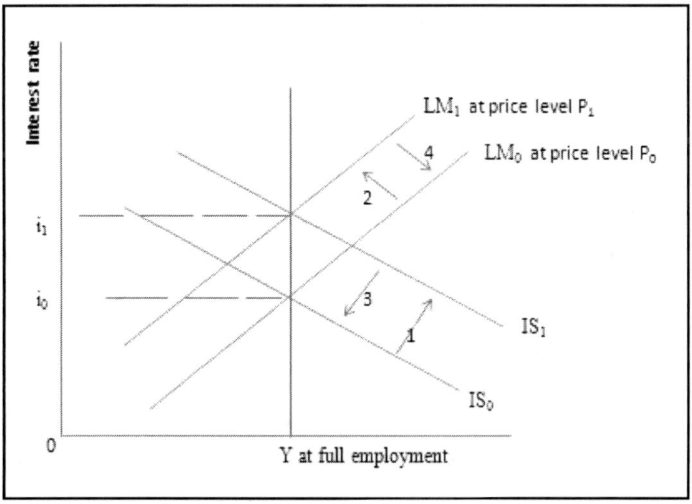

Source: Rosalind, L., & Alexander, R.1982.

Figure-4.11: Shifting of IS Curve and two sector model (Neoclassical case)

An expansionary pure fiscal policy in Keynesian ISLM

Expansionary fiscal policy means an increase in government expenditure or a reduction in tax. Here fiscal policy is pure in the sense that deficit budget of the government is financed by bond selling to the public. There is no role of monetary policy in financing budget deficit. If government expenditure increases IS curve shift to upward. Output and interest rate will increase. As government expenditure encourages production output will increase from initial y_0 to y_1. At this higher level of income more money will be demanded. Since pure fiscal policy is active here money supply will not increase and to get equilibrium in the money market rate of interest will increase from i_0 to i_1 in our figure.

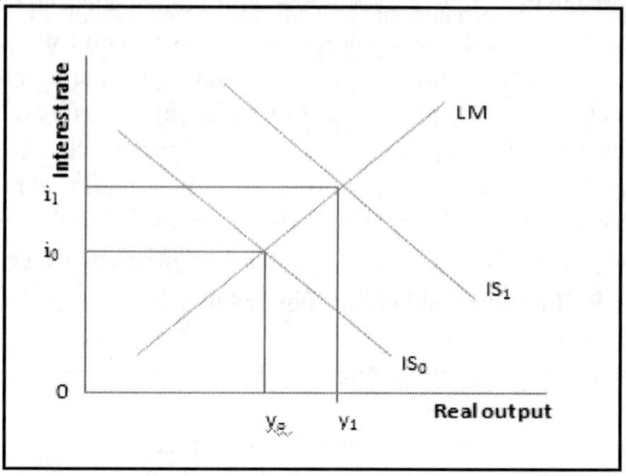

Source: Rosalind, L., & Alexander, R.1982.

Figure-4.12: Pure expansionary fiscal policy (Keynesian case)

The difference between i_0 to i_1 depends on the interest sensitivity of money demand to rate of interest. If money demand is interest inelastic the LM curve will be vertical. Less the sensitivity of money demand to rate of interest steeper the LM curve will be. Therefore, more the demand for money is interest inelastic resulting increase in output (real) will be less. The reason behind this is that investment is negatively related with the rate of interest. As the rate of interest is high investment will be low. Resulting effect of this is low output. This is depicted in the following figure.

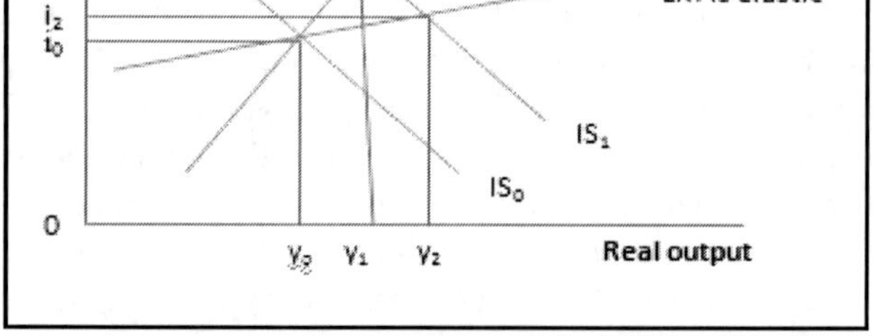

Source: Rosalind, L., & Alexander, R.1982

Figure 4.13: Sensitivity of money demand to rate of interest and LM curve.

The effect of pure expansionary fiscal policy depends on the slope of IS curve. If investment is interest inelastic (investment is autonomous) i.e., IS curve is vertical then output will increase more. If investment is interest elastic or interest responsive the effect of increase in government expenditure or tax cut will increase output less.

Therefore, it can be concluded that fiscal policy will be more effective if

(i) demand for money should be more responsive or sensitive to rate of interest,

(ii) investment is less responsive or sensitive to rate of interest.

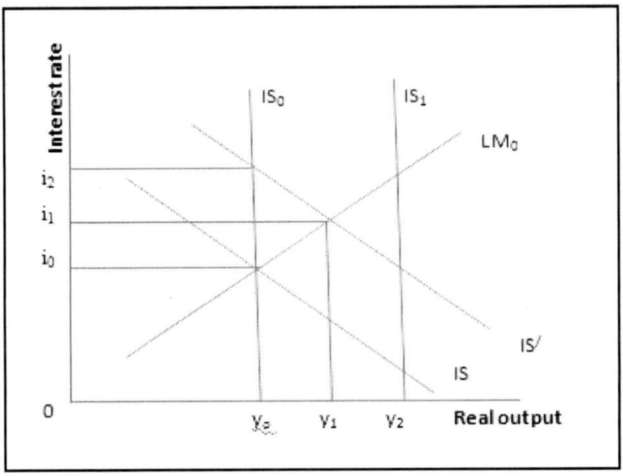

Source: Rosalind, L., & Alexander, R.1982.

Figure 4.14: Sensitivity of investment to rate of interest and IS curve.

An expansionary or tightening monetary policy in Keynesian ISLM

If government takes expansionary monetary policy money supply will increase through open market operation by the central bank in government bonds and as a result of that output will increase and interest rate will fall. In our figure it is depicted very clearly. As money supply increases money market will not clear. Money demand is less than money supply. To get equilibrium in the money market money demand will increases in terms of bond. As demand for bond increases price of bond raises and bond interest rate falls. As a result of decrease in interest rate investment will increase and output will also increase. In case of tightening monetary policy the results will be opposite. Effectiveness of monetary policy depends on sensitivity of money demand to rate of interest and sensitivity of investment to rate of interest. If money demand is less sensitive to interest rate and investment is more interest sensitive.

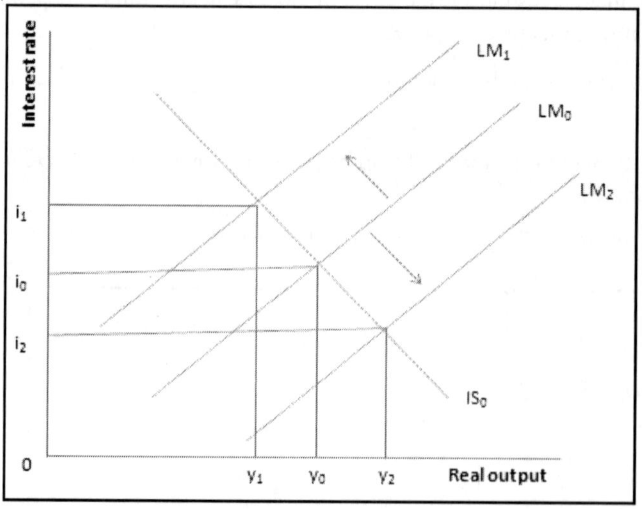

Source: Rosalind, L., & Alexander, R.1982.

Figure 15: Expansionary or tightening monetary policy in Keynesian ISLM.

Crowding out

In the neoclassical model real output is unaffected by fiscal policy. Only interest rate and price level change. When government takes expansionary fiscal policy (increase in government expenditure or reduction in taxes) IS curve shifts upward. As this is financed by selling bonds demand for bonds will increase. As a result of that bond price will increase. This will reduce real money stock. LM curve shifts leftward. To get equilibrium in money market demand for money will reduce resulting increase in real interest rate. Higher rate of interest siphons off private investment and public investment/expenditure will take place in place of private investment. This is called crowding out effect. If expansionary fiscal policy generates from reduction in taxes then higher rate of interest shifts resources from investment to consumption.

The opposite will happen in case of tightening fiscal policy. IS curve will shift leftward. Bond price falls. Real stock of money increases. LM curve shifts rightward. Interest rate would fall.

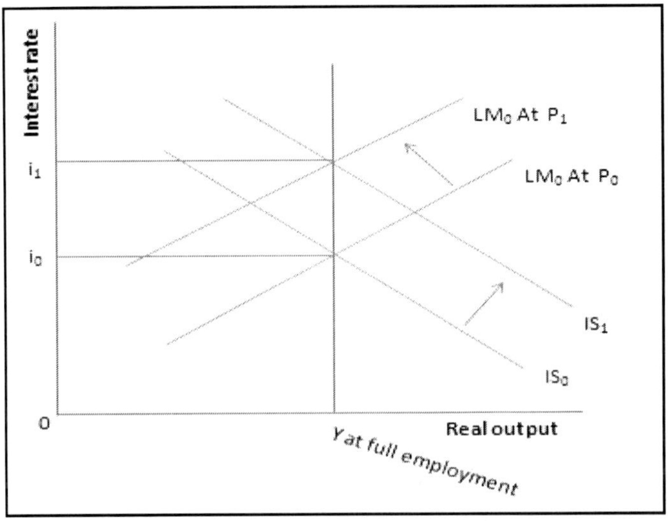

Source: Rosalind, L., & Alexander, R.1982.

Figure 4.16[10]: Crowding out in neoclassical ISLM

An expansionary or tightening monetary policy in Neoclassical ISLM

Figure 4.16: Expansionary or tightening monetary policy in neoclassical ISLM

Problem

Given the ISLM framework consider the effects of

(i) Increase in money supply.

(ii) Increase in Government expenditure.

(iii) Increase in taxes.

Equation for the LM curve:

$$M_0^s = C_0 + C_1Y - C_2r$$

$$Or, r = \frac{C_0}{C_2} - \frac{1}{C_2}(M_0^s) + \frac{C_1}{C_2}$$

where, C_1 implies income sensitivity to money demand, C_2 implies interest rate sensitivity to money demand.

Taking derivative,

$$\frac{\Delta r}{\Delta Y} = \frac{C_1}{C_2}$$

Therefore, Slope of the LM curve = $\frac{C_1}{C_2}$

Equation for the IS curve:

$I + G = S + T$

Since $I = \bar{I} - t_1 r$

where, i_1 implies interest sensitivity to investment and $\bar{I}$ implies autonomous investment.

Since $Y = C + S + T$

$$\text{Or, } S = -C + (Y - T)$$

$$\text{Or, } S = -(a + bY_D) + (Y - T)$$

$$\text{Or, } S = -a + bY_D + Y_D$$

$$\text{Or, } S = -a + (1 - b)Y_D$$

$$\text{Or, } S = -a + (1 - b)(Y - T)$$

Therefore, From the IS curve

$I + G = S + T$

Putting $I = \bar{I} - i_1 r$ and $S = -a + (1 - b)(Y - T)$

We get, $\bar{I} - i_1 r + G = -a + (1 - b)(Y - T) + T$

$$\text{Or, } \bar{I} - i_1 r + G = -a + (1 - b)(Y - T) + T$$

$$\text{Or, } \bar{I} - i_1 r + G = -a + (1 - b)Y - T + bT + T$$

$$\text{Or, } (1 - b)Y = \bar{I} - i_1 r + G + a - bT$$

$$\text{Or, } Y = \frac{1}{1-b}[a + \bar{I} + G - bT] - \frac{i_1}{1-b}r$$

Therefore, Slope of the IS curve

$$\frac{\Delta r}{\Delta Y} = -\frac{(1 - b)}{i_1}$$

where , (1-b) implies marginal propensity to save.

(i) Increase in money supply affects the intercept of the LM equation. Increase in money supply shifts the LM downward and to the right. As a result of that rate of interest falls and income increases. In our figure i_1 an Y_1 respectively.

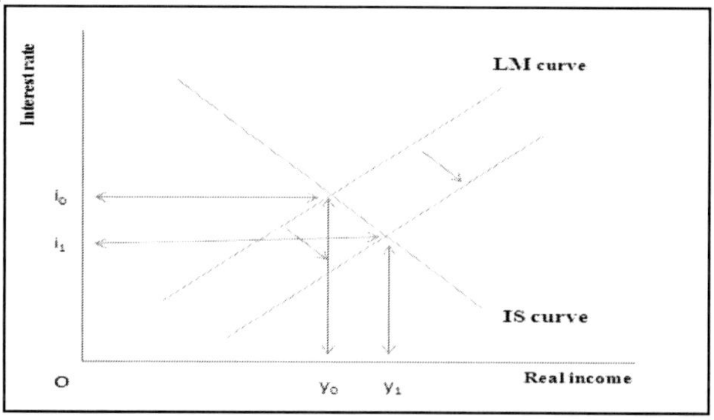

(ii) An interest rate r_0, an increase in government spending increases the total of investment plus government spending from $I_0 + G_0$ to $I_0 + G_1$. To maintain the condition $I + G = S + T$, with a fixed level of taxes, saving must rise from S_0 to S_1, which requires income to be Y_1 instead of Y_0. At interest rate r_0, the equilibrium point in the product market is point B, instead of point A. An increase in government spending shifts the IS schedule to the right from IS_0 to IS_1. From the equation of IS curve we have

$$Y = \frac{1}{1-b}[a + \bar{I} + G - bT] - \frac{i_1}{1-b}r$$

The required increase in income (the horizontal shift in the IS curve) will be

$$\frac{\Delta Y}{\Delta G} = \frac{1}{(1-b)} = \frac{1}{mps}$$

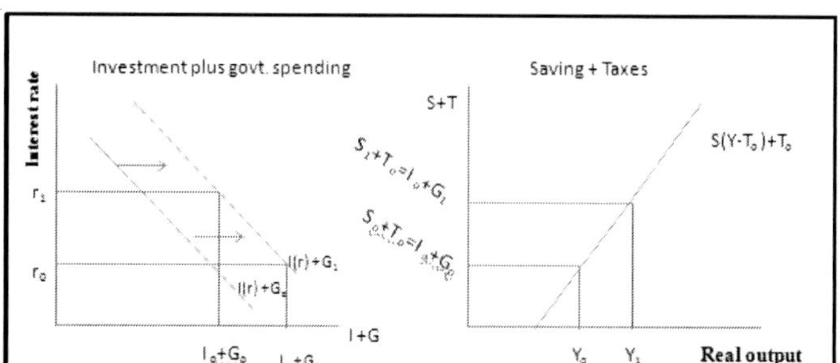

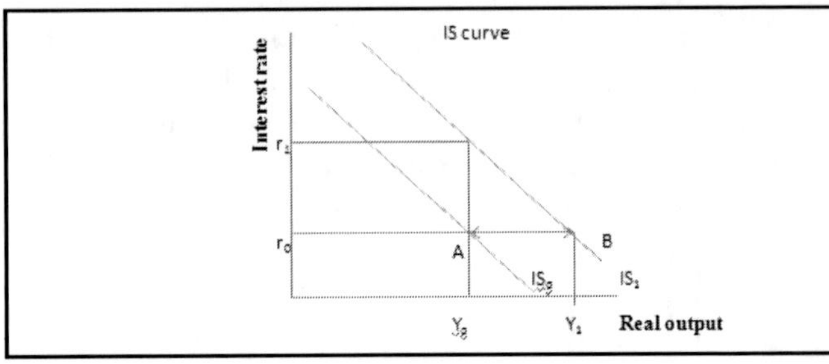

(iii) An increase in taxes shifts the S +T schedule to the left. At r_0 which fixes $I_0 + G_0$, with higher taxes, saving and therefore, income must be lower to maintain the condition I + G = S + T. After the tax increase, an income level of Y_1 (point B) rather than Y_0 (point A) clears the product market for interest rate r_0. The IS curve shifts leftward from IS_0 to IS_1. For a given rate of interest a tax change does not affect the left hand side of the equilibrium condition for the product market

$I(r)+G=S(Y-Y)+T$; Investment and government spending are unchanged. So for equilibrium at the same interest rate, the right-hand side must be unchanged; saving plus taxes must be unchanged. This condition requires that the increase in taxes be exactly balanced by declining in saving,

$$0 = \Delta S + \Delta T$$

Change in saving

$$\Delta S = (1-b)\Delta(Y-T) = (1-b)\Delta Y - (1-b)\Delta T$$

Since $\Delta S + \Delta T = 0$

Or, $(1-b)\Delta Y - (1-b)\Delta T + \Delta T = 0$

Or, $(1-b)\Delta Y - \Delta T + b\Delta T + \Delta T = 0$

Or, $(1-b)\Delta Y = -b\Delta T$

Or, $\Delta Y = -\frac{b}{1-b}\Delta T$

The amount by which the IS curve shifts to the left for a one unit increase in taxes is $-\frac{-b}{1-b}$.

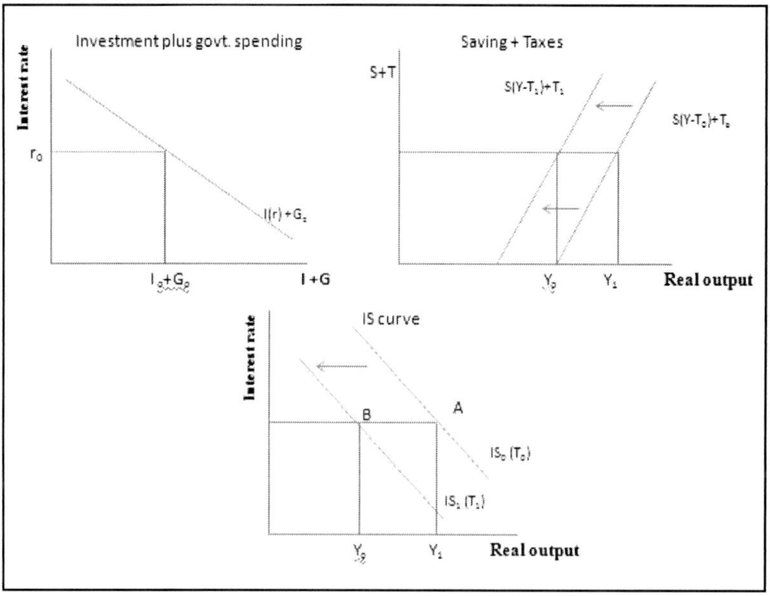
Investment plus govt. spending
Interest rate
r_0
$I(r) + G_1$
I_0+G_0
I + G
Saving + Taxes
S+T
$S(Y-T_1)+T_1$
$S(Y-T_0)+T_0$
Y_0
Y_1
Real output
IS curve
Interest rate
B
A
$IS_0\ (T_0)$
$IS_1\ (T_1)$
Y_0
Y_1
Real output

Chapter - 5

The Mundell –Fleming Model: Money, Capital Flows and the Open Economy

Before going into the deep of the analysis we should have an idea of high-powered money. High-powered money is nothing but equivalent to the foreign exchange reserves with credit creation by central bank of that particular country.

High-powered money = Foreign exchange reserve + Credit creation........(1)

Any change in high-powered money must be equivalent to the change in foreign exchange reserve or change in credit creation or to the change in both the variables in the right hand side.

[Balance of payments consists of two accounts. One is current account and another is capital account. Current account balance shows the summation of net payments to the rest of the world and of the net payments from the rest of the world. It may be surplus or it may be deficit. On the other hand capital account balance shows net capital flows to the country. Net capital flows= other countries' holding of the country's assets – the country's holdings of other countries assets. It also may be surplus or deficit. If current account balance is balanced by capital account balance then balance of payments is equal to zero (BOP=0). If the central bank purchases domestic currency from the foreign exchange reserve market foreign exchange reserves fall by the same amount and vice versa. So change of foreign reserves is equal to BOP.]

Equation (1) can be written as

$$\Delta \text{ High powered money} = \Delta \text{ Foreign exchange reserve} + \Delta \text{ Credit creation} \qquad \text{............... (2)}$$

$$\Delta \text{ High powered money} \equiv \text{BOP} + \Delta \text{ Credit creation} \qquad \text{...............(3)}$$

It is known to us

Domestic money supply = (bank multiplier) multiplied by High powered money

or, Domestic money supply = (bank multiplier) multiplied by *(Foreign exchange reserve + Credit creation)*

or, ΔDomestic money supply = (bank multiplier) multiplied by *(ΔForeign exchange reserve + ΔCredit creation)* ....(4)

From equation (4) it can be concluded that to make the money supply constant change in credit creation should be equal to negative change in foreign exchange reserve. So the effects of foreign exchange reserves or BOP on money stocks can be paralyzed by the central bank. This is the Keynesian understanding of paralyzing of the effect of BOP on money stock by the central bank. But the monetarists do not believe in such understanding.

Mundell-Fleming model (at the start of the 1960s) is an extension of Keynesian open-economy model. According to them net capital flows depends on the difference between the domestic and foreign interest rates. Here it is assumed that expectation about the change of the exchange rate is stagnant.

They reproduced the balance of payments on capital account by the following equation:

[2]Balance of payments on capital account = $\phi\ (i - i_f)$

Balance of payments on capital account is a positive function of the difference between the domestic and foreign interest rates. As the difference increases balance of payments on capital account also increases.

[The balance of payments on current account can be formulated in the following way.

Current Account = Exports is the function of exchange rate + Marginal propensity to import multiplied by income level

Or, $CA = X(e) + fy$

Since

Balance of Payments = Balance of payments on current account + Balance of payments on capital account.

[3]Balance of Payments $X(e) + f(e)y + \phi\ (i{-}i_f)$ ....(5)

Since BOP= ΔFR

$\Delta FR \equiv X(e) + f(e)y + \phi\ (i{-}i_f)$

2. Rosalind, L., & Alexander, R. 1982, pp. 165.
3. Rosalind, L., & Alexander, R. 1982, pp. 166.

In the long-run equilibrium BOP is zero. So equilibrium solution for foreign exchange market is as follows[4]

$$0 \equiv X(e) + f(e)y + \phi\,(i - i_f) \qquad \text{...............(6)}$$

So foreign exchange market is a function of domestic income and interest rate. As import is a positive function of income if income increases current account deteriorates. In the long-run to make BOP=0 deterioration must be counteracted by the enhancement of capital account. The capital account can be improved by increasing the difference between the foreign interest rate and domestic interest rate. Foreign interest rate should be greater than domestic interest rate to improve the capital account.

BOP=0 may have three forms that are depicted in the following figures.

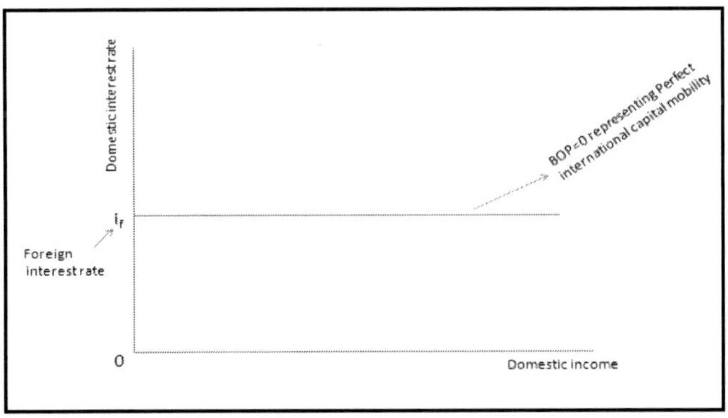

Source: Rosalind, L., & Alexander, R.1982.

Figure-5.1: BOP=0; Representing Perfect International Capital mobility.

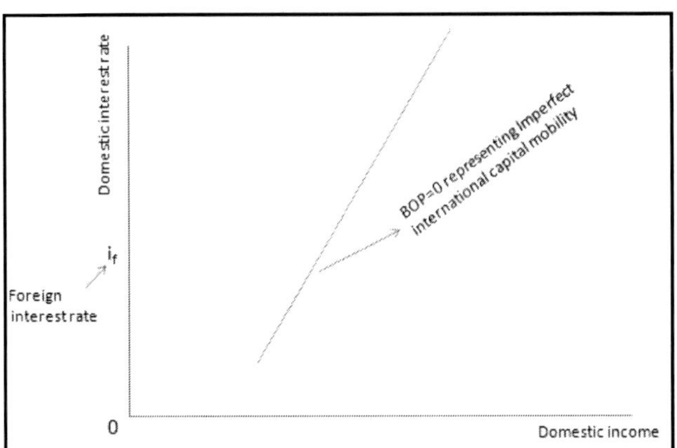

Source: Rosalind, L., & Alexander, R.1982.

Figure-5.2: BOP=0; Representing Imperfect International Capital mobility.

4. Rosalind, L., & Alexander, R. 1982, pp. 166.

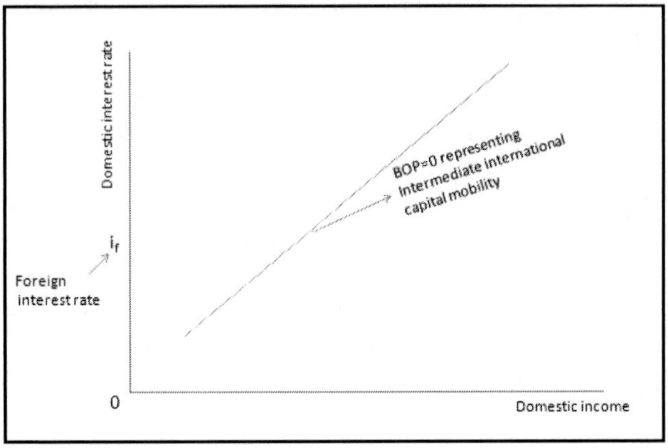

Source: Rosalind, L., & Alexander, R.1982.

Figure-5.3: BOP=0; Representing Intermediate International Capital mobility.

Any point above the BOP=0 represents BOP surplus and any point to the right of BOP=0 represents deficit (foreign rate of interest is higher than the domestic rate of interest). Depreciation of the currency or increase in foreign interest rate shifts the BOP=0 to right and the appreciation of the currency or decrease in the foreign interest rate shifts to the left.

[5]The complete Mundell-Fleming model consists of three equations.

Equation-1

$$0 \equiv X(e) + f(e)y + \phi\,(i - i_f)$$

Equation-2

$$y = \frac{a + I(i) + G_0 X(e)}{s(1-t) + tf(e)} \text{ is the IS function.}$$

Equation-3

$$\frac{M^3}{P} = f(y, i) \text{ is the LM function.}$$

[Goods market equation including foreign sector is as follows

$$y = C + I + G + X - \frac{1}{s}F \qquad \text{...(i)}$$

where y is the level of income, C is consumption, G is government expenditure, X is exports and F is imports, e is the exchange rate.

1. Rosalind, L., & Alexander, R. 1982, pp. 167

As imports depends on domestic income y and e we can write

$$F = f(e)y$$

or, $\frac{1}{e}F = \frac{1}{e}f(e)y$

or, $\frac{1}{e}F$ = marginal efficiency to import y

or, $\frac{1}{e}F = f.y$

or, $\frac{1}{e}F = f.y$ ...(ii)

Aggregate demand equation so that goods market is in equilibrium

$$y = C + I + G_0 + (X–F) \quad \text{...(iii)}$$

Aggregate income equation so that goods market is in equilibrium

$$y = C + S + T \quad \text{...(iv)}$$

Equating equation (iii) and (iv) we get

$$S + T + G_0 + (X - F) \quad \text{...(v)}$$

Savings function can be written as

$$S = - a + s\,(y - T)$$

Investment is a function of domestic rate of interest i.e., i So

$$\mathrm{I} = \mathrm{I}\,(i)$$

T = ty where t is the tax rate.

Now substituting the value of S, T, I in equation (v) we get,

$$\mathrm{I}(i) + G_0 + (X - F) = -a + s(y - ty) + ty$$

or, $\mathrm{I}(i) + G_0 + X(e) - f(e)y = -a + s(y - ty) + ty$

or, $\mathrm{I}(i) + G_0 + X(e) - f(e)y = -a + s(1 - t)y + ty$

or, $\mathrm{I}(i) + G_0 + X(e) - f(e)y = -a + [s(1 - t) + t]y$

or, $\mathrm{I}(i) + G_0 + X(e) = -a + [s(1 - t) + t]y + f(e)y$

or, $a + \mathrm{I}(i) + G_0 + X(e) = [s(1 - t) + t + f(e)]y$

or, $y = \frac{a+\mathrm{I}(i)+G_0+X(e)}{[(s(1-t)+t+f(e)]}$ is the IS function.]

Impact of fiscal policy on the level of income and employment under fixed exchange rates

Depending on the slope of the BOP=0 the impact of fiscal policy is on the level of income under fixed exchange rate. Slope of the BOP represents the sensitivity of BOP to domestic rate of interest. As much as the curve is flat more is the sensitivity of BOP=0 to rate of interest. Therefore, capital inflow depends on the slope of the BOP.

If the government takes expansionary fiscal policy (expansion of government expenditure or cut in tax rate or both) IS curve shifts to the upward.

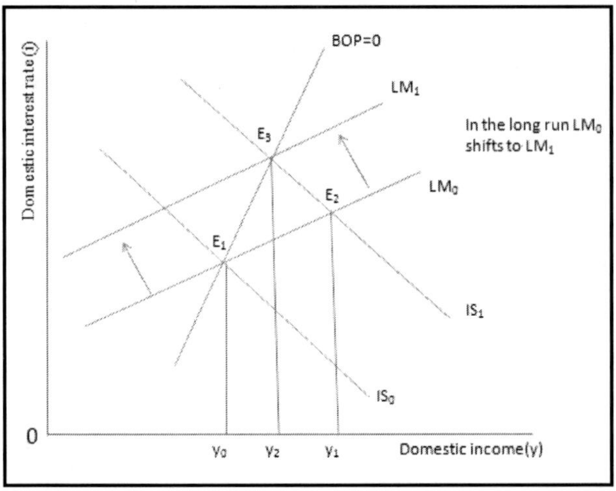

Source: Rosalind, L., & Alexander, R.1982.

Figure- 5.4: Impact of Fiscal Policy.

As a result of that domestic rate of interest is lower than the foreign rate of interest. It creates capital outflow. Due to expansionary fiscal policy income increases from Y_0 to Y_1. Current account deterioration due to increase in real income and capital out flow bring BOP deficit. The new short-run quasi equilibrium is E_2. This BOP deficit can be balanced by central bank by purchasing domestic currency from the foreign exchange reserve market. But persistent BOP deficit cannot be controlled by the central bank as the reserve of the foreign currency declines due to the persistent purchase of domestic currency. So in the short-run central bank can balance the BOP effect on money stock. But in the long-run it is not possible. Money supply will shrink and LM_0 shifts to LM_{-1}. This is the situation where money market, goods market and foreign exchange market are in equilibrium i.e., BOP=0.

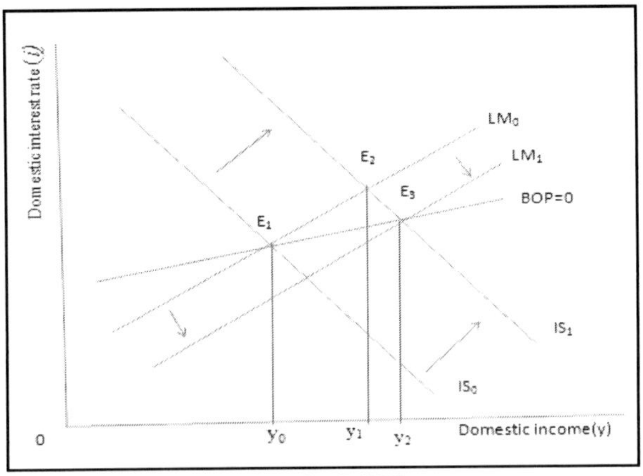

Source: Rosalind, L., & Alexander, R.1982.

Figure- 5.5: Impact of Fiscal Policy.

Now if the BOP=0 is interest elastic the slope of the BOP is less than the slope of LM_0. Due to the expansionary fiscal policy IS_0 curve shifts to IS_1. Income increases from Y_0 to Y_1. Here BOP is surplus depending on new income and higher interest rate. In the short-run income increases but in the long-run it is not possible. Money supply will increase until the foreign rate of interest is equal to the domestic rate of interest i.e., BOP=0. Original fiscal policy will be more effective due to the induced monetary expansion. Now the income level is Y_2 higher than previous Y_1. So the effectiveness of fiscal policy under fixed exchange rate regime depends on the slope of the BOP or the responsiveness of BOP to domestic rate of interest rate.

Impact of monetary policy on the level of income and employment under fixed exchange rates

Impact of monetary policy on the level of income is depicted in the following figure-5.6 and figure-5.7. In figure-5.6 expansionary monetary policies and in figure-5.7 contractionary monetary policies are clearly depicted.

Expansionary monetary policy shifts the LM_0 curve to LM_1. As a result of that domestic rate of interest falls and real income increases. The negative difference between the domestic and foreign interest rates brings deficit in capital account and increase in real income deteriorate current account. As a whole there is BOP deficit. To maintain BOP deficit foreign reserve in the hand of the central bank falls down and in the long run as foreign reserve declines high powered money also declines. As , money supply

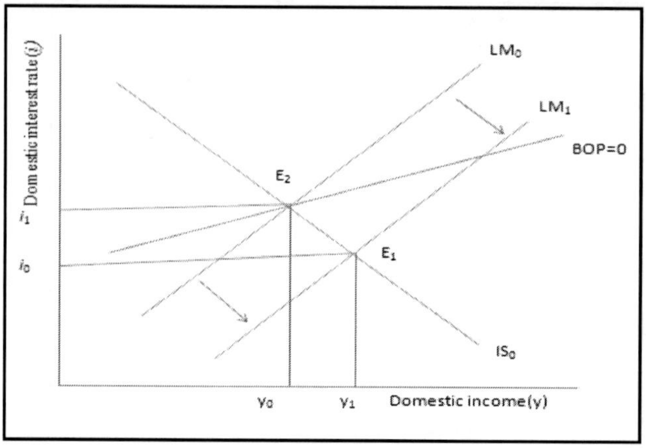

Source: Rosalind, L., & Alexander, R.1982.

Figure-5.6: Impact of Monetary Policy under Fixed Exchange Rate.

will shrink. LM_1 shifts back to LM_0 to its original level where original domestic rate of interest and income and employment are maintained.

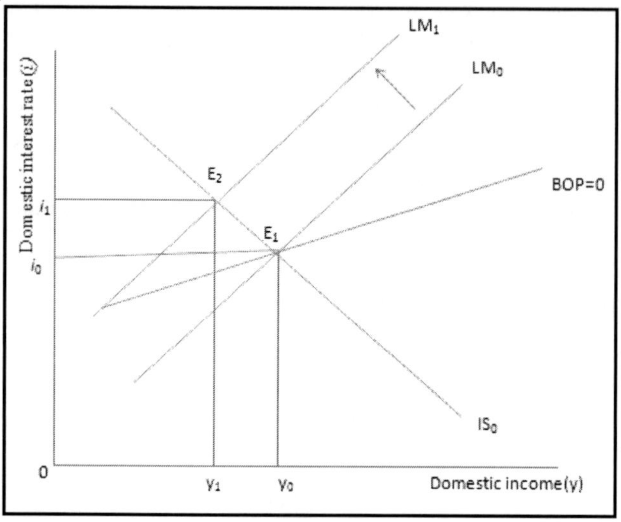

Source: Rosalind, L., & Alexander, R.1982.

Figure-5.7: Impact of Monetary Policy under Fixed Monetary Policy.

Contractionary monetary policy shifts the LM_0 curve to LM_1 in figure-7. As a result of that domestic rate of interest raises and real income declines. The positive difference between the domestic and foreign interest rates brings surplus in capital account and decrease in real income improves current account. As a whole there is BOP surplus. To maintain BOP surplus foreign reserve in the hand of the central bank raises and in the long run as foreign reserve raise high powered money also rises. As $M^s = mH$, money supply will grow. LM_1 shifts back to LM_0 to its original level where original domestic rate of interest and income and employment are maintained.

Impact of monetary policy on the level of income and employment under flexible exchange rates

The basic difference between the fixed and flexible exchange rate regime is that in both short and long-run change in foreign reserve is always constant in flexible exchange rate regime that is there is always domestic autonomy for monetary policy but under fixed exchange rate regime in the short-run there is no domestic autonomy for monetary policy. In the long-run there is domestic autonomy for monetary policy under fixed exchange rate regime.

Under flexible exchange rate regime monetary policy affects the economy through the variation in the real wage rate and in the relative price of domestic to foreign goods. The change in the relative price of domestic to foreign goods comes as a result of change in the exchange rate.

Now suppose the monetary authority adopts expansionary monetary policy. As a result of that LM curve shifts to LM_0 to LM_1. It is clearly depicted in our figure-5.8. As LM_0 shifts to LM_1 domestic rate of interest

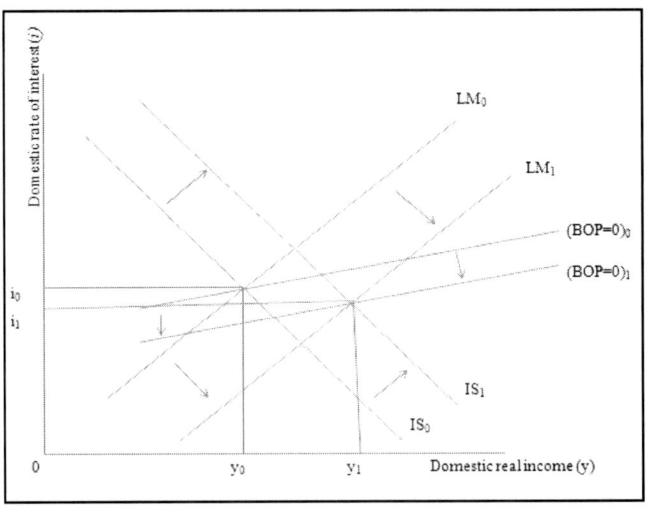

Source: Rosalind, L., & Alexander, R.1982.

Figure-5.8: Impact of Monetary Policy under Flexible Exchange Rate.

falls and the difference between domestic rate of interest and foreign rate of interest is negative. The capital account will deteriorate. As this situation is in the flexible exchange rate regime exchange rate depreciates. Depreciation of the exchange rate lowers the price of export and makes costly the price of import and this situation improves the current account balance. So deterioration of capital account and improvement of current account makes the BOP=0. As the domestic demand shifts to domestic goods and foreign demand also to domestic goods due to the depreciation of the exchange rate shifts IS to the upward and BOP curve towards rightward. Therefore, as a result of monetary expansion income increases from Y_0 to Y_1.

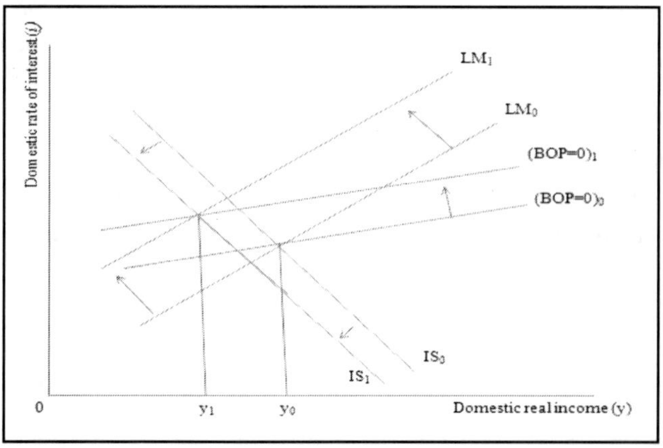

Source: Rosalind, L., & Alexander, R.1982.

Figure-5.9: Impact of Monetary Policy under Flexible Exchanger Rate.

Now suppose the monetary authority adopts contractionary monetary policy. As a result of that LM curve shifts to LM_0 to LM_1 in figure-5.9. As LM_0 shifts to LM_1 domestic rate of interest raises and the difference between domestic rate of interest and foreign rate of interest is positive. The capital account will be in surplus. As this situation is in the flexible exchange rate regime exchange rate appreciates. Appreciation of the exchange rate makes higher the price of export and makes lower the price of import and this situation deteriorates the current account balance. So improvement of capital account and deterioration of current account makes the BOP=0. As the domestic demand shifts to foreign goods and foreigners do not demand for domestic goods due to the appreciation of the exchange rate shifts IS to the leftward and BOP curve upwards. Therefore, as a result of monetary contraction income decreases from Y_0 level to lower Y_1 level.

Impact of fiscal policy on the level of income and employment under flexible exchange rates

Impact of fiscal policy on the level of income and employment depends on the slope of the BOP=0. If it is perfectly interest elastic then impact of fiscal policy on the economy is ineffective. If BOP is interest inelastic or less elastic expansionary fiscal policy has positive effect on the economy.

Now if the government takes expansionary fiscal policy under flexible exchange rate regime IS curve will shift from IS_0 to IS_1. The whole scenario has been depicted in the figure-10. The new equilibrium point is below the equilibrium point necessary to make three markets in equilibrium i.e., money market, goods market and foreign exchange market. So BOP is deficit in the new equilibrium (Capital and current account both are deficits.). It is known to us any point to the right of BOP=0 is deficit. As BOP is deficit exchange rate depreciates and this depreciation makes export price lower and import price higher. Therefore domestic demand as well as foreign demand for domestic goods increase and this situation shifts IS curve further from IS_1 to IS_2. On the other hand depreciation of exchange rate shifts $(BOP=0)_0$ to $(BOP=)_1$ to the rightwards. So income increases from Y_0 to Y_1 and further to Y_2. Therefore, it can be concluded that expansionary fiscal policy does have much more effect on the economy under flexible exchange rate regime.

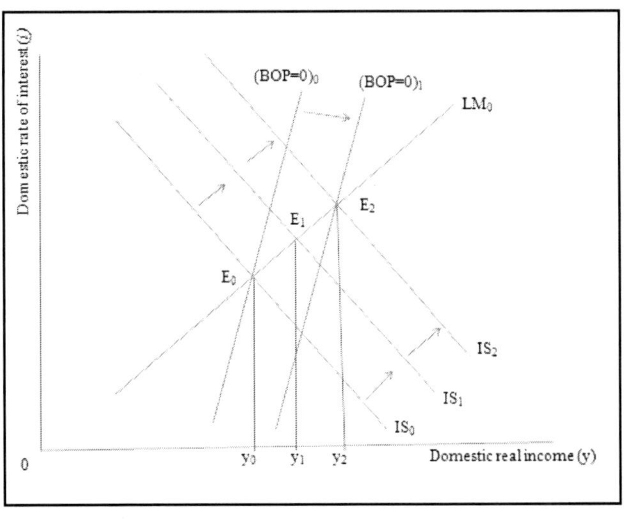

Source: Rosalind, L., & Alexander, R.1982.

Figure-5.10: Expansion Fiscal policy under Flexible Exchange Rate.

Now if the government takes expansionary fiscal policy under flexible exchange rate regime where BOP=0 is perfectly interest elastic. IS curve will shift from IS_0 to IS_1. The whole scenario has been depicted in the figure-5.11. The new equilibrium point is above the equilibrium point necessary to make three markets in equilibrium i.e., money market, goods market and foreign exchange market. So BOP is surplus in the new equilibrium (Capital and current account both are surplus.). It is known to us any point to the left of BOP=0 is surplus. As BOP is surplus exchange rate appreciates and this appreciation makes export price higher and import price lower. Therefore domestic demand as well as foreign demand for domestic goods decrease and this situation shifts IS curve back from IS_1 to IS_0. So income remains unchanged at Y_0. Therefore it can be concluded that expansionary fiscal policy does not have any effect on the economy under flexible exchange rate regime where BOP=0 is perfectly elastic.

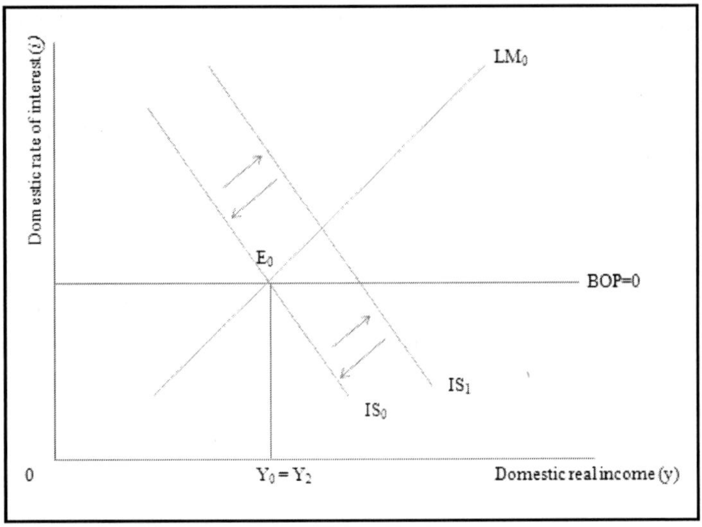

Source: Rosalind, L., & Alexander, R.1982.

Figure-5.11: Impact of Expansionary Fiscal Policy when BOP is perfectly Elastic.

Chapter - 6

Phillips Curve Analysis

The relation between price level and real output is a matter of concern in both neoclassical and Keynesian analysis. Prices are flexible in the neoclassical model and clear the market but in the Keynesian model prices are rigid and remain the market unclear.

Phillips published his article in the year 1958. He took two variables. One is average rate of change of nominal wage rate and another is average rate of change of unemployment. He used UK data over the period 1861-1957. He found a non linear and inverse relationship between the variables concerned. The relationship was stable. It means that the relationship sustains for long period. The concept of price level can be easily introduced in the model. If rate of increase in money wage is same with the rate of increase in the labor productivity then cost of production will not change. So no role of rate of change of price level. If there is a difference between the average rate of increase in nominal wage and average rate of increase in labor productivity the average rate of increase in price level will be equal with the difference.

[6] $$\frac{\dot{P}}{P} = \frac{\dot{W}}{W} - \frac{\dot{Q}}{Q} \text{ where } \dot{P} = \frac{dp}{dt}, \dot{W} = \frac{dW}{dt} \text{ and } \dot{Q} = \frac{dQ}{dt}$$

Policy makers used Phillips curve to reduce unemployment rate permanently. Samuelson and Solow treated the Phillips curve in the same way. But neoclassical thinkers did not believe in that. According to them prices do not have any effect on the real variables. If we see the complete neoclassical model then we find that aggregate supply curve is vertical line and shift in aggregate demand only changes in price level keeping output unchanged. Neoclassical aggregate demand curve can be found by joining all those combinations of output (y) and price level (p). These combinations are found from ISLM intersections at different price level. According to

1. Rosalind, L., & Alexander, R. 1982, pp. 339.

the neoclassical model equilibrium interest rate (i) and output(y) are determined quite independently in the goods market. By equalization of savings and investment equilibrium rate of interest is determined. Equilibrium price level is determined in the money market. Once equilibrium output is determined demand for money balances are required and equilibrium price level equalizes the demand for money balances with the supply of money. Aggregate supply curve is vertical as because price level does not have any effect on supply of output. If prices fall then real wages will rise and it reduces the demand for labor. Until the real wage at its equilibrium level nominal wage will fall. There will be no excess supply of labor. Following figures depict that prices change but equilibrium values of real variables are invariant with changes in equilibrium price level brought about by changes in money supply.

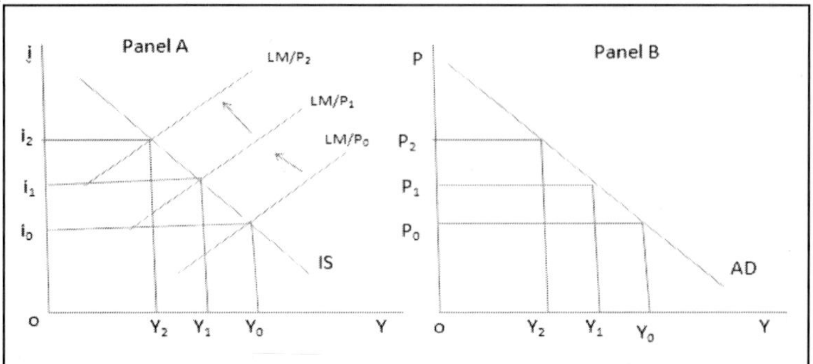

Derivation of Aggregate Demand Curve

Source: Rosalind, L., & Alexander, R.1982, pp. 82.

Figure 6.1: Neoclassical aggregate demand curve.

The aggregate demand function indicates how the volume of real aggregate demand rises as the price level falls. As the price level rises, the real value of the money stock falls, so the LM curve shifts up to the left. This is depicted in panel-A of figure-6.1. Panel-B gives aggregate demand curve which represents the price level and the corresponding level of aggregate demand. It represents simultaneous equilibrium in the goods and money markets. Change in exogenous variables such as government spending or nominal money stock shifts the IS and LM function respectively.

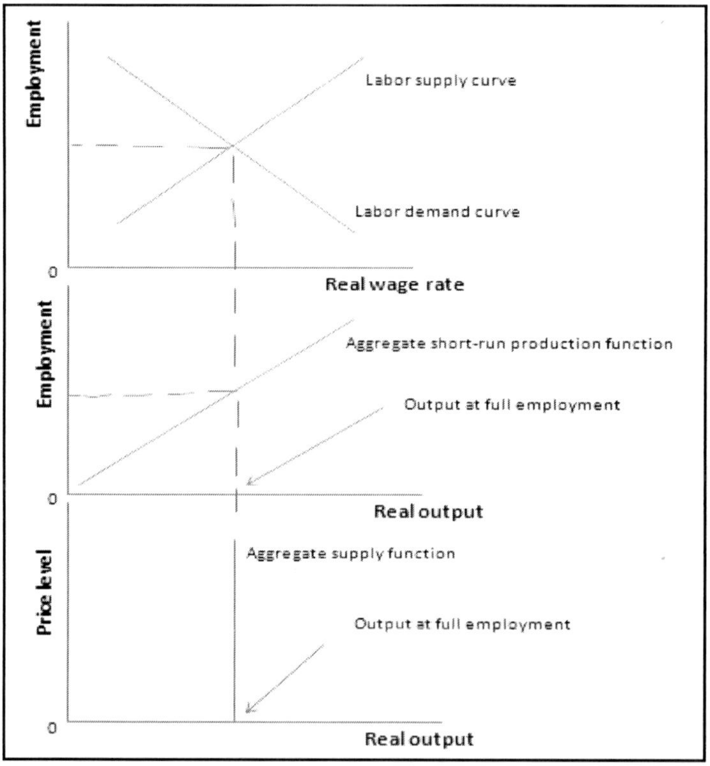

Source: Rosalind, L., & Alexander, R.1982.

Figure 6.2: Neoclassical aggregate supply curve.

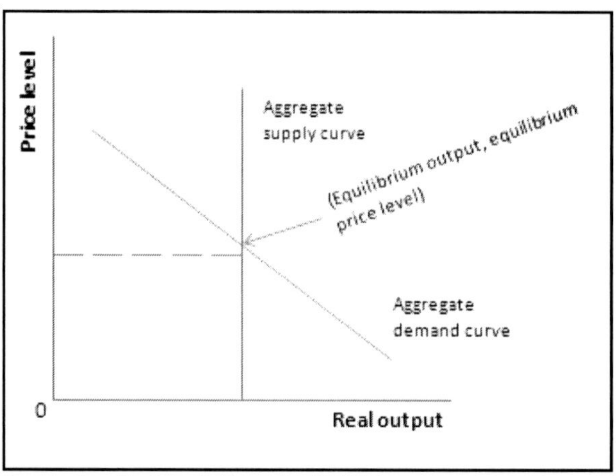

Source: Rosalind, L., & Alexander, R.1982

Figure 6.3: Complete neoclassical model.

Now we try to understand the theoretical background of Phillips relation. Lipsey had a great role here. Keeping other things constant average rate of change of nominal wage i.e.,

$\frac{\dot{W}}{W} = \frac{dW/dt}{dt} = \frac{1}{W}\frac{dW}{dt}$ is a function of excess demand for labor to supply of labor. This can be written as

$$\frac{\dot{W}}{W} = f\left(\frac{Demand\ for\ labor - Supply\ of\ labor}{Supply\ of\ labor}\right)$$

$$\frac{\dot{W}}{W} = f\left(\frac{Employed\ labor + Vacancies) - (Undemployed\ labor + Employed\ labor}{Undemployed\ labor + Employed\ labor}\right)$$

$$\frac{\dot{W}}{W} = f\left(\frac{Vacancies + Undemployed\ labor}{Undemployed\ labor + Employed\ labor}\right)$$

Vacancies and unemployed labor are inversely related. So numerator is a negative part. Therefore, as whole average rate of nominal wage is a function of unemployment and it has an inverse relationship. i.e., $\frac{\dot{W}}{W} = f(U)$.

The Phillips curve crosses the horizontal axis at the frictional unemployment. The frictional unemployment exists in any economy due to people being in the process of moving from one job to another.

Natural Rate Hypothesis: Cynics in his article showed that there is no stable relationship between inflation and unemployment. He made a statistical investigation between inflation and unemployment over the data 1960-1981 in the UK economy. He found that combinations between inflation and unemployment are scattered on the positive quadrant and he concluded that there is no stable relationship. After the Cynics's investigation Phillips curve gets a question mark regarding its policy implication. A new theoretical model developed by Friedman and Phelps supported the Cynics's findings. They said that inflation and unemployment bears a short run relationship but in the long-run there is no trade off. According to Friedman this is because of real wages. In Phillips analysis nominal wages was considered. So he found a stable relationship. Phillips also considered zero expected inflation.

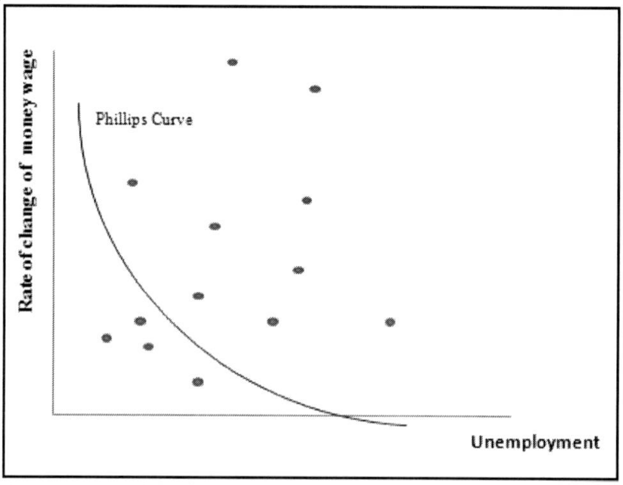

Source: Rosalind, L., & Alexander, R. 1982.

Figure 6.4: Phillips Curve and Cynics observation.

Now we try to understand the inflation and unemployment relationship from Friedman point of view.

[7]According to Friedman average rate of increase in real wage is a negative function of unemployment rate i.e.,

$$\frac{\dot{W}}{W} = f(U)$$

We know that nominal wage = Real wage + Inflation. So

$$\frac{\dot{w}}{w} = \frac{\dot{W}}{W} - \frac{\dot{P}}{P}$$

i.e., Average rate of increase in real wage = Average rate of increase in nominal wage – Average rate of increase in price level or inflation.

As now workers have to calculate real wage from their nominal wage the concept of expectation gets place here. The two terms expected inflation and actual inflation now matter. Without expecting inflation workers could not calculate their real wage from nominal wage.

Since,

$$\frac{\dot{w}}{w} = \frac{\dot{W}}{W} - \frac{\dot{P}}{P}$$

7. Rosalind, L., & Alexander, R. 1982, pp. 343.

Or,

$$\frac{\dot{w}}{w} = \frac{\dot{W}}{W} E\left(\frac{\dot{P}}{P}\right)$$

where, $E\left(\frac{\dot{P}}{P}\right)$ is the expected rate of inflation.

Now,

$$\frac{\dot{w}}{w} = \frac{\dot{W}}{W} E\left(\frac{\dot{P}}{P}\right)$$

$$Or, f(U)\frac{\dot{W}}{W} - E\left(\frac{\dot{P}}{P}\right)$$

$$Or, \ \frac{\dot{W}}{W} f(U) + \alpha E\left(\frac{\dot{P}}{P}\right)$$

[8]This equation is known as expectation augmented Phillips curve. The term á is a parameter. If á is equal to zero then the equation is a Phillips curve. If á is equal to 1 there is no money illusion or in another sense we can say workers are rational. If á is less than 1 and greater than 0, then workers adjust their nominal wage with real wage partially. Workers do have money illusion in the short run. In the short- run they do not be able to take inflation fully into their account when they are calculating their real wage from their given nominal wage.

Now by explaining the following figure we try to prove that in the long-run there is no stable relationship between inflation and unemployment. i.e., there is no trade off between the variables concerned. It is assumed that there is no money illusion. So the expectation augmented Phillips equation will be

$$\frac{\dot{W}}{W} f(U) + E\left(\frac{\dot{P}}{P}\right)$$

When expected inflation is zero the Phillips curve is PC. U_n is the natural rate of unemployment. If government is convinced by the stable Phillips relation then govt. takes expansionary policy and increase money supply. This increase in money supply will increase price level as demand for goods

8. Rosalind, L., & Alexander, R. 1982, pp. 344.

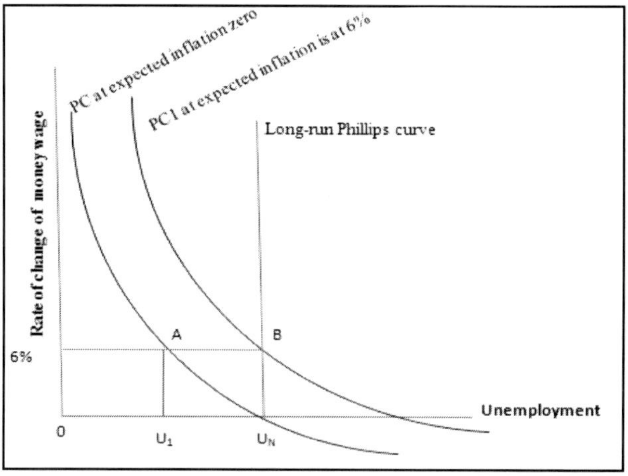

Source: Rosalind, L., & Alexander, R.1982.

Figure 6.5: The Expectation Augmented Phillips Curve.

is increased. As price rises real wage declines and producers will employ more labor to produce more output. Producers will provide higher wage but this wage is less than the increase in price level. As they have no idea about actual inflation they are happy to supply more labor at that high nominal wage. In this way workers are deceived. Now unemployment will be at U_1 and inflation rate will be 6%. So long there is a difference between expected inflation and actual inflation this trade of will persist. Here expected inflation is 0 and actual inflation is 6%. In the long-run when workers remove their money illusion and equal expected inflation with actual inflation then workers ask for higher nominal wage. As a result of that supply of labor declines and it will continue until actual inflation is realized by workers. As soon as the expected inflation is at 6% the Phillips curve shifts to the right. New Phillips curve is now PC1. The economy now at point B and unemployment will at natural rate of unemployment. So rate of unemployment can never be permanently at different level to natural rate of unemployment. This concept is known as *natural rate hypothesis*.

Phillips curve from Keynesian point of view

We have seen that natural rate of hypothesis depends on the adjustment parameter α. According to Friedman there is no trade off between inflation and unemployment in the long-run. In the long-run α is equal to one. Workers do not have any money illusion. They are rational. Keynesian economist[9]

9. J. Tobin, 'Inflation and Unemployment', *American Economic Review,* 62 (1972); reprinted in P. Korliras and R. Thron (eds), *Modern Macroeconomics,* (New York: Harper & Roy, 1979).

Tobin in his analysis argued that if $0 < \alpha \leq 1$ there is a negative relation between the variables concerned in the long run. Even if expected inflation is equal to actual inflation there is a long run relationship. This can be proved in the following manner. Let there is no growth in labor and the economy is in equilibrium at constant price level. In such a situation

$\frac{\dot{W}}{W} = 0$ i.e., Average rate of increase in nominal wage is equal to zero

and expected inflation is also zero, i.e., $E\left(\frac{\dot{P}}{P}\right) = 0$. Now putting these

values in the following equation $\frac{\dot{W}}{W} f(U) + \alpha E\left(\frac{\dot{P}}{P}\right)$

$$Or, 0 = f(U) + \alpha\ 0$$

$$Or, f(U) = 0$$

Now we put $f(U) = 0$ in expectation augmented Phillips curve we get,

$$"\frac{\dot{W}}{W} = \alpha\ E\left(\frac{\dot{P}}{P}\right)$$

Now subtracting $\frac{\dot{P}}{P}$ from both sides we get,

$$\frac{\dot{W}}{W} - \frac{\dot{P}}{P} = \alpha\ E\left(\frac{\dot{P}}{P}\right) - \frac{\dot{P}}{P}$$

Since $E\left(\frac{\dot{P}}{P}\right) = \frac{\dot{P}}{P}$ i.e., expected inflation = actual inflation

$$\frac{\dot{w}}{w} = \alpha \frac{\dot{P}}{P} = \frac{\dot{P}}{P}$$

$Or, \frac{\dot{w}}{w} = (\alpha - 1)\frac{\dot{P}}{P}$ (Rosalind, L., & Alexander, R. 1982, pp. 346-347)

If á is less than one then right hand part of the above equation is negative. There is a long-run trade off between inflation and unemployment. If average rate of increase in price level raises average rate of increase in real wage declines. It is known to us that firms employ workers depending upon the marginal productivity of labor. As real wage falls and it is greater than marginal productivity of labor. Firms get it profitable to employ more labor for their production purposes. So inflation and unemployment has a long-run negative relation. But if á is equal to 1 then there is no long-run trade-off between inflation and unemployment. Long-run relationship will persist just because of Keynesian involuntary unemployment theory. According to Keynesian involuntary unemployment theory wage rigidity (though not full wage rigidity) nominal wage rate will not decline. It results in unemployment and market will not clear. There are several reasons for money rigidity. Such as Money Illusion, Wage Fixation through Contracts, Minimum Wage Laws, Efficiency Wages are among them. Involuntary unemployment is a situation where workers are willing to work at the prevailing market wage rate yet they are unemployed. When workers are not bother about the decline in the real wage rate due to induced inflation but bother about any decline in nominal wage, involuntary unemployment exists. This involuntary unemployment is the key behind the long-run trade-off between inflation and unemployment from Keynesian point of view. Here is the difference between the neoclassical and Keynesian understanding over the Phillips curve.

Adaptive Expectation:

According to Phillips money wages rise more rapidly the greater the amount of excess demand in the labor market (given constant labor productivity) . This can be expressed in the following manner.

$$\frac{\dot{W}}{W} = f\left(\frac{Demand\ for\ labor - Supply\ of\ labor}{Supply\ of\ labor}\right)$$

$$\frac{\dot{W}}{W} = f\left(\frac{Employed\ labor + Vacancies) - (Undemployed\ labor + Employed\ labor}{Undemployed\ labor + Employed\ labor}\right)$$

$$\frac{\dot{W}}{W} = f\left(\frac{Vacancies + Undemployed\ labor}{Undemployed\ labor + Employed\ labor}\right)$$

where, $\frac{\dot{W}}{W} = \frac{dW / dt}{dt} = \frac{1}{W}\frac{dW}{dt}$

Vacancies and unemployed labor are inversely related. So numerator is a negative part. Therefore, as whole average rate of nominal wage is a function of unemployment and it has an inverse relationship. i.e., $\frac{\dot{w}}{w} = f(U)$

So, the Phillips relation is $\frac{\dot{w}}{w} = f(U)$

According to macroeconomic theory excess labor demand is related with real wages. So Phillips relation can be written as $\frac{\dot{w}}{w} = f(U)$

We know that nominal wage = Real wage + Inflation. So $\frac{\dot{w}}{w} = \frac{\dot{W}}{W} - \frac{\dot{P}}{P}$ i.e., Average rate of increase in real wage = Average rate of increase in nominal wage – Average rate of increase in price level or inflation.

As now workers have to calculate real wage from their nominal wage the concept of expectation gets place here. The two terms expected inflation and actual inflation now matter. Without expecting inflation workers could not calculate their real wage from nominal wage.

Since,

$$\frac{\dot{w}}{w} = \frac{\dot{W}}{W} - \frac{\dot{P}}{P}$$

$$Or \frac{\dot{w}}{w} = \frac{\dot{W}}{W} - E\left(\frac{\dot{P}}{P}\right)$$

where, $E\left(\frac{\dot{P}}{P}\right)$ is the expected rate of inflation.

Now,

$$\frac{\dot{w}}{w} = \frac{\dot{W}}{W} - E\left(\frac{\dot{P}}{P}\right)$$

$$Or, f(U) = \frac{\dot{W}}{W} - E\left(\frac{\dot{P}}{P}\right)$$

$$Or, \frac{\dot{W}}{W} = f(U) + \propto E\left(\frac{\dot{P}}{P}\right)$$

This equation is known as expectation augmented Phillips curve. The term α is a parameter. If α is equal to zero then the equation is a Phillips curve. If á is equal to 1 there is no money illusion or in another sense we can say workers are rational. If α is less than 1 and greater than 0, then workers adjust their nominal wage with real wage partially. Workers do have money illusion in the short run. In the short- run they do not be able to take inflation fully into their account when they are calculating their real wage from their given nominal wage.

To have the short- run relationship between inflation and unemployment it is assumed that expectation of inflation is stranded on past period's rate of inflation. It means that if actual rate of inflation gets speed expected inflation is far behind the actual rate of inflation. Therefore, adaptive expectation is a way by which expectations are formed to have short-run trade-off between inflation and unemployment.

"Past error has an important role in calculating expected inflation under adaptive expectation hypothesis.

$$E\left(\frac{\dot{P}}{P}\right)_t - E\left(\frac{\dot{P}}{P}\right)_{t-1} = \gamma\left[E\left(\frac{\dot{P}}{P}\right)_t - E\left(\frac{\dot{P}}{P}\right)_{t-1}\right]$$

where α is greater than zero and less than one

$E\left(\frac{\dot{P}}{P}\right)_t$ implies the rate of inflation expected at time t.

$$Or,\ E\left(\frac{\dot{P}}{P}\right)_t = E\left(\frac{\dot{P}}{P}\right)_{t-1} + \gamma\left[E\left(\frac{\dot{P}}{P}\right)_t - E\left(\frac{\dot{P}}{P}\right)_{t-1}\right]$$

It is distribute lag function and solving we get,

$$Or,\ E\left(\frac{\dot{P}}{P}\right)_t = \gamma \sum_{n=0}^{N} (1-\gamma)^n \left(\frac{\dot{P}}{P}\right)_{t-n}$$

The above equation shows that expected inflation depends on past history of inflation. If γ is very close to 1 then expectation adjusts very quickly.

From the equation of adaptive expectation Phillips curve we get

$$Or,\ \frac{\dot{W}}{W} f(U) + \alpha E\left(\frac{\dot{P}}{P}\right)$$

Putting α =1 we get,

$$\frac{\dot{W}}{W} f(U) + E\left(\frac{\dot{P}}{P}\right)$$

By using mark up price we replace $\frac{\dot{W}}{W}$ by $\frac{\dot{p}}{p}$ and proceed in the following manner.

$P = (1+m)W$ where m is the mark up.

Now we take logarithm of $P = (1+m)W$.

$$Log\ P = (1+m)W$$

Or, $Log\ P = Log(1+m) + Log W$

Now we differentiate

$$\frac{1}{P}\frac{dP}{dt} = \frac{1}{W}\frac{dW}{dt}$$

$$Or, \frac{\dot{P}}{P} = \frac{\dot{W}}{W}$$

Substituting this into

$$\frac{\dot{W}}{W} = f(U) + E\left(\frac{\dot{P}}{P}\right)$$

we get,

$$\left(\frac{\dot{P}}{P}\right)_t = f(U) + E\left(\frac{\dot{P}}{P}\right)_t$$

By substituting $E\left(\frac{\dot{P}}{P}\right)_t = \gamma\sum_{n=0}^{N}(1-\gamma)^n\left(\frac{\dot{P}}{P}\right)_{t-n}$ in the above equation and using Koyck transformation and finally rearranging we get,

$$f(U)_t = (1-\gamma)\left(\frac{\dot{P}}{P}\right)_t - (1-\gamma)\left(\frac{\dot{P}}{P}\right)_{t-1} + (1-\gamma)f(U)_{t-1}$$

$$\text{If } \left(\frac{\dot{P}}{P}\right)_t = \left(\frac{\dot{P}}{P}\right)_{t-1} \text{ then}$$

$$f(U)_t = (1-\gamma)f(U)_{t-1}$$

As time passes we obtain from above equation

$$f(U)_{t+1} = (1+\gamma)f(U)_t = (1-\gamma)^2 f(U)_{t-1}$$

$$f(U)_{t+2} = (1+\gamma)f(U)_{t+1} = (1-\gamma)(1-\gamma)f(U)_t$$

$$= (1-\gamma)(1-\gamma)(1-\gamma)f(U)_{t-1} = (1-\gamma)^3 f(U)_{t-1}$$

and so on.

As t becomes large $(1 - \gamma)^t$ tends to be zero. $f(U)_t$ will be tend to be zero. At stable price level and constant nominal and real wage rate $f(U) = 0$. Here the level of unemployment is the natural rate of unemployment. Under adaptive expectation hypothesis there is no long-run trade- off between inflation and unemployment.

Now we differentiate

$$f(U)_t = (1-\gamma)\left(\frac{\dot{P}}{P}\right)_t - (1-\gamma)\left(\frac{\dot{P}}{P}\right)_{t-1} + (1-\gamma)f(U)_{t-1}$$

with respect to time

$$f^{|}(U)_t \frac{dU_t}{dt} = (1-\gamma)\frac{d}{dt}\left(\frac{\dot{P}}{P}\right)_t \quad \text{here } f^{|}(U)_t < 0$$

Since past cannot be change by current action

$$(1-\gamma)\left(\frac{\dot{P}}{P}\right)_{t-1} = 0 \text{ and } (1-\gamma)f(U)_{t-1} = 0$$

$\frac{d}{dt}\left(\frac{\dot{p}}{p}\right)_t$ is the rate of change of inflation

Dividing both sides of $f^{/}(U)t\frac{dUt}{dt} = (1-\gamma)\frac{d}{dt}\left(\frac{\dot{p}}{p}\right)_t$ by

$$\frac{dUt}{dt} = \frac{(1-\gamma)}{f^{/}(U)t}\frac{d}{dt}\left(\frac{\dot{p}}{p}\right)_t$$

Coefficient of rate of change of inflation is negative as $f^{/}(U)t < 0$

Therefore, unemployment falls in the short-run as inflation accelerates or inflation changes."

(Rosalind, L., & Alexander, R.1982, pp. 350-351)

Rational Expectation Hypothesis

In adaptive expectation workers are predicting inflation depending on the past values of that variable. If there is any error then in the model then that error will intensify as time passes out. In simple we can say error becomes systematic and it is called systematic error repeatable error. If there is systematic error then we should have an understanding that full information is not utilized to make an expectation about the variable.

On the basis of the above criticism of the adaptive expectation hypothesis rational expectation takes place. In rational expectation not only the past information of the variable is used but all information is used to expect the variable. There is no systematic error. Only random error or unsystematic error exists. This type of error has no pattern but random by nature. So the differences or errors between expected and actual inflation are serially uncorrelated. "If expectations are rational then

$$\left(\frac{\dot{P}}{P}\right)_t = E\left(\frac{\dot{P}}{P}\right)_t + \varepsilon_t$$

where ε_t implies serially uncorrelated error term.

When workers have rational expectations then they think about the behavior of the economy. How the economy behaves is the matter of concern. Suppose inflation is because of expansionary monetary policy then movement of money supply should be included at the time of expectation.

If rate of inflation is determined by

$$\left(\frac{\dot{P}}{P}\right)_t = \rho\left(\frac{\dot{M}}{M}\right)_t + \varepsilon_t$$

where $\frac{\dot{M}}{M}$ implies average rate of increase in money supply.

then $$\left(\frac{\dot{P}}{P}\right)_t = \rho\left(\frac{\dot{M}}{M}\right)_t$$

Now we substitute $\left(\frac{\dot{P}}{P}\right)_t$ and $E\left(\frac{\dot{P}}{P}\right)_t$ in the following equation.

$$E\left(\frac{\dot{P}}{P}\right)_t = f(U) + E\left(\frac{\dot{P}}{P}\right)_t$$

$$Or, f(U) = \left(\frac{\dot{P}}{P}\right)_t - E\left(\frac{\dot{P}}{P}\right)_t$$

We get,

$$Or, f(U) = \rho\left(\frac{\dot{M}}{M}\right)_t - \varepsilon_t - \rho\left(\frac{\dot{M}}{M}\right)_t$$

$Or, f(U) = \varepsilon_t$ [Rosalind, L., & Alexander, R.1982, pp.352-353]

Therefore, unemployment is equal to a random error or unsystematic error. It means that there is no short-run trade-off between inflation and unemployment. So under rational expectation hypothesis there is no short-run and long-run relationship between variables concerned.

Chapter - 7

Theories of Business Cycle

1. The Business Cycle

Macroeconomics is a study of aggregate economy. Unlike micro-economics which deals with individual firm and individual consumer macroeconomics deals with all firms, all consumers in an economy. It is a big picture. It is macroeconomics that measures the health of the economy and prescribes medicines in terms of policies (monetary or fiscal policies). There are some leading economic indicators that tell us about the health of the economy. In one framework we can represent all that is called business cycle. An economy has three major goals. One is economic growth, second one is prevention of unemployment and the third one is inflation under control.

Business cycle is visualization of economic conditions. It is a graph that shows how society is dealing to meet those goals. Business cycle is measured by two components. One is real GDP that is measured along vertical, axis and another is time that is measured along horizontal axis. Figure 7.1 depicts the business cycle.

The line which fluctuates over time is real GDP over time. The upward rising straight line is the growth trend line. This trend line economy wants to achieve with the full employment of all available resources. Real GDP can increase over time. It is called expansion. Real GDP can continue up to the peak. It is the highest level real GDP before the economy meets with contraction.

Real GDP can decrease over time. It is called contraction. Real GDP can continue up to the trough. It is the lowest level of real GDP before the economy meets with expansion. This up and down in business cycle will continue for months, quarter or year. For developed countries it may stay for 18 years. For developing countries it may stay for 8 years. There are two reasons. One is static effects like change in consumer behavior and another is shocks like natural disaster etc.

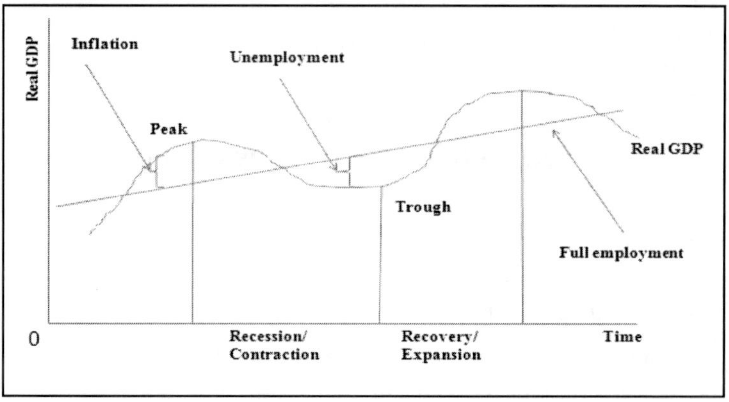

Source: Internet

Figure- 7.1: The Business cycle

There are five phases of business cycle. Phases are given below.

1. Depression or contraction,
2. Recovery,
3. Prosperity or full employment,
4. Boom or inflation or over full employment,
5. Recession or a turn from prosperity to depression,

In our figure from peak to trough is called depression or contraction. In this period output, aggregate demand, employment decline. At trough unemployment is maximum. After trough expansion or recovery starts and it will continue up to peak. Where the real GDP line crosses the growth trend line is called full employment. Inflation is visualized by the space between the peak and growth trend line. Excessive unemployment is found by the space between the growth trend line and trough. Recession is period of time during which the aggregate level of economic activity starts declining. There is contraction or slowing down in business activities.

2. Samuelson's Model of the Trade Cycle

Before going to spread some light on Samuelson's model of trade cycle we have to understand the fundamental background of the theory. Keynes described static fluctuation in his model. According to Keynes investment plays an important role to generate fluctuation. Firms do investment just because of profit expectation. Change in investment makes change in aggregate demand. If aggregate demand increases it will increase income, output and employment. Keynes's multiplier theory explained the whole mechanism. But Keynes failed to spray light on cyclical fluctuation. Professor Paul Samuelson explained the cyclical fluctuation in business cycle through multiplier and accelerator theory. He tried to provide a clear idea of five different types of fluctuations through multiplier-accelerator interaction.

Increase in autonomous investment affects income and income increases by a multiplier. Multiplier is a reciprocal of (1-marginal propensity to consume). On the contrary increase in income caused by increase in autonomous investment raises investment. This increase in investment is called induced investment. It is induced in the sense that changes in investment are because of changes in income. As a result of multiplier-accelerator model aggregate demand changes more than single multiplier effect.

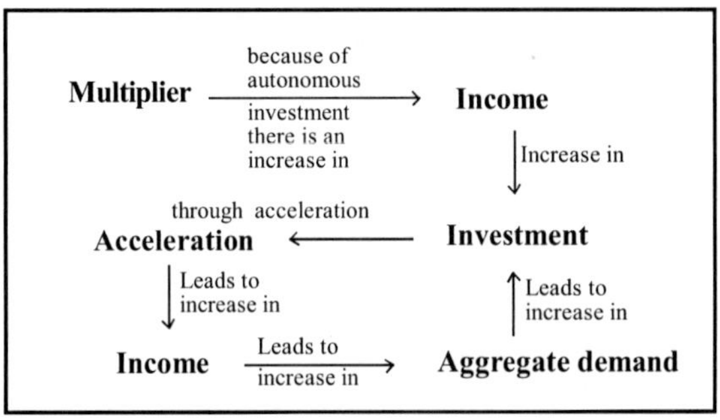

Figure-7.2: Multiplier-accelerator interaction procedure.

The Samuelson[10] model is as follows.

$$Y_t = G_t + C_t + I_t$$

where Y_t implies national income at time t, G_t represents government expenditure at time t, C_t is the consumption at time t and I_t shows investment at time t.

$$C_t = C\ autonomous + cY_{t-1}$$

$$I_t = I\ autonomous + \gamma(Y_{t-1} - Y_{t-2})$$

where C is marginal propensity to consume and γ accelerator or capital output ratio.

10. Paul A. Samuelson, "Interactions between the Multiplier Analysis and Principle of Acceleration ," *The Review of Economic Statistics,* May 1939, reprinted in *Reading in Macroeconomics, (ed)* M.G. Mueller.

Now from equation we get, $Y_t = G_t + C_t + I_t$ we get,

$$Y_t = G_t + C_{autonomous} + cY_{t-1} + I_{autonomous} + \gamma(Y_{t-1} - Y_{t-2})$$

$$Or, \quad Y_t = I + C_{autonomous} + cY_{t-1} + I_{autonomous} + \gamma(Y_{t-1} - Y_{t-2})$$

$$Or, \quad Y_t = I + C_{autonomous} + I_{autonomous} + (c + \gamma)Y_{t-1} - Y_{t-2}$$

Therefore, national income at period *t* depends on previous two periods weighted national income. Weights depend on marginal propensity to consume and capital output ratio or accelerator. The value of *mpc* is less than 1 and greater than 0. The value of accelerator is greater than zero. Professor Samuelson explained five types of fluctuations which are given with example in the appendix (table-1 to table-5 and figure-1 to figure-5). Five cases are given below.

Multiplier and Acceleration Interaction Effect on Income

Case-1: Interaction Effect on Income (*mpc*=0.5 and accelerator=0)

When there is no accelerator effect then there is no cycle. Only static fluctuations are there depending on multiplier effect. The cycle less income path is given below.

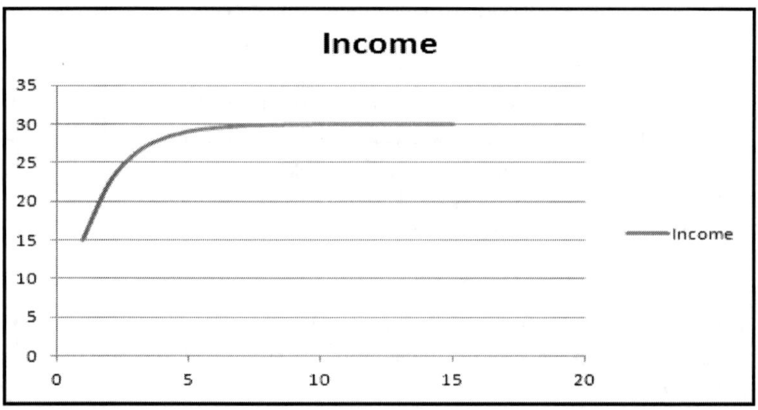

Source: Author's own.

Case-2: Interaction Effect on Income (*mpc*=0.5 and accelerator=1)

When accelerator is 1 and *mpc* is ½ then damped oscillation is there and fluctuations are around static multiplier. The following figure depicts the situation.

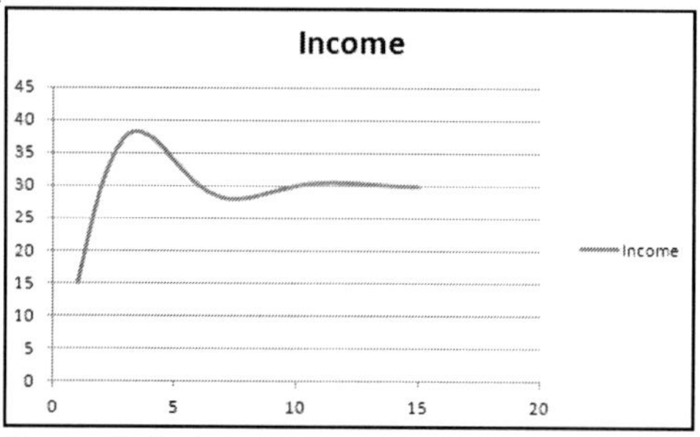

Source: Author's own.

Case-3: Interaction Effect on Income (*mpc*=0.5 and accelerator=2)

Multiplier and acceleration interaction effect on income depicts cycles of constant aptitude when *mpc*=0.5 and accelerator=2. The following figure shows fluctuations around static equilibrium with fixed tendency.

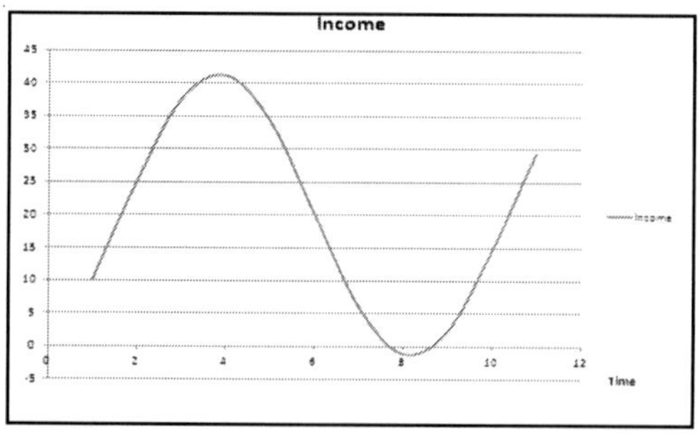

Source: Author's own.

Case-4: Interaction Effect on Income (mpc=0.5 and accelerator=3)

Multiplier and acceleration interaction effect on income depicts explosive cycles when *mpc*=0.5 and accelerator=3. The following figure shows explosive cycles.

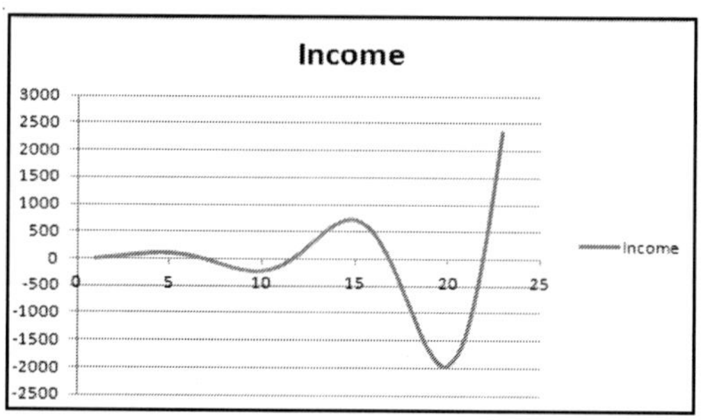

Source: Author's own.

Case-5: Interaction Effect on Income (*mpc*=0.5 and accelerator=4)

When there accelerator is 4 with *mpc* 0.5 then there is cycle less explosive income path. The cycle less explosive income path is given below.

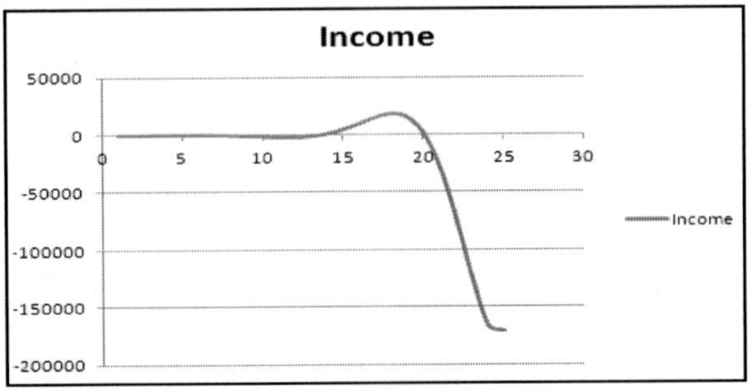

Source: Author's own.

In above mentioned five fluctuations there are only two cycles. One is case 3 (cycles of constant aptitude) and another is case 4(explosive cycles).

Multiplier- Acceleration Interaction Effect on Income has a merit. In this model income grows faster than multiplier or accelerator model unaccompanied. It removes the shortcomings of Keynes's static fluctuation model. It not only represents dynamic fluctuations but also provide direction to stabilize the economy. Explosiveness of the cycle depends on the value of capital output ratio. Larger the value of accelerator greater is the chance of explosiveness.

There are number of loopholes in the Samuelson's model. He did not say anything about the time span of dissimilar cycles. In his model marginal propensity to consume and capital output ratio are constant. Though in reality they are not constant, they are changeable. The major unclear part of the Samuelson's model is that there is no trend in income path. Fluctuations are around the static level. But in reality there are trends in income path. If we see USA or UK economy then we find that there are trend in income path though there are oscillations. J.R. Hicks in his book *A Contribution to the Theory of the Trade Cycle* cleared this loophole found in multiplier-accelerator interaction model of Samuelson.

Multiplier and Acceleration Interaction Effect on Income (Calculated in terms of crores)

Table-7.1: Interaction Effect on Income (mpc=0.5 and accelerator=0)

Period (1)	*Initial Consumption (2)*	*Induced investment (3) [Column5Xmpc)*	*Induced net in national (4) [Column 3-column2] X accelerator*	*Total Income (5) C2+C3+C4*
1	15	0	0	15
2	15	7.5	0	22.5
3	15	11.25	0	26.25
4	15	13.125	0	28.125
5	15	14.0625	0	29.0625
6	15	14.53125	0	29.53125
7	15	14.76563	0	29.76563
8	15	14.88281	0	29.88281
9	15	14.94141	0	29.94141
10	15	14.9707	0	29.9707
11	15	14.98535	0	29.98535
12	15	14.99268	0	29.99268
13	15	14.99634	0	29.99634
14	15	14.99817	0	29.99817
15	15	14.99908	0	29.99908
mpc=0.5 and accelerator=0				

Source: Author's own.

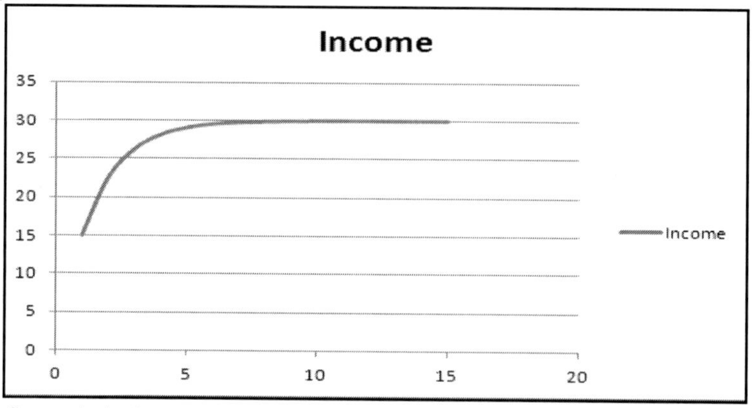

Source: Author's own.

Figure-7.3: Graphical presentation of interaction between multiplier and accelerator(mpc=0.5 and accelerator=0)

Table-7.2: Interaction Effect on Income (mpc=0.5 and accelerator=1)

Period	*Initial Consumption*	*Induced investment*	*Induced net in national*	*Total Income*
1	15	0	0	15
2	15	7.5	7.5	30
3	15	15	7.5	37.5
4	15	18.75	3.75	37.5
5	15	18.75	0	33.75
6	15	16.875	–1.875	30
7	15	15	–1.875	28.125
8	15	14.0625	–0.9375	28.125
9	15	14.0625	0	29.0625
10	15	14.53125	0.46875	30
11	15	15	0.46875	30.46875
12	15	15.23438	0.234375	30.46875
13	15	15.23438	0	30.23438
14	15	15.11719	–0.11719	30
15	15	15	–0.11719	29.88281
mpc = 0.5 and accelerator = 1				

Source: Author's own.

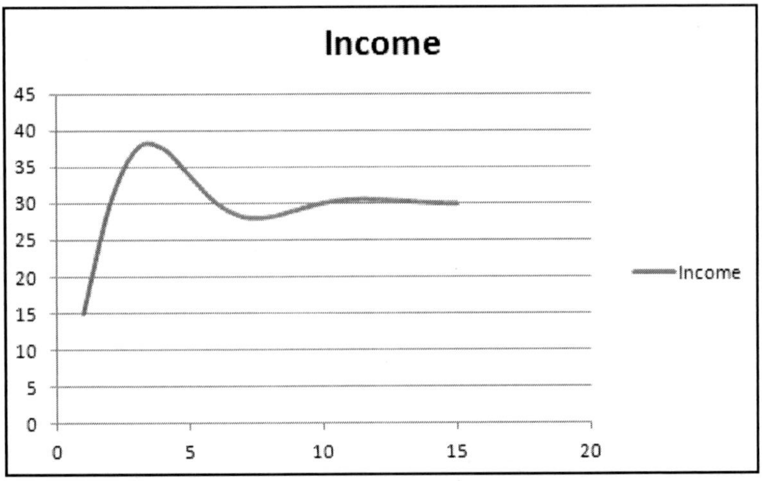

Source: Author's own.

Figure-7.4: Graphical presentation of interaction between multiplier and accelerator(mpc=0.5 and accelerator=1)

Table-7.3: Interaction Effect on Income (mpc=0.5 and accelerator=2) Hicks's Model of the Trade Cycle:

Period	Initial Consumption (2)	Induced investment (3) [Column5Xmpc)	Induced net in national(4) [Column3-column2]X accelerator	Total Income (5) C2+C3+C4
1	10	0	0	10
2	10	5	10	25
3	10	12.5	15	37.5
4	10	18.75	12.5	41.25
5	10	20.625	3.75	34.375
6	10	17.1875	–6.875	20.3125
7	10	10.15625	–14.0625	6.09375
8	10	3.046875	–14.2188	–17188
9	10	–0.58594	–7.26563	2.148438
10	10	1.074219	3.320313	14.39453
11	10	7.197266	12.24609	29.44336
mpc=0.5 and accelerator=2				

Source: Author's own.

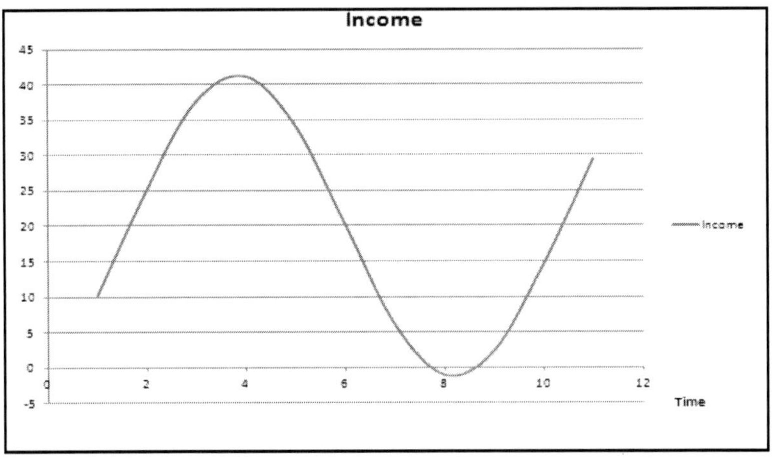

Source: Author's own.

Figure-7.5: Graphical presentation of interaction between multiplier and accelerator(mpc=0.5 and accelerator=2)

Table-7.4: Interaction Effect on Income (mpc=0.5 and accelerator=2)

Period	*Initial Consumption*	*Induced investment*	*Induced net in national*	*Total Income*
1	15	0	0	15
2	15	7.5	22.5	45
3	15	22.5	45	82.5
4	15	41.25	56.25	112.5
5	15	56.25	45	116.25
6	15	58.125	5.625	78.75
7	15	39.375	-56.25	-1.875
8	15	-0.9375	-120.938	-106.875
9	15	-53.4375	-157.5	-195.938
10	15	-97.9688	-133.594	-216.563
11	15	-108.281	-30.9375	-124.219
12	15	-62.1094	138.5156	91.40625
13	15	45.70313	323.4375	384.1406
14	15	192.0703	439.1016	646.1719
15	15	323.0859	393.0469	731.1328
16	15	365.5664	127.4414	508.0078
17	15	254.0039	-334.688	-65.6836
18	15	-32.8418	-860.537	-878.379
19	15	-439.189	-1219.04	-1643.23
20	15	-821.616	-1147.28	-1953.9
21	15	-976.948	-465.996	-1427.94
22	15	-713.972	788.9282	89.95605
23	15	44.97803	2276.851	2336.829
24	15	1168.414	3370.309	4553.723
25	15	2276.862	3325.342	5617.203
mpc=0.5 and accelerator=3				

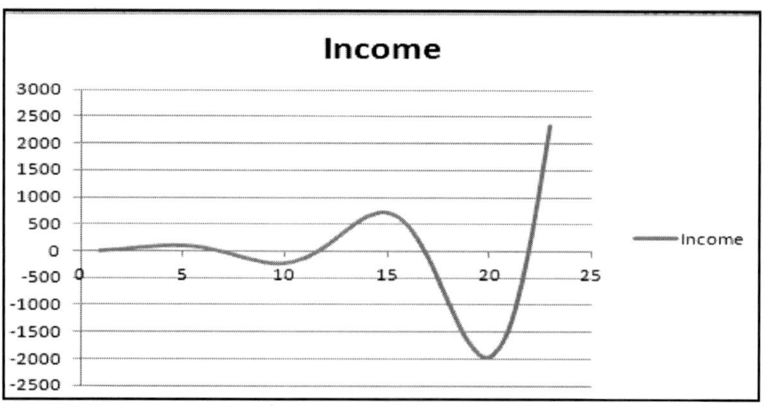

Source: Author's own.

Figure- 7.6: Graphical presentation of interaction between multiplier and accelerator(mpc=0.5 and accelerator=3)

Table-7.5: Interaction Effect on Income (mpc=0.5 and accelerator=4)

Period	*Initial Consumption*	*Induced Investment*	*Induced Net in National*	*Total Income*
1	15	0	0	15
2	15	7.5	30	52.5
3	15	26.25	75	116.25
4	15	58.125	127.5	200.625
5	15	100.3125	126.5625	241.875
6	15	120.9375	82.5	218.4375
7	15	109.2188	-46.875	77.34375
8	15	38.67188	-282.188	-228.516
9	15	-114.258	-611.719	-710.977
10	15	-355.488	-964.922	-1305.41
11	15	-652.705	-1188.87	-1826.57
12	15	-913.286	-1042.32	-1940.61
13	15	-970.305	-228.076	-1183.38
14	15	-591.691	1514.458	937.7673
15	15	468.8837	4242.297	4726.181
16	15	2363.091	7576.827	9954.918
17	15	4977.459	10457.47	15449.93
18	15	7724.966	10990.03	18730
19	15	9364.998	6560.126	15940.12
20	15	7970.062	-5579.74	2405.319
21	15	1202.66	-27069.6	-25852
22	15	-12926	-56514.5	-69425.5
23	15	-34712.8	-87147.1	-121845
24	15	-60922.4	-104839	-165746
25	15	-82873.1	-87802.6	-170661
mpc = 0.5 and accelerator = 4				

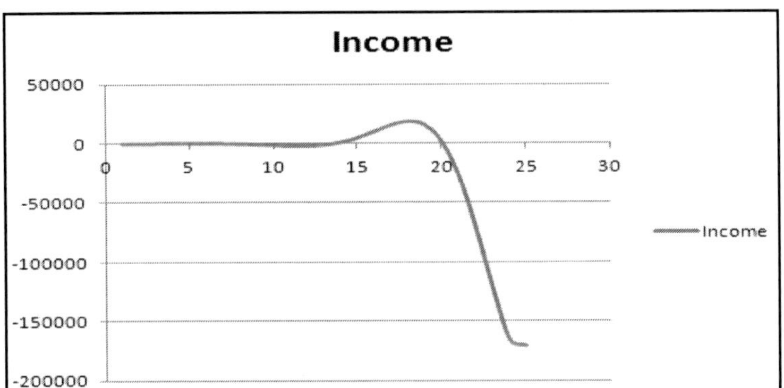

Source: Author's own.

Figure-7.7: Graphical presentation of interaction between multiplier and accelerator (mpc=0.5 and accelerator=4)

Table-7.6: Interaction Effect on Income (mpc=0.2 and accelerator=2)

Period	*Initial Consumption*	*Induced investment*	*Induced net in national*	*Total Income*
1	10	0	0	10
2	10	8	16	34
3	10	27.2	38.4	75.6
4	10	60.48	66.56	137.04
5	10	109.632	98.304	217.936
6	10	174.3488	129.4336	313.7824
7	10	251.0259	153.3542	414.3802
8	10	331.5041	160.9564	502.4605
9	10	401.9684	140.9286	552.897
10	10	442.3176	80.69841	533.016
11	10	426.4128	-31.8096	404.6032
			mpc=0.8 and accelerator=2	

Source: Author's own.

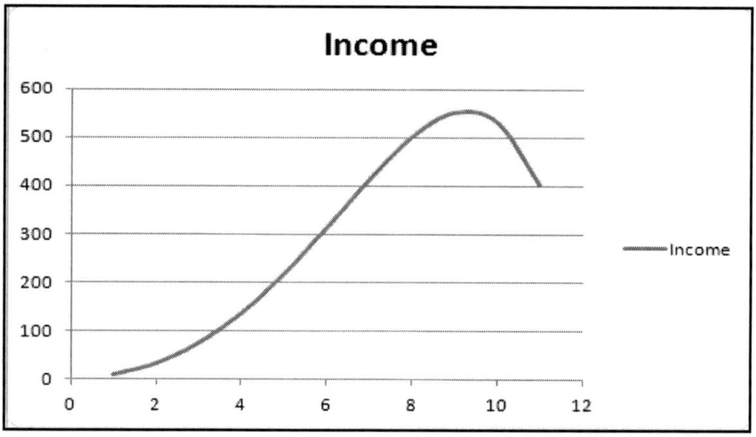

Source: Author's own.

Figure-7.8: Graphical presentation of interaction between multiplier and accelerator(mpc=0.2 and accelerator=2)

Table-7.7: Interaction Effect on Income (mpc=0.8 and accelerator=2)

Period	*Initial Consumption*	*Induced investment*	*Induced net in national*	*Total Income*
1	10	0	0	10
2	10	2	4	16
3	10	3.2	2.4	15.6
4	10	3.12	-0.16	12.96
5	10	2.592	-1.056	11.536
6	10	2.3072	-0.5696	11.7376
7	10	2.34752	0.08064	12.42816
8	10	2.485632	0.276224	12.76186
9	10	2.552371	0.133478	12.68585
10	10	2.53717	-0.0304	12.50677
11	10	2.501353	-0.07163	12.42972
mpc=0.2 and accelerator=2				

Source: Author's own

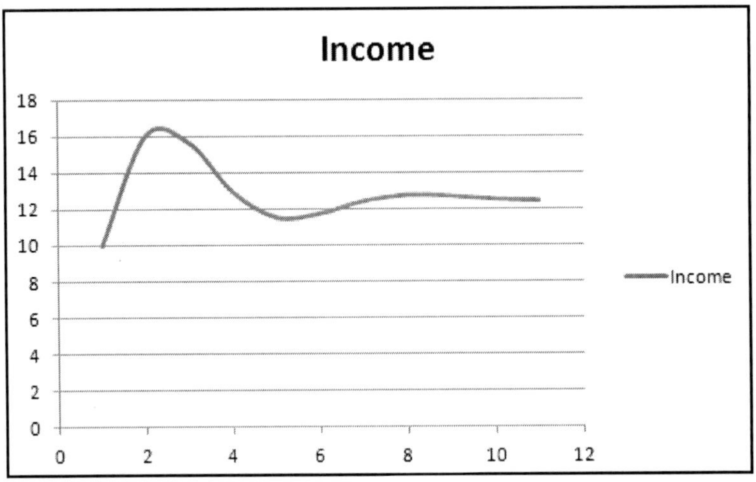

Source: Author's own

Figure-7.9: Graphical presentation of interaction between multiplier and accelerator(mpc=0.8 and accelerator=2)

Samuelson's article is very short and formal. It presents a linear second-order difference equation producing either stable or diverging path. He did not say anything about the time span of dissimilar cycles. The major unclear part of the Samuelson's model is that there is no trend in income path. Fluctuations are around the static level. But in reality there are trends in income path. J.R. Hicks in his book *A Contribution to the Theory of the Trade Cycle* makes some important changes to the model: by adding a floor and a ceiling to a linear model, he creates a piecewise-linear framework that can construct bounded fluctuations. Moreover, the model shows how a growth process can be coupled with the business cycles. In the cycle hypothesis displayed by Hicks', growth is immensely significant: Hicks holds, as does Harrod, that we should approach the business cycle as an issue of a growing economy. In other words, we should consider not variances simply, however changes as they happen about a rising pattern. In this way, Hicks' model of the business cycle stands for a significant step towards combining a theory of cyclical fluctuations with the factors of economic growth.

The procedure of growth is clarified as far as the multiplier and accelerator which work with a period lag. According to Hicks, "the theory of the acceleration and the theory of multiplier are the two sides of the theory of the fluctuations, just as the theory of demand and the theory of supply are the two sides of the theory of value."

According to Hicks autonomous investment represents the expansion of factors. It is because of expansion of population and technological enhancement. Thus, the useful concepts which play an important part in Hicksian model of business cycle are autonomous investment, induced investment, the warranted rate of growth (The growth path of real income maintaining equilibrium in the goods market requires that the economy should grow at a steady exponential rate to maintain. The rate of growth is called warranted rate of growth.) and the connection of the multiplier with the accelerator.

Hicks in his theory of trade cycle made a difference between autonomous investment and induced investment. Autonomous investment is a function of changes of output such as changes in public investment (railway infrastructure, roads etc) and induced investment is a function of changes of output generated from autonomous investment. He assumed autonomous investment has a increasing rate if there is no external factor to disturb.

Hicks agreed that the fundamental causation of the cycle lies in the multiplier-accelerator relationship. In his model there is an effective ceiling that represents the full employment level. Here he got the idea from Harrod's natural rate of growth (Natural rate of growth is equal to the rate of growth of the labor force in the absence of technical progress.). The effective floor which was found in the business cycle depends on the trend levels of autonomous investment.

Assumptions to develop Hicks theory of the trade cycle

(i) Autonomous investment is increasing at a regular rate

(ii) Coefficients of the saving and investment are such that an upward displacement from the equilibrium path will tend to cause a progress away from equilibrium. Here movement may be delayed or lagged.

(iii) Beyond the full employment level of output it is impossible to expand output.

(iv) On the downward motion of the economy down swing capital output ratio plays an indirect role as a constraint.

(v) Since consumption and induced investment work in lagged way multiplier and accelerator functioning act in lagged way

(vi) There are ceilings and floors and oscillations are within the wrap though accelerator is greater than 1.

(vii) It is assumed that multiplier and accelerator are constants. As they are constants function of consumption and function of investment are also constants.

The Model

Hicks explained his trade cycle on the basis of the following figure.

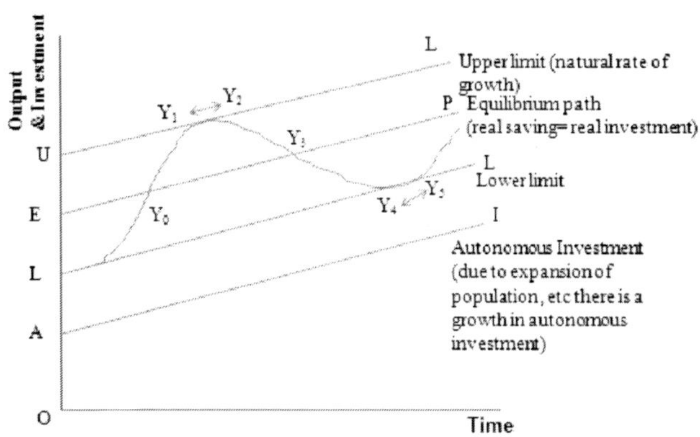

Source: Internet

Figure-7.10: Graphical representation of Hicks Trade Cycle.

In this figure Line AI shows autonomous investment, this is assumed to be growing at a constant rate. It grows because of population growth, technological change etc. As time passes governments' routine activities increase such as construction of road, etc. EP exhibits the equilibrium path of output which relies on autonomous investment. This equilibrium path is constructed by applying 'super multiplier' (mathematical combination of multiplier and accelerator.). It is the warranted rate of growth where real saving is equal to real investment. LL presents the lower equilibrium path of output. It is also the floor. UL depicts the full employment ceiling indicating utmost growth when dearth of resources occurs. It is supposed that this path is above the equilibrium path EP and it is also assumed that it grows at the same rate as autonomous investment grows. UL line is based on the Harrod's natural rate of growth.

In our figure we have shown that growth of an economy starts from Y_0 and touches the full employment level at $Y_{1.}$ It continues up to Y_2 at the full employment level for some time. The growth path of income falls through Y_3 and touches LL line at Y_4. The growth path continues on that line for some time (up to Y_5) and then it turns up. The rate of increase of output (Y_0 to Y_1) is much larger than rate of decline of output (Y_2 to Y_4).

Up to Y_0 the economy moves along equilibrium path of output and employment EP. Suppose at Y_0 there is a rupture of autonomous investment (suppose there is an invention). This will cause a annoyance and the path of income travels progressively away from EP to UL. Though the burst is short lived and autonomous investment goes down back to its previous level, yet on account of the multiplier and acceleration interaction moves the economy from Y_0 to Y_1.

However, the uphill growth cannot continue forever and finally arrive at the ceiling UL at point Y_1. As soon as the increase of output punches the point Y_1 the cycle arrives at the top of the boom. It has to come down. It does not drop with a collapse straight away but moves stealthily along the ceiling for some time following lagged effects and adjustments of induced investments.

As long as lagged effects of induced investment is there the growth path of output creeps along the full employment path. After that it travels down and downward movement starts.

Downward movements do not stop at the warranted rate of growth or equilibrium growth path. Since current investment is less than the level of investment that is required to maintain output at equilibrium level movements do not bring to an end at EP line.

Now, the downward spiral is not rapid without any floor. The downward movements become gradual along $Y_2Y_3Y_4$. It has a floor and it cannot move beyond this floor just because multiplier < 1and disinvestment is delimited by replacement.

Hicks in his business cycle showed that upward movement and downward movement are not similar. As because of investment composites of the difference between autonomous investment and the constant rate of depreciation. If upward and downward activities of accelerator were identical then the economy would have a sharp drop.

As because of investment in gross cannot go down to zero, output cannot go down indefinitely to autonomous investment line. The bend must have a floor. After reaching LL it does not move up immediately. It creeps along the LL line on account of the existence of surplus capacity. As there is autonomous investment and multiplier growth path of income does not fall below Y_4. Once surplus capability is worn out, the positive acceleration effect becomes functioning once more. It means that autonomous investment generates income through multiplier which will in turn lead to an increase in investment that is called induced investment and the accelerator is triggered off with multiplier and it moves the economy towards the upper limit again. The cyclical process will be shown again in this way.

Critical Evaluation of Hicks' Theory:

Consequently, we find that Hicks gives an attractive clarification of defining moments of business spin through accelerator. Since the framework has a roof and a base it must swing between these two breaking points. Hicks' great contribution to the theory of business cycle is that it explained how surplus capacity delays the upswing. Hicks in his model nicely represented cyclical fluctuation with in a framework that has upper and lower boundary.

Hicks theory of business cycle was critically criticized by Kaldor, Duesenberry, Lundberg, Smithies and others.

According to Kaldor, Hicks in his theory used accelerator in inflexible form. Multiplier and accelerator functioning which is based on that thanking would be unacceptable if accelerator is not rigid.

Hicks assumed that multiplier is constant over the period. He got the idea for Keynesian static model of business cycle. But Hicks's assumption on this point is not true as because in reality marginal propensity to consume varies over time. Friedman in his empirical research proved that marginal propensity to consume varies to cyclical changes in business cycle.

Capital output ratio is constant at different types of swings in the trade cycle. Constancy of capital output ratio is an assumption on the validity of the Hicks theory. But in reality capital output ratio changes depending on technological change and others. Lundberg suggested that constant capital output ratio should be kept aside to have an understanding the business cycle in a realistic way.

Professor Smithies in his article said that basis of growth must be within the system. Hicks in his theory mentioned that changes in autonomous investment due to independent factors are responsible for upward trend in output. So according to him Hicks's theory of trade cycle is incomplete.

According to Duesenberry Hicks in his business cycle showed the importance of the effect of multiplier-accelerator interaction but it was mechanical. Human judgment, business expectations have no role to play.

From Hicks's theory of business cycle we found that contraction part is much longer than expansion part of the cycle. In reality we have an understanding just opposite of that view. Specially, after war we have seen that expansion period is longer than contraction period.

Hicks in his model confuses the role of money. He says that contraction period from 1922 to 1923 was because of monetary factors. But he in his model mentions that basic reason for the downward movement of the output is the multiplier-accelerator interaction effect. Monetary factors do not have any role to play.

According to Dernburg and McDougall no one can split trend of full employment from the growth path of output. They said that full employment depends upon available resources with the country. If capital stock which is one of the resources on which full employment depends raises then full employment level will be at variance.

Professor Nicholas Kaldor supposes the implement of accelerator misleading in that it assumes nonexistence of excess capacity in capital-goods industries and permanent nature of demand for capital goods. In Kaldor's observation the confirmation is on the opposing. Industries subject to cyclical fluctuations retain excess capacity as a normal practice for they face changeable demand.

Professor Harrod has distrusted that autonomous investment is likely to be progressing in a bend. The chance is more that the depression delays it. In his investigation of the American business cycles in the nineteenth century Readings Feels noted down that the renewals were not due to the wearing out of excess capacity; the upward movements did not wait for induced investment dropping to zero. Rather despite of the survival of excess capacity growth initiated in many cases.

There are number of weakness in the Hicks's theory of trade cycle. In spite of these loopholes this theory has a fundamental. He nicely explained fluctuations of growth path with upper and lower limit. According to Dernburg and McDougall, "The Hicks's model serves as a useful framework of analysis which, with modification, yields a fairly good picture of cyclical fluctuation within a framework of growth. It serves especially to emphasize that in a capitalist economy characterized by substantial amounts of durable equipment, a period of contraction inevitably follows expansion. Hicks's model also pinpoints the fact that in the absence of technical progress and other powerful growth factors, the economy will tend to languish in depression for long periods of time."

Nicholas Kaldor's Model of the Trade Cycle

Nicholas Kaldor[11] was a Cambridge economist. He presented a business cycle depending on Keynes' concept of investment and saving functions. Keynesian understanding of saving and investment functions depends on the linear form of investment and saving functions. Kaldor kept himself aside from this linear understanding of investment and saving functions. He introduced nonlinear form of investment and saving curve. According to him if income increases investment or saving will not increase proportionately. Erratic changes could be found in saving or investment due to changes in income. Kaldor crossed linear relationship between income and saving or investment on the basis of following reasons as presented through our following figure-7.11.

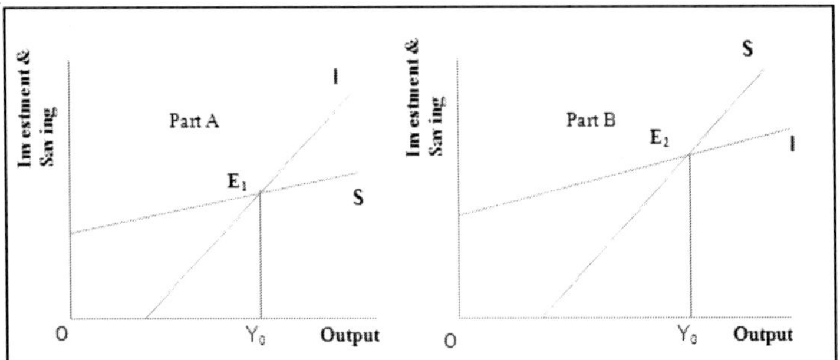

Source: Internet.

Figure-7.11: Linear Saving & Linear Investment Function

11. "A Model of the Trade Cycle", E.J. March 1940. Reprinted in his *Essays on Economic Stability and Growth*, 1960.

Along the vertical axis we measure investment & saving and along the horizontal axis we measure output. The figure has two parts, part A and part B. In part A intersection between investment and saving represents equilibrium at point E_1. If any disturbance is created in the economy then it will impact on investment & saving and output will increase to infinity or decrease to zero. If planned investment is greater than planned saving then output will increase more and more. It will create hyperinflation in the economy. In the same way if saving is greater than investment output will decline. It will decline up to zero. This situation presented in part A depicts non stability in the economy. So any disturbance in the economy that deviates (from point E_1) investment from saving will make the economy unstable.

Now if we consider the B part of our Figure-7.11 then we find that any disturbance in the economy changes the equilibrium point E_2 in the short-run but in the long-run the economy gets the previous equilibrium point. If investment is greater than saving (to the left of point $E\text{-}_2$) then income will increase till the previous equilibrium point E_2 is reached. If saving is greater than investment (to the right of point $E\text{-}_2$) then income will decline till the previous equilibrium point E_2 is reached. So in case of linear investment and saving function business cycle will not generate as because business cycle is a dynamic process and it push the economy towards new equilibrium. That is the reason behind the Kaldor's understanding of nonlinear investment function and nonlinear saving function in building business cycle.

Kaldor's nonlinear investment and saving function are shown in figure-7.12 and 7.13.

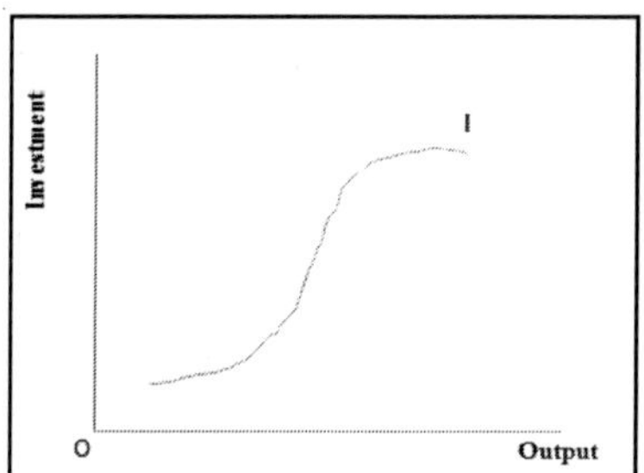

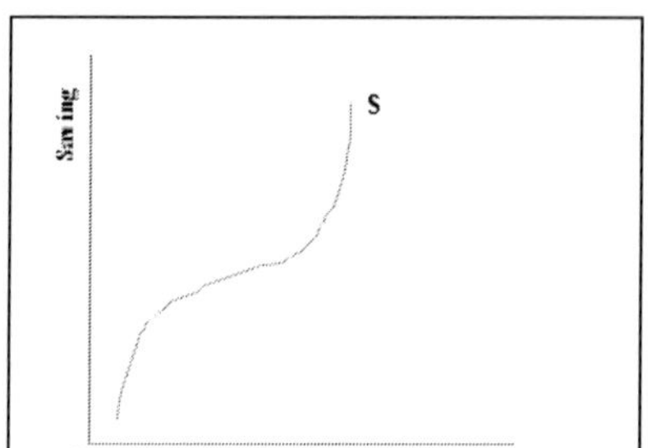

Source: Internet.

Figure-7.12: Nonlinear Investment Function

Figure-7.13: Nonlinear Saving Function

In Figure-7.12, it is clear that at low income investment function is near about parallel to horizontal axis to some extend as because in the recession investment increases very slowly or constant. In the boom investment is also parallel to the horizontal axis as because in the boom investment becomes constant or very slow. Now we consider the economic reasoning of this. According to Kaldor investment is a function of income (Y) and capital stock (K). Investment is positively related to income and negatively related to capital stock. If capital stock is high then investment is low. At the beginning of the investment curve (I) the curve is flat as capital stock is high increase in income will not be capable to increase investment to rise. Until capital stock is exhausted investment will not take place. As capital stock is totally exhausted investment curve will be steeper. In the boom inflation is high. As a result of that expected demand will be low and excess capacity of the economy will increase i.e., capital stock will increase. So in prosperity investment curve will be flat again. In another way we could say that in recession and progression marginal propensity to invest declines.

Mathematical representation

$$I = f(Y,K), \frac{dI}{dY} > 0 \frac{dI}{dK} < 0$$

In Figure-7.13, it is clear that at low income saving function is near about parallel to vertical axis to some extend as because in the recession saving increases very quickly as marginal propensity to save is high. In the boom saving is also parallel to the vertical axis as because in the boom saving becomes more at that period. Now we consider the economic reasoning of this. According to Kaldor saving is a function of income (Y) and capital stock (K). Saving is positively related to income and positively related to capital stock. If capital stock is high then saving is high. At the beginning of the saving curve (S) the curve is vertical as mps is high even at low income. In the boom inflation is high. As a result of that expected demand will be low and excess capacity of the economy will increase i.e., capital stock will increase. So in prosperity saving curve will be vertical again. In another way we could say that in recession and progression marginal propensity to save increases.

Mathematical representation:

$$S = f(Y,K), \frac{dS}{dY} > 0 \frac{dS}{dK} > 0$$

$$\frac{dS}{dY} > \frac{dS}{dK}$$

According to Kaldor when there is inequality between investment and saving business cycle will emerge. If investment is greater than saving economic activities are found and economic expansion takes place. But this situation will not stay for long time. In another way if investment is less than saving then economic activities reduce and recession will start. Kaldor says that recession will continue for long if investment is not taken place. Now we use our Figure-7.14 to clarify the economic understanding. In our figure both the nonlinear functions intersect with each other. Points A, C and B are the three equilibrium points. Point C is unstable but points A and B are stable points in short-run.

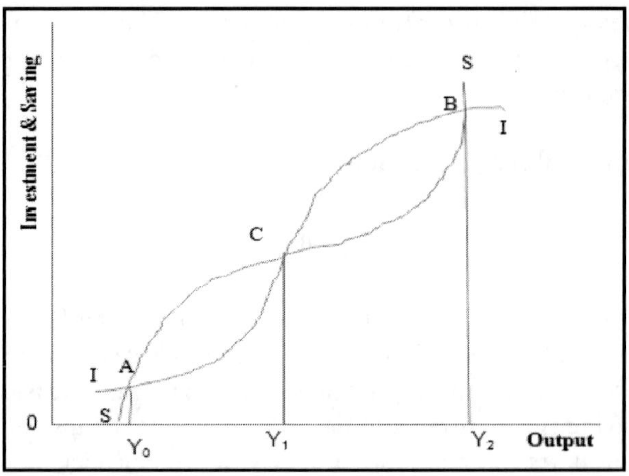

Source: Internet.

Figure-7.14: Interaction of Nonlinear Investment and Saving Function

To the left of Y_0 investment is greater than saving. So economy moves towards point A and gets equilibrium. Suppose for some economic activities national income is at a point between Y_0 and Y_1. Here saving is greater than investment. As a result of that economic contraction will take place and the economy comes back to point A. Similarly if we consider the part beyond point B then we find that saving is greater than investment and economic contraction will take place. Economy comes back to point B at Y_2 income. It is assumed that for some economic actions national output is at a point between Y_1 and Y_2. Here investment is greater than saving. As a result of that economic expansion will take place and the economy goes to point B. Therefore, it is clear that when national output is between points A and

C equilibrium moves to short-run equilibrium point A and when national output is between points C and B equilibrium moves to short-run equilibrium point B.

Following three figures (Figure-7.15 to Figure-7.17) depicts the contraction of the business cycle. These three stages in Kaldor analysis clear the concept of contraction in the trade cycle. Suppose the economy is at point B. At point B income is high. At this high income level investment is more than saving. If investment is high capital stock is also high. High capital stock reduces marginal efficiency of capital (MEC). This falling MEC reduces marginal propensity to invest. On the contrary Marginal

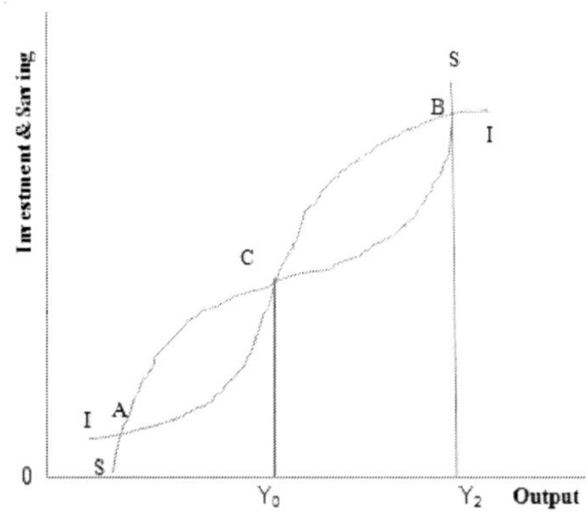

Source: Internet

Figure-7.15: First Stage of Economic Contraction (MEC declines, MPI declines and MPS increases: Upward shifting of saving curve)

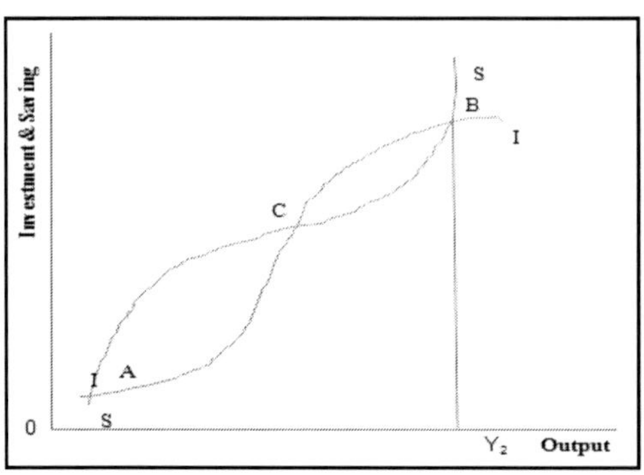

Source: Internet

Figure-7.16: Second Stage of Economic Contraction (MEC declines, MPI declines and MPS increases: Upward shifting of saving curve)

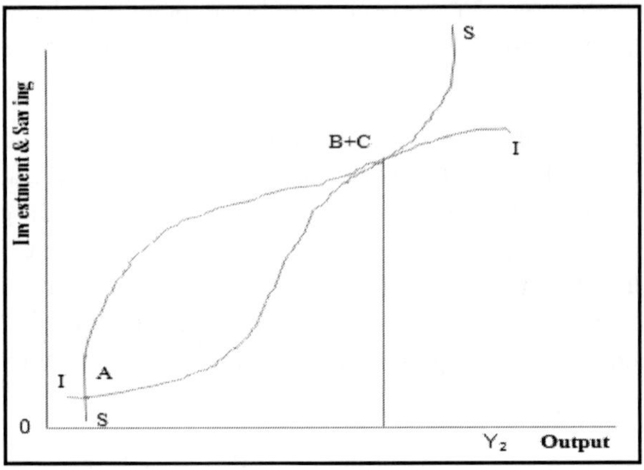

Source: Internet.

Figure-7.17: Third Stage of Economic Contraction (MEC declines, MPI declines and MPS increases: Upward shifting of saving curve.)

efficiency of saving increases at the same time. That is why beyond point B saving curve is upward rising and investment curve is downward sloping. As saving curve shifts upward and investment curve shifts downward points C & B close to each other. After some time B and C coincide with each other. When points B and C meet each other there is no possibility of having investment more than saving and contraction starts. This contraction pulls point (B + C) to A at low income level.

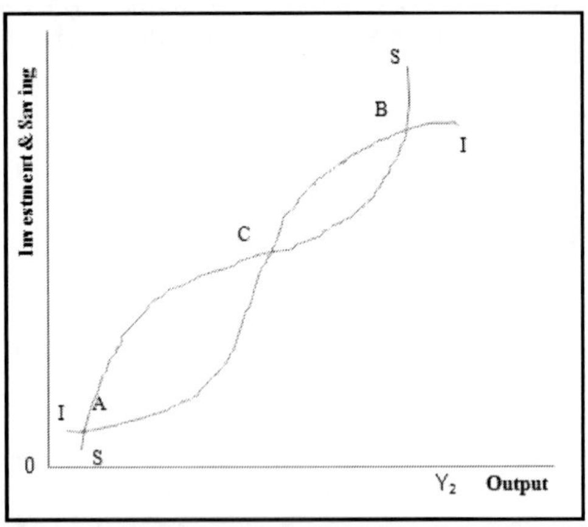

Source: Internet.

Figure-7.18: First Stage of Economic Expansion (MEC increases, MPI increases and MPS declines: Downward shifting of saving curve.)

Following three figures (Figure-7.18 to Figure-7.20) depicts the expansion of the business cycle. These three stages in Kaldor analysis menifest the concept of expansion in the trade cycle. Suppose the economy is at point A. At point A income is low. At this low income level investment

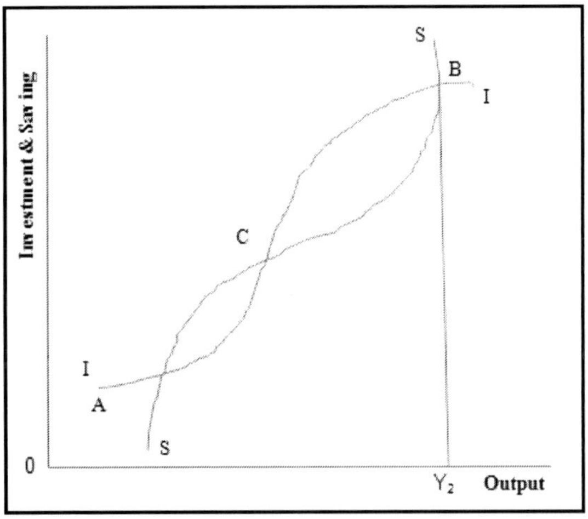

Source: Internet

Figure-7.19: Second Stage of Economic Expansion (MEC increases, MPI increases and MPS declines: Downward shifting of saving curve)

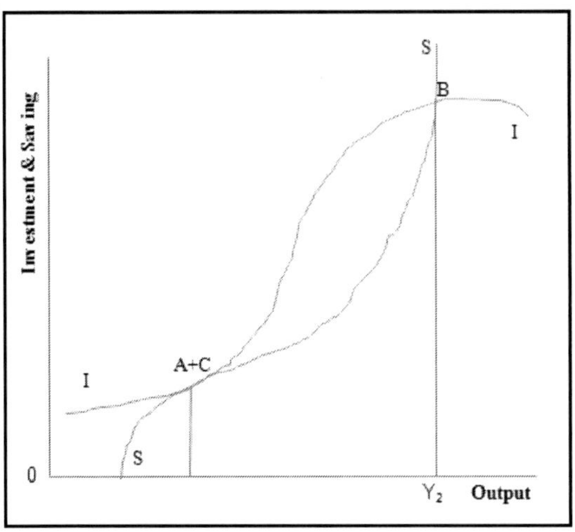

Source: Internet

Figure-7.20: Third Stage of Economic Expansion (MEC increases, MPI increases and MPS declines: Downward shifting of saving curve)

is less than saving. At point A economy will stay for some time. Now economy starts to use excess capacity of capital stock. As capital stock is being used investment begins to rise. As capital stock declines marginal propensity to save decreases. As saving curve shifts downward and investment curve shifts upward points A & C close to each other. After some time A and C coincide with each other. When points A and C meet each other investment is more than saving and expansion starts. This expansion shifts point (A+C) to B at high income level.

In this way contraction and expansion continues in an economy and cyclical process generates. Kaldor's trade cycle model is self generating. Kaldor observed cycles in his model are not of same duration. According to him expansion and contraction are not symmetrical positively. Slope of investment and saving have important role in Kaldor's business cycle. Monetary factors and acceleration principle do not have any role in explaining business cycle as far as his understanding over the trade cycle is considered.

Chapter - 8

Consumption

About Consumption

We should have a clear idea about the term 'consumption'. According to Adam Smith "consumption is the sole end and purpose of all production". Consumption is a service that is provided by a good. Individual's expenditure on that good is called consumption expenditure. There are durable goods and non durable goods. The length of time is short for non-durables and the length of time is long for durable goods. Vegetables are non-durable and buses are durables goods.

In macroeconomic theory consumption has a great role. In Solow growth model saving rate is important for economic well being. Saving is a part of income that is not spent on consumption. In short saving is the negative consumption. In IS-LM model consumption is very important. Slope of the IS curve depends on the marginal propensity to consume. Without consumption Keynes's aggregate demand cannot be calculated. So it is not astonishing that aggregate consumption theory is the most important region of macroeconomic study. In this chapter we discuss about different approaches to explaining consumption of well-known economists.

The Absolute Income hypothesis:

In john Maynard Keynes's General Theory published in 1936 primary importance was given to disposable income. There are three important suppositions in the theory of consumption formed by Keynes. One is marginal propensity to consume, 2nd one is average propensity to consume and third one is that income is the main determinant of consumption though the rate of interest has some important role in determining consumption theoretically.

Marginal propensity to consume (*mpc*) implies change in consumption due to one unit change in income. Its value lies between zero and one. If it is constant as income rises then consumption function is linear. On the other hand if *mpc* falls as income rises consumption function is non-linear.

In this theory of consumption average propensity to consume declines as income rises. It is because as income rises marginal propensity to save increases.

Keynesian consumption function is given below. In this function *a* is the autonomous consumption and *b* is the *mpc*. Autonomous consumption *a* determines the intercept on the vertical axis and *mpc* determines the slope of the consumption function.

$$C = a + by$$[12]

$$Or, C/y = a/y + by/y$$

$$Or, APC = C/y = a/y + b$$

According to classical economists if interest rate is higher it supports savings. As it supports savings it automatically discourages consumption. But this thought was not accepted by Keynes as he believed that theoretically classical economists were true but his experience did not support that.

The following figure depicts the Keynesian consumption function with the three properties that are assumed by Keynes.

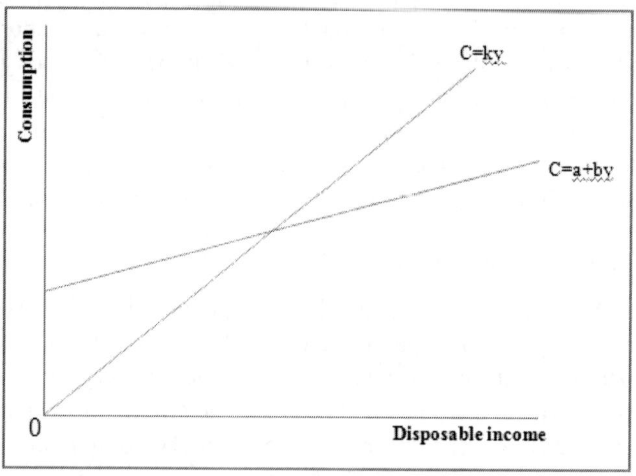

Source: Internet

Figure - 8.1: Proportional Consumption Function

12. Mankiw N. Gregory (2010), "Macroeconomics" 7th Edition, Worth Publishers, pp. 458.

The verification on consumption proclaimed so far discloses that, while there appears to be some stable connection between consumption and income over the long run, in the short run current income alone offers a pitiable explanation of consumption performance. The insufficiency of absolute income hypothesis was apparent by the start of the 1950s and inspired the seek for another theories. Two theories, the permanent income hypothesis (PIH) and the life-cycle hypothesis (LCH) have been accepted over the absolute income hypothesis. Both these theories consider the household's preference of consumption and saving over a long time horizon.

Irving Fisher and choices involving different periods of time

Keynes in his theory of consumption relates consumption with current income. But it has some shortcomings. Current consumption depends on present as well as future level of income. If present consumption is high then future consumption will be low. If we consider two periods- period 1 and period 2 that cover the whole life of an individual then period 1's consumption depends on period 2's consumption. If consumer consumes more at period 1 he has to consume less at period 2. He has to borrow from future income. If consumer consumes more at period 2 he has to save at period 1 and that save will be used for consumption. For simplicity two periods are considered here. In this example individual's choices involve two periods of time. Irvine Fisher gave importance on this issue – issue of choices involving different periods of time.

Now we develop Fisher's model of consumption.

Y_1 => Income at period 1

Y_2 => Income at period 2

C_1 => Consumption at period 1

C_2 => Consumption at period 2

S=> Savings at period 1 used for period 2

r => Interest rate prevails in the economy

All variables are real.

Now $S=Y_1-C_1$[13]

$C_2=(1+r)S+Y_2$ Or, $C_2=(1+r)[Y_1-C_1]+Y_2$ Or, $C_2 = (1+r)Y_1+(1+r)C_1+Y_2$

or, $C_2+(1+r)C_1=(1+r)Y_1+Y_2$

or, $C_1+C_2/(1+r)=Y_1+Y_2/(1+r)$

13. Mankiw N. Gregory (2010), "Macroeconomics" 7th Edition, Worth Publishers, pp. 462.

The left hand side of the above equation is total consumption (consumption of two periods) and the right hand side is the total income (income of two periods). $C_2/(1+r)$ is the 2nd period consumption used at 1st period and $Y_2/(1+r)$ is the 2nd period income used at 1st period income.

If all income earned at period 2 is consumed at period 1 then total income at period 1 would be

$Y_1 + Y_2/(1+r)$. If all income earned at period 1 is saved for period 2 then total income at period 2 would be $(1+r)Y_1 + Y_2$. If an individual likes to consume more than Y_1 at period 1 he has to borrow from period 2 and if an individual likes to consume more than Y_2 he has to save the income earned at period 1.

If income increases consumer consumes normal goods more than previous income. On the other hand if real interest rate increases consumption at period1will reduce and consumption at period 2 will increase. It should be noted here that increase in real interest rate impacts consumption through two effects. One is income effect and another is substitution effect. Two effects run in opposite direction. So to inspire or discourage saving relative size of income and substitution effects have a role when interest rate increases.

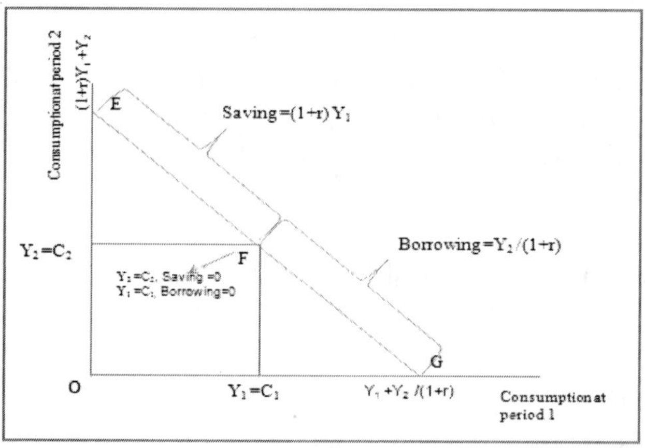

Source: Internet.

Figure 8.2: Fisher's Intertemporal Budget line.

In Figure-8.2, the consumer's intertemporal budget con-straint is shown by the line EFG. It displays the alternative combinations of period 1 and period 2 consumption. These alternative points the consumer can choose.

If at point F he consumes his entire income in both the periods ($Y_1 = C_1$ and $Y_2 = C_2$, Saving = 0, Borrowing = 0). At point E, $C_1 = 0$ and $Y_1 = S$. Nothing is consumed at period 1.

Therefore $C_2 = (1 + r)Y_1 + Y_2$. Thus if he decides points between E and F, he swallows less than his income in period 1 and he saves the remaining part for period 2.

At point G, $C_2 = 0$. This means that the consumer borrows the maximum possible amount against Y_2. This means that C_1 is $Y_1 + Y_2/(1 + r)$. Thus if he decides any point between F and G, he swallows more than his income in period 1 and borrows to fill the gap. There are other attainable points on the EFG budget line.

Life-Cycle Hypothesis and Franco Modigliani

In Fisher's model of consumption function we have seen that consumption of individuals depend on life time income. This is the fundamental base of Franco Modigliani's life-cycle hypothesis. There is a systematic distribution of income in life-cycle hypothesis. People save their income when it is high and spend that income when income is low. So income moves from the time of high income to the time of low income.

Now we illustrate the model with the following example.

Let an individual lives N years, his wealth is W and his service period is T with income Y per year.

Therefore, his total income is W+TY. If he likes to distribute his income equally over his life time then his consumption will be

$$C=(W+TY)/N$$

$$\text{Or, } C=(1/N)W+(T/N)Y$$

$$\text{Or, } C=\alpha W+\beta Y$$ [14]

where α marginal propensity to consume out of wealth and β marginal propensity to consume out of income. $C=\alpha W+\beta Y$ is the Modigliani' consumption function. But it is short-run consumption function. In the long-run wealth increases as income increases. So average propensity to consume will not decline. The Life-Cycle consumption function is graphically represented in the following figure.

14. Mankiw N. Gregory (2010), "Macroeconomics" 7th Edition, Worth Publishers, pp. 472.

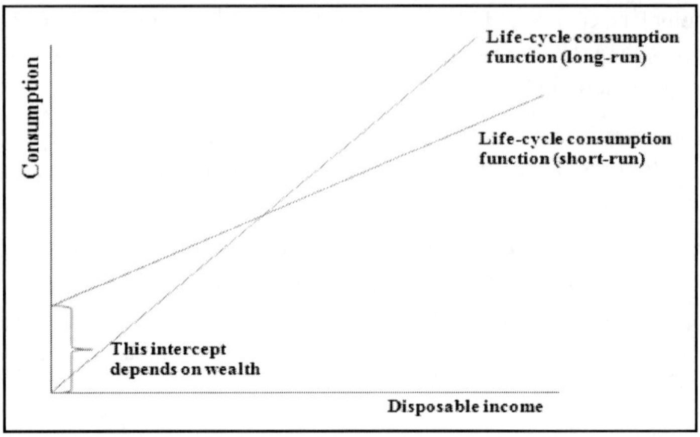

Source: Internet.

Figure -8.3: Life-Cycle Consumption Function.

If the consumer equally distributes consumption over her life, consumer will save and build up wealth during her working years and then dissave and run down her wealth during retirement. Income and consumption curve over the life-cycle of a consumer is given below.

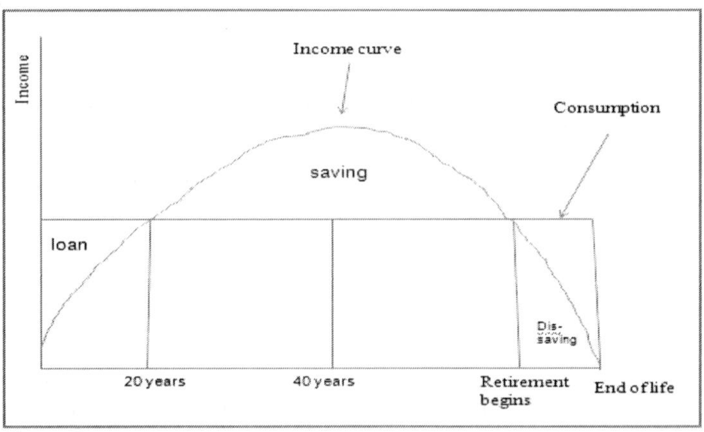

Source: Internet.

Figure-8.4: Consumption and income curve over the Life-Cycle.

Permanent-Income Hypothesis

Permanent income hypothesis was explained by Milton Friedman in his book published in 1957. In Franco Modigliani's life-cycle hypothesis consumer's income follows a regular pattern. Consumer earns in his service period and savings out of his earning spends in his retirement life. On the basis of Modigliani's understanding of income pattern Friedman said individual's income does not follow a regular pattern rather individual's income has two parts. One is temporary or random and another is fixed part.[15]

According to Friedman

$$Y = Y^P + Y^T$$

Y=> Current income

Y^P => Permanent income or average income

Y^T => Transitory income or deviation from average income

Friedman's understanding of consumption function is as follows.

$$C = k\, Y^P$$

where k is a constant that measures the portion of permanent income consumed.

According to Keynes average propensity to consume declines as income rises. Unlike the Keynesian understanding according to Friedman understanding average propensity to consume deciles as current income rises when transitory income is positive and APC increases as current income falls when transitory income is negative.

$$APC = C/Y = k\, Y^P/Y$$

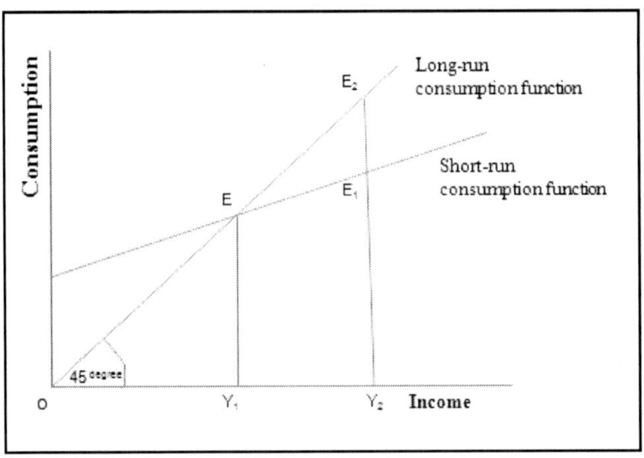

Source: Internet.

Figure -8.5: Permanent Income Consumption Function.

15. Milton Friedman, A Theory of the Consumption Function (Princeton, NJ: Princeton University Press, 1957)

In 1946 Kuznets showed in his article that consumers spend a fixed portion of his income on consumption. Over the period of his study 1869 to 1938 (time series analysis) he proved this with empirical analysis. Friedman also supported this and he said that in short-run income fluctuates because of transitory income. As transitory income rises Average propensity to consume falls and as transitory income falls average propensity to consume rises. In the long-run there is a constant average propensity to consume. It supports the Kuznets understanding.

In our figure point E shows that at income Y_1 short-run consumption function is equal to long- run consumption function. But at income Y_2 long-run consumption is more than short-run consumption as because in the short-run people think that high income will not persist for long time. So they consume less portion of their income. As in the long-run high income persists people consume more. So there is a difference between E_1 and E_2 at income level Y_2.

Chapter - 9

Investment

About Investment

Investment appertains to the accumulation of real capital goods over time by firms. Real capital goods are of two types. One is fixed capital (plant, machinery, etc.) and another is working capital (raw materials, manufactured inputs, etc).

In aggregate demand investment is a smaller component. But investment is a crucial element in aggregcate supply. It is crucial in the sense that this investment is used to form capital assets. Formation of capital requires sacrifice of labor and other resources that could be used for present consumption in alternative way.

If the capital stock bigger over time, the enlarge in capital stock per period of time is known as net investment. Gross investment is the addition of replacement investment and net investment.

By saving the people as a whole is releasing from present consumption wealth which can be transformed into capital goods and hence into extra future consumption. The procedure of capital accumulation or net investment entangles net savings in aggregate by members of the community.

The Multiplier

The multiplier presents a measure of the degree of changes in national income stimulated by a given change in autonomous spending. Aggregate spending is divided into autonomous and induced spending. In a closed economy autonomous spending is of two types. One is autonomous investment spending and another is autonomous consumption spending. Induced expenditure or spending depends on national income. Consumption function can be stated as $C=a+bY$. *a* is the autonomous consumption and *b* $(0<b<1)$ is the marginal propensity to consume.

Therefore, Aggregate expenditure in a closed economy can be stated as

E=C+I (without considering government expenditure)

$$\text{or, } E = a + bY + I = bY + (a+I)$$

In equilibrium planned expenditure equals national income (Y).

Therefore, E= bY+(a+I), Or, Y= bY+(a+I), Or, Y(1-b)=(a+I), Or, Y=(a+I)/ (1-b)

Change in Y due to change in autonomous consumption (a) or autonomous investment (I) is equal to Y(1-b) i.e., income multiplied by marginal propensity to save or one minus marginal propensity to consume.

Change in income due to change in autonomous investment depends on marginal propensity to consume. Marginal propensity to consume changes the slope of the aggregate expenditure curve. If *mpc* is zero the aggregate expenditure curve is horizontal. If *mpc* is low aggregate expenditure curve will be upward but not too much steep. If *mpc* is high aggregate expenditure curve will be upward and steeper.

The line (C+I) shifts upward to $(C+I)'$ as a result of an increase in autonomous consumption. The new equilibrium point shifts from point A to E. Here marginal propensity to consume is zero. So (C+I) curve is parallel to horizontal. Here change in autonomous consumption is equal to change in real income i.e., (Y_0 to Y_1)

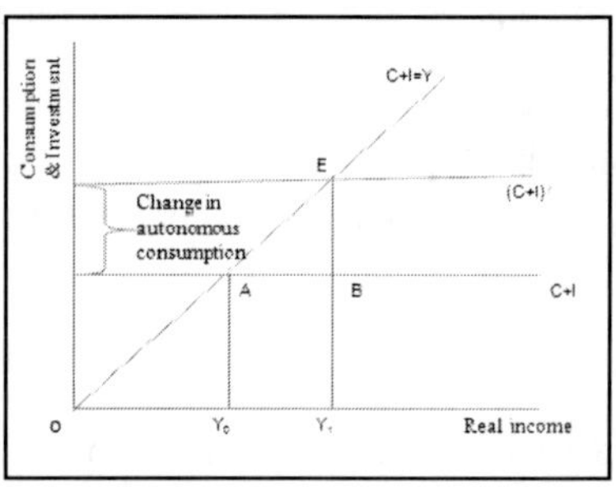

Source: Internet

Figure-9.1: Effects of Multiplier when* mpc *is 0

The line (C+I) shifts upward to $(C+I)'$ as a result of an increase in autonomous consumption. The new equilibrium point shifts from point A to E. Here marginal propensity to consume is zero. So (C+I) curve is parallel to horizontal. Here change in autonomous consumption is equal to change in real income i.e., (Y_0 to Y_1) is more than in autonomous consumption.

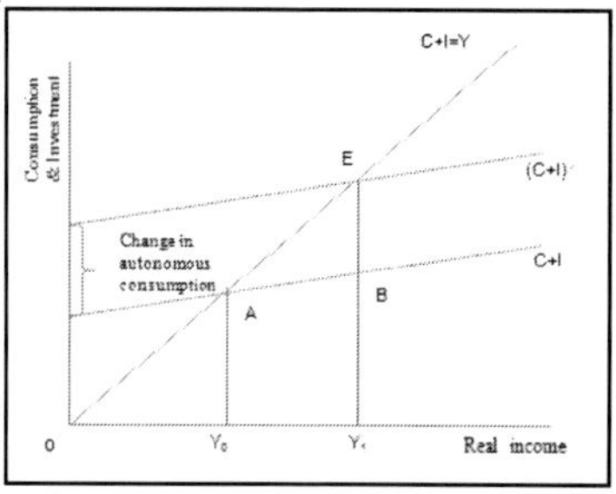

Source: Internet.

Figure-9.2: Effects of Multiplier when* mpc *is greater than 0 but not too much

The line (C+I) shifts upward to (C+I)′ as a result of an increase in autonomous consumption. The new equilibrium point shifts from point A to E. Here marginal propensity to consume is greater than zero but not too much high. So (C+I) curve is upward rising. Here change in real income i.e., (Y_0 to Y_1) is more than change in autonomous consumption.

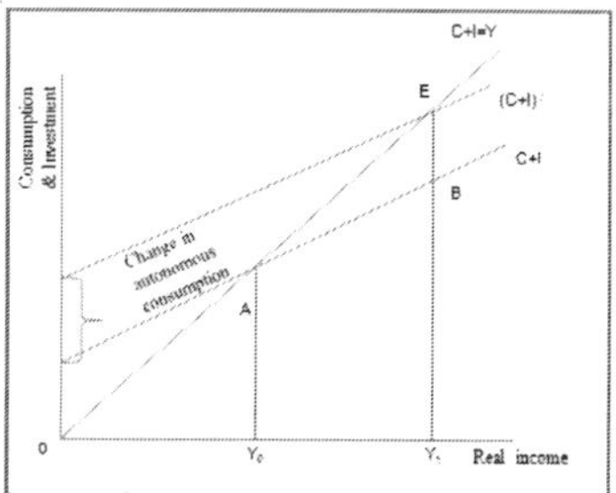

Source: Internet.

Figure-9.3: Effects of Multiplier when* mpc *is too high, such as 0.85

The line (C+I) shifts upward to (C+I)′ as a result of an increase in autonomous consumption. The new equilibrium point shifts from point A to E. Here marginal propensity to consume is greater than zero and much high. So (C+I) curve is upward rising and steeper. Here change in real income i.e., (Y_0 to Y_1) is much more than change in autonomous consumption.

Table- 9.1: Derivation of the Multiplier

MPC (Change in consumption due to one unit change in income)	***1-MPC = MPS***	***Multiplier Coefficient***
0	1	1
0.5	0.5	2
0.6	0.4	2.5
0.7	0.3	3.34
0.8	0.2	5
0.9	0.1	10
1	0	Infinity

Source: Author's own.

It is clear from the table that as marginal propensity to consume increases multiplier coefficient also increases. As marginal propensity to consume decreases multiplier coefficient increases. When *mpc* is 0 multiplier coefficient is one and when *mpc* is one (i.e., total income is used for consumption purposes) multiplier coefficient is infinity.

Table- 9.2: Forward Functioning of Multiplier

Period	*Increment in Investment*	*Increment in Income*	*Increment in Consumption*	*Increment in Saving*
t	200	200	100	100
t+1		100	50	50
t+2		50	25	25
t +3		25	12.5	12.25
t+4		12.5	6.25	6.25
t+5		6.25	3.12	3.12
		0	0	0
To end with	200	400	200	200

Source: Author's own.

The above table depicts the forward functioning of multiplier. It is assumed that *mpc* is constant with value 0.5. If investment is increased by \$200 million then it has an immediate effect on production and it will increase income by amount \$200 million. It will have immediate increase in consumption and consumption will increase by amount \$ 100 million. This increment in consumption again will increase production and income by amount \$ 100 million. This process will continue until increment in income would be \$ 400 million. The following figure shows the forward functioning of multiplier.

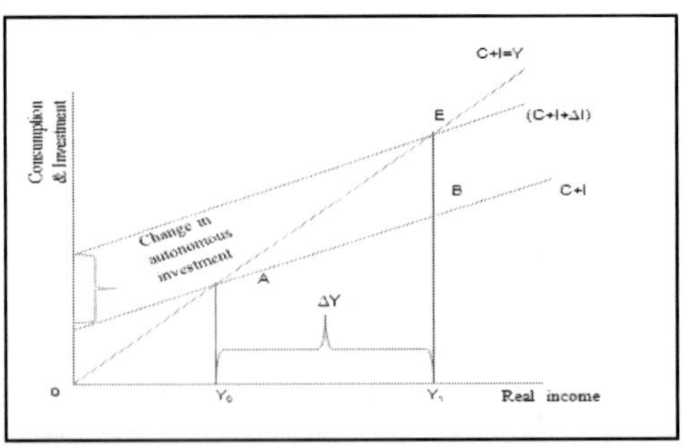

Source: Internet.

Figure-9.4: Forward Functioning of Multiplier

In the above figure consumption and investment are measured along the vertical axis and real income is measured along the horizontal axis. Here slope of the aggregate expenditure curve is 0.5 as marginal propensity to consume is 0.5. As investment changes by the amount "I aggregate expenditure curve shifts to (C+I+"I). New equilibrium is at point E. Due to the increase in autonomous investment real income increases twice times of the increase in investment. Due to the value of *mpc* (0.5) income increases double of change in investment.

Assumptions of Investment Multiplier

Keynes assumed following assumptions for smooth functioning of investment multiplier.

Assumptions

Autonomous Investment has a role in Keynesian multiplier. Induced investment does not have any role in this concept.

Keynes considered lump-Sum Taxes. There is no proportional relationship between income and tax rate. If amount of tax increases as income increases then generated income has a little effect on production.

If there is a demand for consumer goods in the market consumer goods will be supplied. It means there is availability of goods depending on effective demand.

There is always addition in investment and it is necessary for the smooth functioning of multiplier process.

According to Keynes net investment should be positive. Gross investment is an addition of replacement capital and net investment. Gross investment is positive even when net investment zero. So positive net investment is mandatory for successful multiplier process.

Marginal propensity to consume should be constant. Keynes considered his model in the short-run. As Keynes assumed in the short-run people's propensity to consume does not vary with change in income.

Foreign imbalances are not considered in Keynesian multiplier process. Economy is considered to be closed.

Time Lag is not considered in the multiplier process. Increment in consumption instantly generates production or income.

Involuntary unemployment has a role in the multiplier process. Keynes considered the economy in the short-run. In the short-run there is always unutilized resources and this resources should be used for the fulfillment of effective demand.

Accelerator Theory of Investment

Change in capital stock is related with change in output in the following way.

$$K_t - K_{t-1} = v(Y_t - Y_{t-1})$$

$$\text{Or, } I_t = v(Y_t - Y_{t-1})$$

where K_t is the capital stock at time t, K_{t-1} is the capital stock at time (t-1), Y_t is the output at time, Y_{t-1} is the output at time (t-1) and v is the capital output ratio.

Assumption of acceleration principle:

(*a*) There is no excess capacity in the economy,

(*b*) Capital assets are easily available,

(*c*) Change in output makes change in capital stock at the same year. No time lag adjustment is there,

(*d*) Capital assets are divisible.

Following hypothetical table clears the concept of acceleration principle.

Accelerator Theory of Investment

Period	*Output*	*Required Capital Stock*	*Replacement Capital*	*Net Investment*	*Gross Investment*
t-1	500	1500			
t	550	1650	300	150	450
t+1	600	1800	330	150	480
t+2	650	1950	360	150	510
t+3	700	2100	390	150	540
t+4	750	2250	420	150	570
t+5	800	2400	450	150	600
t+6	850	2550	480	150	630
t+7	900	2700	510	150	660
t+8	950	2850	540	150	690
t+9	950	2850	570	0	570
t+10	900	2700	570	-150	420
	Capital output ratio = 3		Depreciation = 0.2		

Source: Author's own.

Required Capital Stock = Output X Capital Output Ratio

Replacement Capital = Required Capital Stock at previous period X Depreciation

Net Investment = Change in Output X Capital Output Ratio

Gross Investment = Replacement Capital + Net Investment

At period (t-1) output is 500. To produce that amount of required capital is 1500 (output multiplied by 3). At period t output is 550 and to produce that amount of output required capital is 1650. Replacement capital at that period is 300 (1500 multiplied by 0.2). Net investment at period t is equal to change in required capital. Gross capital at period t is equal to net investment plus replacement capital. Mathematically net investment is negative at period (t+10). But practically it is not possible. Replacement capital may be reduced to make net investment non negative. Our table shows the method through which change in output affects investment.

Influence of Fiscal Policy and Monetary Policy on Investment

Fiscal policy and monetary policy both affect investment. Fiscal policy affects private investment through two distinct channels. On the one plane it may affect the level of future anticipated demand for output, while on the cost side changes in tax can alter the cost of capital services. The latter has been the major tool whereby governments have tried directly to control the level and opus of investment.

As with consumption, monetary policy affects investment by inducing a process of portfolio alteration. A boost in the money supply relative to interest- bearing financial assets stimulates a switch into the latter type of assets, including equity. Asset prices increase and interest rates and dividend yields also fall. A continuously sloppy monetary policy which escorts to inflation and high nominal interest rates may well slow down investment. Fiscal policy also affects interest rates. Government budget deficits financed by bond issues raise interest rates and so inhibit private-sector investment. Interest rate rises if government budget deficits is financed by issuing bonds and reduce private-sector investment.

Tobin's q Ratio

There is a relationship between investment and fluctuations in the stock market. So investment has a role in a stock market. Actually investor gets incentive from stock prices.

Tobin's q is the ratio between a physical asset's market value and its replacement value. It was introduced in 1968 by James Tobin and William Brainard, although the use of the letter 'q' did not appear until Tobin's 1969 article "A general equilibrium approach to monetary theory". Tobin writes one, the numerator, is the market valuation: the going price in the market for exchanging existing assets. The other the denominator, is the replacement or production cost: the price in the market for the newly produced commodities. We believe that this ratio has considerable macroeconomic significance and usefulness, as the nexus between financial markets and markets for goods and services.

If Tobin's q is less than 1, the market value is less than the recorded value of the assets of the company. This suggests that the market may be undervaluing the company. John Mihaljevic points out that "no straightforward balancing mechanism exists in the case of low Q ratios. i.e., when the market is valuing an asset below its replacement cost. In the case of stock market as a whole, rather than a single firm, the conclusion that assets should be liquidated does not typically apply. A low q ratio for the entire market does not mean that blanket redeployment of resources across the economy will create value. Instead, when market-wide Q is less than parity, investors are probably being overly pessimistic about future assets returns." Lang and Stulz found out that diversified companies have a lower q- ratio than focused firms because the Tobin's discoveries show us that movement in stock prices will be reflected in changes in consumption and investment, although empirical evidence reveals that his discoveries are not as tight as one would have thought. This is largely because firms do not blindly base fixed investment decisions on movements in stock price; rather they examine future interest rates the present value of expected profits. Other influences on q. Tobin's q measures two variables-the current price of capital assets as measured by accountants or statisticians and the market value of equity and bonds but there are other elements that may affect the value of q, namely speculation, reflecting etc. The intellectual capital of corporations, that is, the unmeasured contribution of knowledge, goodwill, technology etc. that a company may have but are not recorded by accountants. some companies seek to develop ways to measure intangible assets such as intellectual capital.

Tobin's q-ratio is as follows

$$q = \frac{\textit{Market Value of Installed Capital.}}{\textit{Replacement Cost of Installed Capital.}}$$

$$q = \frac{\textit{The value of the economy's capital as determined by the stock market.}}{\textit{The price of that capital if it were purchased today.}}$$

Stock: The shares in the ownership of corporations.

Stock Market: The market in which shares are traded.

The value of Tobin's q may be greater than 1 or less than 1. If the value of the economy's capital as determined by the stock market is more than the replacement cost of installed capital then Tobin's q is greater than 1. In the same way if the replacement cost of installed capital is greater than market value of installed capital then Tobin's q is less than 1.

In the event that the marginal product of capital surpasses the expense of capital, at that point firms are winning benefit on their introduced capital. These benefits make the organizations increasingly attractive to possess new capital, which raises the market estimation of these organizations' stock, inferring a high estimation of q. Additionally, if the marginal product of capital misses the mark regarding the expense of capital, at that point firms are causing misfortunes on their introduced capital, suggesting a low market esteem and a low estimation of q.

Numerical Example:

Let Tata Company has \$80 million of assets, 20 million shares outstanding and a current share price of \$5.

Solution

The **Tobin's Q ratio** is a measure of firm assets in relation to a firm's market value. The formula for Tobin's Q is:

Tobin's Q = Total Market Value of Firm / Total Asset Value of Firm

Tobin's Q is:

Tobin's Q = (20,000,000 X \$5) / \$80,000,000 = 1.25

Problem:

I = \$ 110; C =\$ 70 + 0.70 Y.

(*a*) Find the equilibrium level of income,

(*b*) Find the equilibrium level of income when there is a \$ 30 increase in autonomous investment.

(*c*) Establish the multiplier effect of the \$ 30 increase in autonomous consumption.

Solution:

(*a*) We know that Y=C+I

Or, Y=\$ 70 + 0.70 Y + \$110

Or, Y-0.70Y=\$70 + \$110

Or, 0.30Y=\$180

Or, Y=\$180/.30=\$600

Therefore, equilibrium level of income is \$600.

(*b*) There is a \$ 30 increase in autonomous investment.

Therefore, Y=C+I= \$ 70 + 0.70 Y +(\$110+\$30)

Or, Y=\$210/.30 = \$700

The equilibrium level of income is \$700 when there is a \$ 10 increase in autonomous investment.

(*c*) The equilibrium level of income increases by \$ 100 (from ₹600 to ₹700) as a result of a \$30 increase in investment. As a result of autonomous investment there is a multiplier effect (“Y/”I) of 100/30.

Problem:

(*a*) Find out the multiplier when the marginal propensity to consume is 0.70, 0.60 and 0.50.

(*b*) What is the relationship between the marginal propensity to consume and the value of the multiplier?

(*c*) If the multiplier value is 5 what affect a \$40 decrease in autonomous spending has upon equilibrium income.

Solution:

(*a*) The multiplier m equals 1/(1-marginal propensity to consume). The value of multiplier is 3.33 when the MPC is 0.70; The value of multiplier is 2.5 when MPC is 0.60; and 2 when MPC is 0.50.

(*b*) Consumption and disposable income has a relation. If income increases consumption also increases. The value of multiplier is directly related with marginal propensity to consume. If marginal propensity to consume increases the value of multiplier also increases.

(*c*) We know that the decline in income equals Change in investment multiplied by the multiplier. The decrease in equilibrium income is ₹200.

Chapter - 10

Case Studies

CASE STUDY - 1

DETERMINANTS OF INFLATION: EVIDENCE FROM BANGLADESH

Introduction

The emergence of substantial inflation figure in Asia and Bangladesh in particular has led to widespread studies about its causes. Persistent price increases are among the most serious problems affecting every economic unit. That is why very country is saddle with the responsibility of ensuring stability in general price level as one of core macroeconomic objectives to achieve economic development.

Inflation is generally used to describe a situation of rapid, persisted and unacceptably high rises in the general price level in an economy, resulting to general loss of purchasing power of the currency. Inflation causes serious discomfort for consumers, investors, producers and the government (Asogu, 1990). Long term inflation occurs when the money supply grows at a faster rate than the output of goods and services. This situation occurs when there is more money than is needed to accommodate nominal growth in output, consumers and businesses want to purchase more goods and services than can be produced with current resources (labour, materials, etc.) causing upward pressures on prices. Over a short term, inflation can occur from various shocks in the economy. Food and energy price shocks are common examples of this type of inflation in Bangladesh. A price of a commodity such as fuel may rise suddenly and sharply, relatively to other commodities prices response, may result to short term increase in overall prices

Inflation in Bangladesh has been accelerating from beginning and has become a major concern to the government. Several policies were introduced to control inflation in the economy and despite these policies, inflationary trends continue to fluctuate. Government needs to control high levels of unpredictable inflation since it can severally disrupt the economy. The tools governments normally use include monetary policy (i.e. increase or decrease in the money supply and interest rate), fiscal policy (changes in the amount of taxes and government spending) and various controls on prices, tariffs, etc. Many nations choose monetary policy as their primary tool since it has proven to be effective, less disruptive to the market operations and easier and quicker to implement since adjusting the money supply does not require legislative approval as would be for instance changing the tax structure.

The three major explanations of inflation include fiscal, monetary, and balance of payments aspects. Monetary aspect, inflation is considered to be due to an increase in money supply, in fiscal aspect, budget deficit are the fundamental causes of inflation. However, the fiscal aspect is closely linked to monetary explanations of inflation since government deficit are often financed by money creation in developing countries. In the balance of payment aspect, emphasis is placed on exchange rate. That is the collapse of exchange rate brings about inflation either through higher import prices and increase in inflationary expectation, which are often accommodated or through an accelerated wage indexation mechanism (Akinbobola, 2012).

However, efforts by various governments to curb inflationary tendencies, the problems and its effects continued unabated. Studies reveal growth in money supply, government deficit financing, exchange rate decreased agricultural and industrial production among other were responsible for inflationary pressure in Bangaladesh. And the most significant effect of inflation is its impact on government revenues and non-performance of the economy. Inflation also makes budgeting and future planning difficult for economic agents imposes a drag on productivity, particularly when firms are forced to shift resources away from products and services, thereby discouraging investment and retarding growth (Orubu, 2009).

Milton Friedman (1963) wrote Inflation is always and everywhere a monetary phenomenon. The Quantity Theory of Money leads us too agree that the growth in the quantity of money is the primary determinant of the inflation rate. John Maynard Keynes (1936) argued that demand determines output, which, in turn, determines employment and prices. At full employment of men and capital, excessive demand for goods and services drives up the general level of prices causing inflation. The biggest challenge in macro-economic management is reining the inflation. The inflation rate of Bangladesh in the last five years, starting from FY 2004-05 is above 6 percent and in 2010 is 8.44 percent, with the non-food inflation close to 5.37 percent and food inflation 10.34 percent. The gap between the targeted GDP growth rate and the achieved GDP growth in the last twenty years revealed that increase in average inflation may be one of the major reasons (Bangladesh Economic Update, 2010).

The high inflation rate has become a serious concern in the industrial and emerging market economies globally. Inflation constitutes one of the factors responsible for poverty, low standard of living and growth in Bangladesh. Hence, the paper is to investigate into the root causes of inflation in Bangladesh.

Theoritical Issues and Literature Review

Inflationary discourse still remains the most contentious Macroeconomic studies which have theoretical basis in the perspective of both the Monetarist and the Keynesian schools of thought. Most economist before Keynes had underscored the relationship between the amount of money supply and the level of general prices, however, with varying degree of emphasis. The quantity theory of money states that the general price level changes in direct proportion to a change in the level of money supply.

Keynes (1936) posited that inflation is caused by a situation of excess aggregate demand over aggregate supply when there is no excess capacity, a situation in which the economy operates at full employment of resources. Furthermore, there are strong arguments that fiscal deficits are major cause of inflation. Abolo (1997) among other researchers contented that evidence points to fiscal deficits as major cause of inflation.

The argument that price inflation is significantly determined by the process mark-up on the costs of firm's production process has been advanced in the models of Goacher (1986) and Gordon (1984) believed that inflation could result from the cost of imported goods rising independently of the demand for them in the domestic economy.

Most recently, there is an emerging trends of literature on inflation came to be known as the political economy approach to macroeconomic policy Selialia (1995).These recent theories of inflation have shifted attention away from traditional direct economic causes of inflation, such as money creation, towards political and institutional determinants of inflationary pressures because being theoretical and put emphasis almost exclusively on industrial countries.

There are relatively large literature dealing with relations between monetary indicators and other macroeconomic variables. Doroshenko, (2001), consider relation between both money supply and inflation and between money supply and inflation and found a long-run relationship between money growth and inflation. Clemens and Alex (2002) empirically estimate the relationship between exchange rate accommodation and the degree of inflation persistence using a non-linear autoregressive inflation equation for ten European countries for the period 1974-1998..Thier results provide supportive evidence for the existence of a positive link between exchange rate accommodation and inflation persistence for most of the smaller and more dependant exchange rate mechanism countries, even when mean level shift in inflation are appropriately accounted for.

Mahamadu and Philip (2003) explore the relationship between monetary growth, exchange rate, and inflation in Ghana using Error Correction Mechanism The result confirms the existence of a long run equilibrium relationship between inflation, money supply, exchange rate and real income. In line with theory, the finding demonstrates that in the long run, inflation in Ghana is positively related to the money supply and exchange rate and negatively related to real income.

In Nigeria, there have been several studies on causes on inflation. For instances Oyejide (1972),

Odusanya and Atanda (2010) analyzed the dynamics and simultaneous inter-relationship between inflation and its determinants in Nigeria between 1970 and 2007 examined using the Augmented Dickey Fuller (ADF) and unit root test. The result reveals that inflation rate, growth rate of real output, money supply and real share of fiscal deficit are stationary at levels, while, other incorporated variables-real share of import, exchange rate and interest rate are stationary at first difference. Adeyeye and Kola also examined the causes and effects of inflation in Nigeria between 1969 and 2009 and what could be done to ameliorate the negative effects on the economy. The time series variables properties on some selected variables were examined using ADF unit root test and co- integration analysis. The result reveals that money supply, growth rates, gross domestic product growth rate and expenditure revenue ratio are not spurious but exchange rate of dollar to Naira was non-stationary. The study also revealed that the GDP growth rate is counter inflationary as against inflationary factors. It is sufficed to say that causes of inflation is one of the most highly treated subject in economic researches and literature. Bangladesh Bank, IMF and CPD (2007) explored that both demand and supply side factors constitute the relevant sources of inflation in Bangladesh. Among these are M2 growth, private sector credit growth, market capitalization growth, growth of government borrowing, remittance growth, exchange rate change, market syndicate. Taslim (1980) used regression models for explaining the inflationary process of Bangladesh. He explored that one year lagged money supply had significant positive effect on inflation. However, the introduction of wage variable as an additional independent variable resulted in dramatic fall of statistical significance of coefficients of other variables in the regression model.

Estimation of the Models: Augmented Dickey-Fuller (ADF) unit root test was applied in checking the order of integration of the series. The results of the estimates are reported in Table- A.

Table-A: Results Of Augmented Dickey-Fuller Tests For Unit Root of variables concerned

					Mackinnon Critical Value			
Variable	*Ex-ogenous*	*ADF Test Statistic*	*Prob.* value*	*Lag length*	*1%*	*5%*	*10%*	*Inference*
Inflation (It) at level	none	-5.54	0	0	-3.63	-2.95	-2.61	I(0)
Interest rate (rt) at 1st difference	none	-3.58	0.01	0	-3.63	-2.95	-2.61	I(1)
Exchange rate (Et) at 1st difference	none	-5.82	0	0	-3.64	-2.95	-2.61	I(1)
Govt.expenditure (Gt) at 1st difference	none	-6.07	0	0	-3.65	-2.95	-2.61	I(1)
Money supply (Mt) at 1st difference	none	-4.05	0.0072	0	-3.64	-2.95	-2.61	I(1)

Source: Author's own.

It is important to note that the mixture of both I(0) and I(1) variables would not be possible under the Johansen procedure. This therefore, gives a good justification for using the bounds test approach, or ARDL model, which was proposed by Pesaran et al (2001).

Methodology: The ARDL model can be specified as follows:

$$I_t = \alpha_0 + \alpha_1 E_t + \alpha_2 M_t + \alpha_3 R_t + \alpha_4 G_t + \varepsilon_t \qquad ...(1)$$

Where I is Inflation, E is exchange rate, M is money supply, R is interest rate and G is govt. expenditure. ε is a white noise process and t is the time period. The equation (1) is my model and from this model the ARDL model can be specified.

Estimation Techniques: The methodology used in this study is based on the autoregressive distributed lag (ARDL) model which does not involve pre-testing variables. This methodology is used to examine the cointegration relationship among $I_t = E_t + M_t + R_t$ and G_t variables.

ARDL framework for the above equation is given as

$$\Delta I_t = \alpha_0 + \sum_{i=1}^{n} \alpha_{1i} \Delta I_{t-1} + \sum_{i=1}^{n} \alpha_{2i} \Delta E_{t-1} + \sum_{i=1}^{n} \alpha_{1i}$$

$$\Delta M_{t-1} + \sum_{i=1}^{n} \alpha_{4i} \Delta R_{t-1} + \sum_{i=1}^{n} \alpha_{5i} \Delta G_{t-1}$$

$$+\beta_1 I_{t-1} + \beta_2 I_{t-1} + \beta_3 M_{t-1} + \beta_4 R_{t-1} + \beta_5 I_{t-1} + \varepsilon t \qquad ...(2)$$

The ARDL model testing procedure starts with conducting the bound test, which states the null hypothesis of zero cointegration, i,e.

$$H_0 + \beta_1 = \beta_2 = \beta_3 = \beta_4 = \beta_5 = 0$$

against the alternative hypothesis of the existence of cointegration, i.e.

$$H_0 \neq \beta_1 \neq \beta_2 \neq \beta_3 \neq \beta_4 \neq \beta_5 \neq 0$$

The statistic underlying the procedure is the F-statistic which is used to test the significance of lagged levels of the variables, in order to establish the existence of cointegration. Two sets of critical values are reported in Pesaran and Pesaran (1997), Pesaran et al (2001) or Narayan (2004). The critical values are divided into upper and lower critical bounds. The upper critical values assume that all the series are I(1) while the lower critical values assume that all the series are I(0). In the bound testing approach, the calculated F-statistic is compared with the critical values provided by Pesaran and Pesaran (1997), Pesaran et al (2001) or Narayan (2004). However, due to the limited number of sample observations, the critical values in this paper are extracted from Narayan (2004). If the computed F-statistic falls outside the critical bound, a conclusive inference can be made without considering the order of integration of the underlying regressors. For instance, if the F-statistic is higher than the upper critical bound, then the null hypothesis of no cointegration is rejected. Alternatively, if the F-statistics is lower than the lower critical bound, then the null hypothesis of nocointegration cannot be rejected. If however the calculated F-statistic lies within the lower and upper bounds, then the test is said to be inconclusive. In this context, the unit root tests should be conducted to ascertain the order of integration of the variables. If all the variables are found to be I(1), then the decision is taken on the basis of the upper critical value. On the other hand, if all the variables are I(0), then the decision is based on the lower critical bound value.

Once cointegrating relationship is ascertained, the error correction estimates of the ARDL model are obtained. The diagnostic test statistics of the selected ARDL model can be examined from the short run estimates at this stage of the estimation procedure. Similarly, the test for parameter stability of the model can be performed. The error correction representation of equation (2) can be specified as follows:

$$\Delta I_t = \alpha_0 + \sum_{t=1}^{n} a_{1i}\Delta I_{t-1} + \sum_{t=1}^{n} a_{2i}\Delta E_t + \sum_{t=1}^{n} a_{3i}$$

$$\Delta M_{t-1} + \sum_{t=1}^{n} a_{4i}\Delta R_{t-1} + \sum_{t=1}^{n} a_{5i}\Delta G_{t-1} + \gamma ECTt - 1 + \varepsilon t$$

where ECM is the error correction term which measures the speed of adjustment, and ã is the coefficient of the error correction term, which is expected to be negative and statistically significant to further confirm the existence of a cointegrating association.

Sources of data: The time series data were derived from various secondary sources such as: Indian Financial Statistics etc. The macroeconomic data covers between 1976- 2010. Base period is 2000. Log of variables has been used in my research work. The data gathered were subjected to various econometric tests with the aid of E-views.

Empirical Analysis

Bound test Cointegration Results: In order to perform the bound testing procedure, equation (2) using the ARDL approach to cointegration, to examine the long run relationships among the variables in equation (1). A lag length of 2 was chosen as the maximum lag length based on the AIC and SIC. This is also consistent with Pesaran and Shin (1999) who recommended choosing a maximum lag length of 2 for small sample annual data. The F-statistic and critical bounds values for testing the null of no cointegrating relationship are reported in Table-1.

Table 1: Bounds Test for Cointegration Analysis

Critical Value	*Lower Bound Value*	*Upper Bound Value*
1%	3.74	5.06
5%	2.86	4.01
10%	2.45	3.52

Source: Author's own.

Note: Computed F-statistic: 6.47 (Significant at 0.05 marginal values). Critical Values are cited from Pesaran et al. (2001), Table CI (iii), Case 111: Unrestricted intercept and no trend.

Table 2: Bounds Test Results

Variables	*F-Statistic*	*Probability*	*Inference*
I_t, E_t, M_t, R_t, G_t	6.47	0.0018	Cointegration

Source: Author's own.

The estimated coefficients of the long-run relationship between I_t, E_t, M_t, R_t, G_t are expected to be significant.

Table- 3: Long-run estimated coefficients based on equation (2)

Dependent variable: d(log Inflation)

Variables	*Coefficient*	*Standard Error*	*T-Ratio*	*Probability*
Constant	5.91	2.73	2.16	0.03
E_t	-8.49	2.49	-3.4	0.001
M_t	0.88	0.67	1.3	0.2
R_t	0.9	0.7	1.28	0.2
G_t	2.24	0.85	2.61	0.01
R^2=0.30, Adjusted R^2=0.20, Log likely hood=-13, F-Stat=3.13, AIC-1.07, SIC=1.29				

Source: Author's own.

The calculated F-statistic when inflation is the dependent variable is 6.47, which is higher than the upper bound critical value at the 5 percent level of significance (4.01). This implies that the null hypothesis of no cointegration is rejected at the 5 percent level and that there is indeed a cointegration relationship among the inflation and its determinants.

Long Run and Short Run Dynamics: There is a long run association as far as bound test is concerned. Results are given in table -3. The results suggest that exchange rate has negative effect on inflation, money supply and interest rate have no significant effect on inflation, and government expenditure has positive effect on inflation.

Table-4: Error Correction Representation for the Selected ARDL Model

Dependent Variable: D (INFLATION)				
Variable	**Coefficient**	**Std. Error**	**t-Statistic**	**Prob.**
C	-0.016047	0.253381	-0.063333	0.9501
D (INFLATION (-1))	0.805913	0.38762	2.079129	0.0507
D (INFLATION (-2))	0.360397	0.274169	1.314506	0.2036
D (EXCHANGE RATE(-1))	7.030518	4.16613	1.687542	0.107
D (EXCHANGE RATE(-2))	1.571135	3.728362	0.421401	0.678
D (MONEY SUPPLY(-1))	0.03849	2.538937	0.01516	0.9881
D (MONEYSUPPLY(-2))	1.714355	2.706644	0.633388	0.5337
D (INTERESTRATE(-1))	-3.793734	1.997255	-1.899474	0.072
D (INTEREST RATE (-2))	3.327917	1.712781	1.94299	0.0662
D (GOVT EXPENDITURE (-1))	-6.579168	2.170203	-3.031591	0.0066
D (GOVT EXPENDITURE (-2))	1.420193	1.370513	1.036249	0.3125
ECT (-1)	-1.962548	0.494318	-3.970214	0.0008
R-squared	0.774936	Mean dependent var		0.00759
Adjusted R-squared	0.651151	S.D. dependent var		0.633897
S.E. of regression	0.374401	Akaike info criterion		1.153018
Sum squared resid	2.803524	Schwarz criterion		1.702669
Log likelihood	-6.448292	Hannan-Quinn criter.		1.335212
F-statistic	6.26034	Durbin-Watson stat		1.811603
Prob(F-statistic)	0.000211			

Source: Author's own.

It is clear from the above table on the basis of F-statistic that the null hypothesis is accepted i.e, there is no serial correlation.

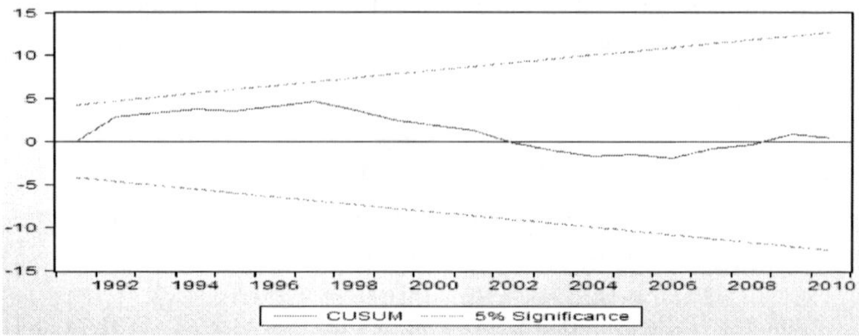

Source: Author's own.

Figure 2: CUSUM Test for stability of parameters:

The diagnostic test statistics indicates that there is no evidence of serial autocorrelation in the disturbances. The coefficient of determination (R^2) indicates that the model is reasonably accurate in prediction, and 77 percent of variation in the dependent variable is accounted for by the independent variables. The stability of the regression coefficients are evaluated using cumulative sum (CUSUM) test. The regression equation appears to be stable as the CUSUM test statistics lies within the 5% critical bound as shown in the Figure-2.

Short-run Causality Test (Wald Test F-statistic)

Table-6: Short run causality between inflation and exchange rate

Wald Test:			
Test Statistic	***Value***	***df***	***Probability***
F-statistic	1.598022	(2, 20)	0.2271
Chi-square	3.196043	2	0.2023

Source: Author's own.

Exchange rate at lag 1 and exchange rate at lag 2 cannot jointly cause inflation because null hypothesis i.e., c(4)=c(5)=0 is accepted. Therefore, there is no short run causality running form exchange rate to inflation.

Table-7: Short run causality between inflation and money supply

Wald Test:			
Test Statistic	***Value***	***df***	***Probability***
F-statistic	0.216421	(2, 20)	0.8073
Chi-square	0.432843	2	0.8054

Source: Author's own.

Money supply at lag 1 and money supply at lag 2 cannot jointly cause inflation because null hypothesis i.e., c(6)=c(7)=0 is accepted. Therefore, there is no short run causality running form money supply to inflation.

Table-8: Short run causality between inflation and interest rate

Wald Test:			
Equation: Untitled			
Test Statistic	***Value***	***df***	***Probability***
F-statistic	2.472744	(2, 20)	0.1097
Chi-square	4.945488	2	0.0844

Source: Author's own

Interest rate at lag 1 and interest rate at lag 2 can jointly cause inflation because null hypothesis i.e., c(8)=c(9)=0 is rejected. Therefore, there is a short run causality running form interest rate to inflation.

Table-9: Short run causality between inflation and govt. expenditure

Wald Test:			
Equation: Untitled			
Test Statistic	***Value***	***df***	***Probability***
F-statistic	5.941915	(2, 20)	0.0094
Chi-square	11.88383	2	0.0026

Source: Author's own

Govt. expenditure at lag 1 and govt. expenditure at lag 2 can jointly cause inflation because null hypothesis i.e., c(10)=c(11)=0 is rejected. Therefore, there is a short run causality running form govt. expenditure to inflation.

Conclusion & Policy Implication: This paper has estimated the impact of exchange rate, money supply, interest rate and government expenditure on inflation of Bangladesh by using time series data from 1976-2010 by employing Bound Testing approach. The analysis demonstrates that in the long-run, exchange rate has negative effect on inflation, money supply and interest rate have no significant effect on inflation, and government expenditure has positive effect on inflation.

While in the short-run, the results indicate directional causality taking inflation as dependent variable and exchange rate, money supply, interest rate and government expenditure. It is manifest that inflation is sensitive to changes both interest rate and government expenditure. Therefore, the government should realise effective macro-economic policies. The policy implication is that in Bangladesh to lessen inflation momentum the government will have to pursue a monetary and fiscal policy which matches with the actual scenario of real sectors and monetary sectors. Govt. spending should be prudently utilized.

There is a recommendation that further study should be carried out using different sets of variables with appropriate mathematical models to detect determinants of the inflation in Bangladesh.

References

Adeyeye, E.A. and T.O.Fakiyesi (980) "Productivity price and incomes Board and Anti inflationary policy in Nigeria in the Nigerian economy under the military. Proceedings of the 1980, Annual Conference of Nigerian Economic Society, Ibadan.

Adeyeye and Kola (2012) "Empirical Analysis of the causes and effects of Inflation in Nigeria" Journal of Economic and Sustainable Development, www.iiste.org, vol.3, no.11. Pp35-40.

Akibobola,T.O(2012)"The dynamics of money supply, exchange rate and inflation in Nigeria" Journal of Finance and banking,vol. 2 no.4, pp117-141

Asogu, J. O. (1991) "An econometric Analysis of the nature and causes of Inflation in Nigeria" Economic and Financial Review, Vol.29, no.2.

Aris, M. J. (1992) "Wage inflation" in current issues on Macroeconomics, London, Macmillan Education ltd.

Batini,N. (2004)"Achieving and Maintaining Price Stability in Nigeria, IM working paper,04- 97,Washington DC.

Edwaikhide et al (1994)"Exchange rate, Money supply and Inflation in Nigeria: An Empirical Investigation "African Journal of Economic Policy", vol.2 pp57-73.

Eihner, A. S. (1973) "A theory of the determinantion of mark-up under oligopoly" Economic Journal, December 1973.

Friedman, Milton (1963) *Inflation: Causes and Consequences*. New York: Asia Publishing House.

Fuller, T. M. and Ikhide, (1998)'An Economic Analysis of Nigerian Consumer Price Index" Journal of Economics, \vol.24(2), pp1-15.

Goaecher, D. J. (1986) An introduction to Monetary Economic, London Financial Training Publication ltd.

International Monetary Fund, 2007, Bangladesh: Selected Issues (IMF Country Report No. 07/230, June 2007), pp. 16-23.

Jhingan, M. L.(2004) Monetary Economics, 6th ed. Vrinda Publications Ltd.

Keynes, J. M. (1936) The General Theory of Employment, Interest and Money. Published for the Royal Economic Society by Macmillian Press Ltd, London and Basingstoke.

Mahamadu, B. and Philip, A. (2003) " Monetary Growth, Exchange rates and Inflation in Ghana: An Error Correction Analysis, Working Paper, WO/BOG- 2003/05

Odusunya, I. A. and A. A. Atanda (2010): Analysis of inflation and its determinants in Nigeria , Pakistan Journal of Social Sciences, volume 7, No.2 Pp 97-100.

Okpara and Nwoaha (2010)" Government Expenditure, Money supply, Prices and output Relationship in Nigeria: An Econometric Analysis" International Research Journal of Finance and Economic Issues 54.

Oruba, C. O.(2009) "Inflation in Nigeria: Concept, Measurement and Control", Bullion,

Central Bank of Nigeria,Vol. 33(1)

Osakwe, J.O. (1983) "Government Expenditure, Money supply and prices, 1970-1980,CBN Economic and Financial Review, Vol.21, no.2.

Oyejide, T. A. (1972) "Deficit Financing, Inflation and capital Formation: The analysis of the Nigerian economy, 1957-1970" NJESS, ol.14.

Owoye, O. (2007) "Money Targeting, Money Demand and Real GDP growth in Nigeria: Do rule Apply? Journal of Business and Public Affairs Vol.1 (2) pp1-20.

Pesaran, M.H., Y. Shin. & Smith R. (2001) "Bounds testing approaches to the analysis of level relationships", *Journal of Applied Econometrics,* Vol. 16 :pp 89-326.

Selialia, F.L. (1995) The Dynamics of Inflation in Lesotho, Unpublished M.A Thesis,University College, Dublin.

Taiwo, J. K. (2011) "Econometric Analysis of the cuases and effects of Inflation", MSc Thesis, Department of Mathematics, University of Abuja, Nigeria.

Taiwo, J. K. and Adeyeye (2012) "Empirical analysis of the effects and causes of Inflation in Nigeria" Journal of Economics and Sustainable Devlopment, Vol.3, no.11, www.iiste.org

Taslim, M. A., 1980, 'Inflation in Bangladesh: A Re-examination of the Structuralist Monetarist Controversy'. *The Bangladesh Development Studies*, X (1), 100-116.

CASE STUDY - 2

EMPIRICAL EVIDENCE OF TWIN DEFICITS HYPOTHESIS IN THE CONTEXT OF INDIAN ECONOMY – A TIME SERIES ANALYSIS

Introduction

Like any developing countries India has been facing fiscal deficit and it is a matter of concern. Fiscal deficit and trade deficit have varied between 3 percent to 7 percent and between 0 percent to 6.8 percent respectively during the last three decades. It is necessary to reduce the two deficits. As far as the twin deficit is concerned there is a close relation between two deficits. Since these two deficits are behind the primary reason for poor economic health of any economy, empirical research on causal relationship between the two variables are matter of concern in the economy of India.

"The twin deficits hypothesis (TDH hereafter) are said to exist if the government budget deficit, through its effect on national saving and consumption, leads to a current account deficit. In a Mundell-Fleming framework, it is argued that an increase in budget deficit would induce upward pressure on interest rates, causing capital inflows and appreciation of exchange rates. Hence, an increase in current account deficit emerges. On the contrary, the Ricardian Equivalence Hypothesis (REH hereafter) states that shifts between taxes and budget deficits do not matter for the real interest rate, the quantity of investment, or the current account balance, negating any link between the two deficits (Magazzino, 2012)." (Cosimo Magazzino, 2012, pp.65-66) . In Jun, 2019 India current account deficit is 2 percent of nominal GDP. The data was high (all-time) of 2.2 percent in Jun 2004 and low (all-time) of -6.8 percent in Dec 2012.Balance of payment crisis, Asian crisis and financial crisis were found in Indian economy during the period 1990 to 2013. The balance of payment calamity in 1990s affected the economy of India very badly. Oil led crisis i.e., increase in oil prices affected current account and the current account affected the budget deficit.

There are mixed results regarding the twin deficit hypothesis. Some found no causal relationship, some found unidirectional causal relationship or bidirectional causal relation.

So it is important to empirically examine if the current account deficit is responsible to carry the Indian economy in deficit or if the budget deficit is responsible to keep the economy in deficit. It is also significant to find the out the causal direction in the Indian economy.

The article is organized in seven sections: Section II: Literature Survey and about the Indian economy, Section III: Theoretical Framework, Section IV: Variables, Data, Stationarity and Cointegration, Section V: The VAR Model, Section VI: Impulse Response and Variance Decomposition, Section VII: Conclusion.

Literature Survey

Anoruo, E. and Ramchander, S. (1998) in their article using VAR found causal association between budget deficit and trade deficit in India. Trade deficit causes budget deficit as far as their findings are concerned. Long-run association was not the matter of their research.

Anita Ghatak and Subrata Ghatak (1996) found by using multicointegration analysis and estimation of the rational expectations model both invalidate the RE hypothesis in India.

Baharumshah, Lau (2009) in his study gave focus on structural break and twin deficit in East Asian Countries and results supported the causality running from fiscal deficit to trade deficit.

Afonso et al. (2018) studied 193 countries (data period 1980–2016) using fixed effect model. The results find the presence of fiscal policy diminishs the effect of budget deficit on current account deficit.

Aghevli and Sassanpur (1982) argued that heavy public expenditure would direct to a corrosion of the trade deficit in Iran.

Anoruo, E. and Ramchander, S. (1998) in their article using VAR found causal association between budget deficit and trade deficit in India. Budget deficit is caused by trade deficit as far as their findings are concerned. Long-run association was not the matter of their research.

Anita Ghatak and Subrata Ghatak (1996) found by using multicointegration analysis and estimation of the rational expectations model both invalidate the RE hypothesis in India.

Asrafuzzaman, Amit Roy and Sanat Das Gupta (2013) in their article based on the data set 1972-2012 and using VAR model found current account deficit causes budget deficit in the economy of Bangladesh.

Badinger et al. (2017) examined the role of fiscal rules in the association between fiscal and current balances in 73 countries using data period of 1985–2012. Twin deficits hypothesis was confirmed in the findings.

Baharumshah, Lau (2009) in his study gave focus on structural break and twin deficit in East Asian Countries and fiscal deficit caused trade deficit.

Basu, S. and Datta, D. (2005) in the article "Does Fiscal Deficit Influence Trade Deficit? An Econometric Enquiry" discovered Twin deficit was not applicable in the economy of India during their study period.

Bhat and Sharma (2018) investigate the relationship between budget deficit and current account deficit for India using data period from 1970–1971 to 2015–2016. They used ARDL approach. The Keynesian proposition was accepted. Long-run relationship between the two deficits was found in their results.

Bose and Jha (2011) examined the twin deficits hypothesis in India. It is found that there is a causal relationship among exchange rate, interest rate and fiscal deficit. No variables affect current account deficit. It is also found that oil price has an effect on other variables concerned.

Baharumshah et al. (2006) investigated the hypothesis for four countries of ASEAN using cointegration. He found that his results support Keynesian proposition and there is a causal linkage between budget deficits to current account deficit.

Cosimo Magazzino, (2012) used numerous time series techniques to examine the connection between current account and budget deficits in Italy. His study period was 1970-2010. It was found that trade balance Granger-caused budget deficit but cointegration between the variables concerned was absent.

Enders and Lee, (1990) using variety of samples found no stable long-run causal relationship between budget deficit and current account deficit. Their findings supported Recardian Equivalence Hypothesis.

Feldstein (1992) argued that the gap in savings that enlarges trade deficit is because of fall in private savings. Increased budget deficit has no role. The budget deficit tends to increase real interest rates and as a result crowding out of private investment takes place. Net exports also decline. In the early 1980s this was the explanation behind the high current account deficit.

Garg and Prabheesh(2017) by using ARDL approach examined the twin deficits in India. They found support in favor of twin deficit hypothesis.

Goyal and Kumar (2018) examined the relation between the current account and budget deficit, and the exchange rate, using VAR model for

India over the study period 1996Q2 to 2015 Q4. Ricardian hypothesis was not accepted in their research.

Kulkarni and Erickson (2006) empirically studied the twin deficits hypothesis using comparative study. There study focused on Pakistan, India and Mexico. The results showed that budget deficit caused the trade deficit. Study showed that Pakistan is marked by the absence of unidirectional relationship.

Khalid, A.M. and Guan, T.W. (1999) in the article titled "Causality Tests of Budget and Current Account Deficits: Cross Country Comparisons" used the data of twin deficit over the period 1985 to 2001 found that twin deficit hypothesis is applicable in the context of Indian Economy.

Litsios and Pilbeam (2017) examined twin deficits hypothesis in Greece, Portugal and Spain and they used ARDL model. The findings supported inverse association between saving and current account deficit.

Hakro, A.N., (2009) examined the twin deficit hypothesis in the economy of Pakistan and found granger causality running from fiscal deficit to trade deficit during 1948 to 2005.

Islam and Wetzel (1991), based on time-series data in Ghana, reveal that the rising budget deficit is associated with the deterioration in the trade deficit.

Islam, M.F., (1998) examined the theory of twin deficit in the context of Brazilian economy over the period 1973-1991 and found two ways causal relationship between fiscal and trade deficit variables.

Mansur (1989) has done a comprehensive study in Philippines. The findings indicate that budget deficits led to a deterioration of the current account deficit in the economy of Phillippines. One of the major arguments is that the weak management of fiscal policy and monetary policy worsen the CAD, because most of the policy instruments may define the relationship between the budget deficit and the trade deficit.

Nigeria and Alam *et al.*(2014) found bi-directional causality between budget deficit and current account deficit in Bangladesh.

Osoro et al. (2014) in his paper empirically investigated the proposition of twin deficits. He used VECM. Results showed that budget deficit causes current account deficit in direct and indirect way. It is also found a positive association among current account deficit, interest rate and GDP.

Parikh, A. and Rao, B. (2006) in their statistical investigation found fiscal deficit causes trade deficit and there was long-run connection between the variables concerned over the period 1970 to 2000.

Ratha (2011) investigated the hypothesis in India over the period 1998 to 2009 and his results showed that twin deficits exist in the short-run. There is no causal relation in the long-run. Recardian Equivalence Hypothesis was found in the long-run.

Ratha, A. (2012) found that in the short-run Mundell-Fleming functioning is applicable but in the long-run the Ricardian Equivalence Hypothesis (REH) holds well in the economy of India over the period of study.

Rosensweig and Tallman (1993) stated that there is a strong causal relation between trade deficit and budget deficit.

Sakyi and Opoku (2016) for Ghana; Cardoso and Domenech, found that fiscal deficits cause the current account deficits of 94 economies. The twin deficits hypothesis in recent years becomes debatable in the developed as well as in the developing economies.

Saeed and Khan (2012) in their article tested Ricardian Equivalence hypothesis in Pakistan using data from 1972 to 2008. The results showed that there is unidirectional causality. Ricardian Equivalence hypothesis was not applicable in Pakistan.

Rajasekar & Deo (2016) find the long-run connection and bidirectional causality between trade deficit and budget deficit in India.

Vamvoukas (1999) using the econometric methodology including cointegration, VECM and Granger causality test discovers the association between these two deficits in a small open economy. Vamvoukas's findings suggest that BD effects the CAD.

Zaidi (1985) used data from different countries such as South Korea, the Philippines, Thailand, Greece, and Brazil and found diverse results. While bidirectional causality was established between BD and the CAD in South Korea and the Philippines, a one way directional causality from the CAD to BD was established in Thailand and Greece. In the case of Brazil, there is no a significant relationship between the two deficits.

So the past study represents incongruous results between the causal relationship of fiscal deficit and trade deficit the Indian Economies point of view.

About Indian Economy

"By 1990-91 the Indian economy was quite weak, it was burdened with heavy debt rising interest costs and deficits. India traditionally had a current account deficit with significant portion of the imports being that of oil and petroleum products. The weak economic situation further worsened with the Gulf-war which led to rise in oil prices coupled with drying up of credit lines and investors pulling out money. The country's foreign exchange reserves had depleted significantly and the level of reserves was only sufficient to finance imports of another three weeks. India had to arrange for emergency funds from the IMF to avoid default on external obligations. In response to the crisis the government headed by Prime Minister Narasimha Rao commenced on the path of economic liberalisation whereby the economy was opened up to foreign investment and trade, the private sector was encouraged and the system of quotas and licenses were dismantled. Fiscal policy was re-oriented to cohere with these changes. In order to augment the receipts the government undertook to reform both the direct and indirect taxes and for the first time the country embarked on the policy of disinvestment. The measures proposed above to meet the crisis are often referred to as the New Economic Policy of 1991. These measures could broadly be classified under three heads viz. liberalization, privatization and globalization. Under liberalization many industries were freed from the licensing requirement, the investment limit in small scale industries was enhanced, free determination of interest rates by commercial banks and abolition of restrictive trade practices. With privatization, the government invited the private sector to own and manage part of Public Sector Enterprises And among the measures for globalization included reducing tariffs, partial convertibility of the currency and increasing limits of foreign investment in India. In addition to the above, the government also brought in reform in the tax structure and reduce the non-capital expenditure like subsidies. The reforms were calibrated to bring about revenue neutrality in the short term and to enhance revenue productivity of the tax system in the medium and long term. The overall thrust was to decrease the share of trade taxes in total tax revenue, increase the share of domestic consumption taxes by transforming the domestic excises into a VAT, and increase the relative contribution of direct taxes. The share of direct taxes as part of total revenue receipts rose from 15 percent in 1991-92 to 20 percent in 1996-97 and to 26 percent in 2000-01, correspondingly the share of indirect taxes fell from 61 percent in 1991-92 to 54 percent in 1996-97 and to 45 percent in 2000-01.

Correspondingly significant efforts were also made to reduce subsidies and cut down the non-capital expenditure. However, given the large debt burden meant that the interest component would not reduce significantly or at a rapid pace as desired. The proportion of interest to total revenue expenditure rose form 32 percent in 1991-92 to 37 percent in 1996-97 and stood at 36 percent in 2000-01, over the same period share of subsidies fell from 15 percent in 1991-92 to 10 percent in 1996-97 and was maintained at 10 percent in 2000-01.

The economic policy had fairly significant positive impacts on the revenue and primary deficits as well. The new economic policy brought with itself a fresh approach, the government not only liberalized the licensing it also began with the disinvestment of the public enterprises and it's holding. This had a twin effects; firstly, it lead to lowering the capital expenditure and secondly, it increased the capital receipts. Thus post 1991 there was steady decline in the primary deficit as percentage of GDP, it fell 3.95 percent in 1990-91 to 0.51 percent in 1996-97.However the interest burden continued to mount and thus the difference between the fiscal and primary deficits rose from 3.66 percentage points in 1990-91 to 4.19 percentage points in 1996-97."(S. Gupta and K. Singh, 2016, pp.66)

Most of the time current account deficit interchanges trade deficit. The largest component of current account deficit is the trade deficit. But there are differences. Current account deficit means a country's spending on imports is more than its earning from exports. On the other hand if country's imports (total value) go beyond the total value of exports, the country's has trade deficit. India's trade balance data is available from January, 1957 till date with average deficit 367.7 $ mn. It was all-time high

Table-1: Trend of Fiscal and Trade Deficit in the Indian Economy

Year	*Fiscal Deficit (as percentage of GDP)*	*Year*	*Fiscal Deficit (as percentage of GDP)*	*Year*	*Trade balance $ billion*	*Year*	*Trade balance $ billion*
1990-91	7.61	2006-07	3.3	1990-91	-5.9	2006-07	-59.3
1991-92	5.39	2007-08	2.5	1991-92	-1.5	2007-08	-88.5
1992-93	5.19	2008-09	6	1992-93	-3.3	2008-09	-118.4
1993-94	6.76	2009-10	6.5	1993-94	-1.1	2009-10	-109.6
1994-95	5.52	2010-11	4.8	1994-95	-2.3	2010-11	-118.6

(*Contd...*)

1996-97	4.1	2012-13	5.1	1996-97	-5.7	2012-13	-190.3
1997-98	4.8	2013-14	4.5	1997-98	-6.5	2013-14	-135.8
1998-99	5.1	2014-15	4.1	1998-99	-9.2	2014-15	-137.7
1999-00	5.4	2015-16	3.9	1999-00	-12.8	2015-16	-118.6
2000-01	5.7	2016-17	3.5	2000-01	-6	2016-17	-183.4
2001-02	6.2	2017-18	3.2	2001-02	-7.6	2017-18	-162.1
2002-03	5.9	2018-19	3	2002-03	-8.7	2018-19	-183.5
2003-04	4.5	2019-20	3	2003-04	-14.3	2019-20	
2004-05	4			2004-05	-28		
2005-06	4			2005-06	-46.1		

Source: Indiabudget.gov.in

in March, 1977 (258.9$ mn) and touched the bottom in October, 2012 (-20.2$ bn). In August, 2019 total Exports of India arrived at 26.1 $ billion. Year on rear there was a decrease of 6.0 percent. In August, 2019 total imports of India arrived at 39.6 $ billion. Year on rear there was a decrease of 13.4 percent.

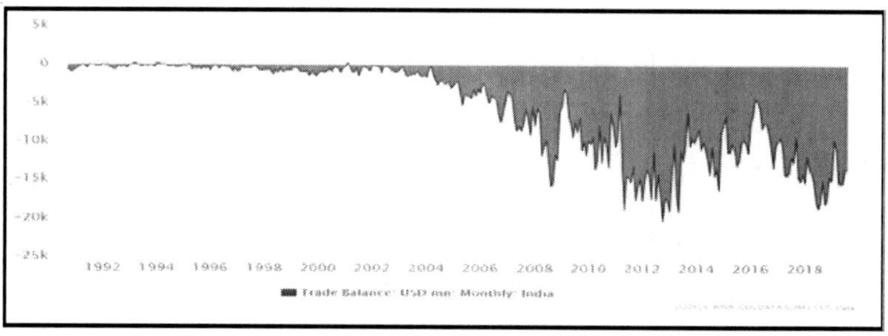

Source: www.ceicdata.com

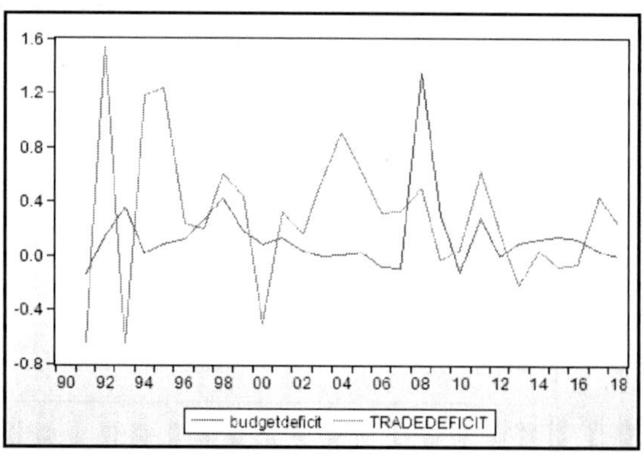

Source: Author's Estimation

Table-2: Descriptive Statistics

	Fiscal Deficit	Trade Deficit
Mean	395829.4	-355420.3
Median	234501.0	-125725.0
Maximum	1100425.	-3350.000
Minimum	45850.00	-1286948.
Std. Dev.	353053.7	402560.9
Skewness	0.841704	-0.791371
Kurtosis	2.288339	2.239538
Jarque-Bera	4.036221	3.725745
Probability	0.132906	0.155226
Sum	11479052	-10307189
Sum Sq. Dev.	3.49E+12	4.54E+12

Source: Author's Estimation

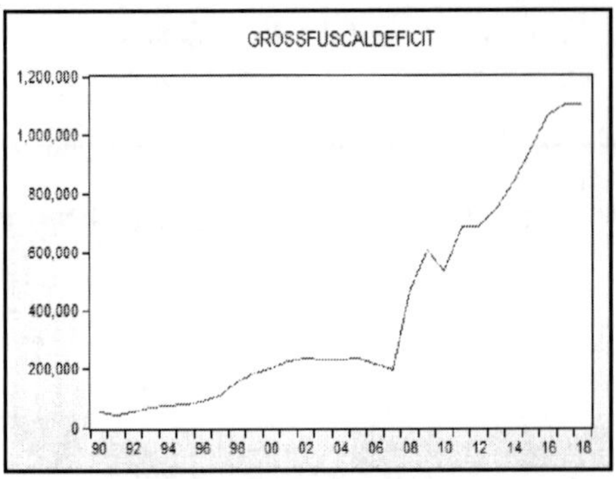

Source: Author's Estimation

Figure- 2: Gross Fiscal Deficit

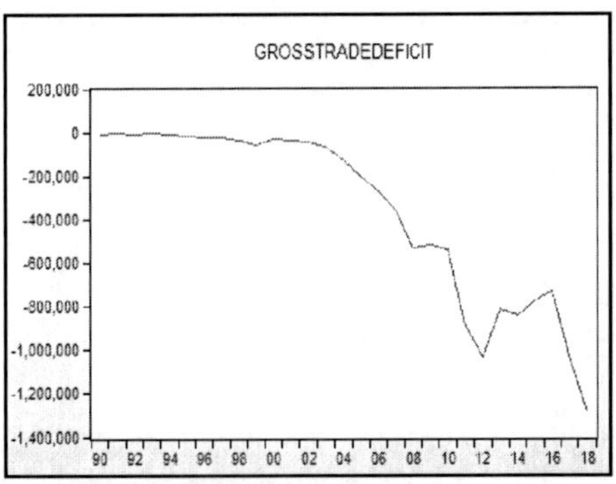

Source: Author's Estimation

Figure-3: Gross Trade Deficit

The Theoretical Framework

A current account deficit in the USA (at the regime of President Reagan) was explained by the Twin deficits hypothesis in the decades of 1980 and 1990 (Abell, 1990; Darrat, 1988; Markin & Narayan, 2013). At that time in USA fiscal expansion was high and it lead to depreciation of the currency. As a result of that current account deficit expanded. The identity of national income (open economy) is the fundamental root of making out the association of fiscal and trade deficit.

National Income Identity can be written as follows:

Y=C+I+G+(X-M)

where Y=> Gross domestic income,

C=> Consumption expenditure of the house holds

I=> Investment expenditure

X=> Total export of goods & services

M=> Total import of goods & services

Current Account = Total export + Net factor income from abroad – Total import

= Total receipts from abroad – Total payment from abroad

Savings in an open economy can be written as

Savings = Investment + Current account

Or, Savings=Private Savings + Government savings = Investment + Current account

Or, (Income – Consumption expenditure – Tax paid to the government) + (Tax earned by the government - Government expenditure – Transfer of payment) = Investment + Current account

Or, Private Savings + (Tax earned by the government - Government expenditure – Transfer of money) = Investment + Current account

Or, Current account = (Private Savings – Investment) + (Tax earned by the government - Government expenditure – Transfer of payment)

Current account = Saving deficit + Fiscal deficit

[In another way we can say

Current account = Capital Account + Fiscal policy]

If Private Savings, Investment are constant or unchanged over time then fluctuations in fiscal deficit is responsible for fluctuations in current account. On the other if private savings and investment are changing over time changes in fiscal deficit can be balanced by changes in saving deficit. In such a situation fiscal deficit does not effect on current account (Barro, 1974, 1989; Suresh and Tiwari, 2014).

According to Keynes huge borrowing by the government leads to fiscal deficit. As govt. expenditure is high aggregate demand is high. Increase in aggregate demand raises price level. Nominal interest rate will increase and as a result of that capital inflow would take place. Exchange rate would appreciate. Import will increase as the price of imports is less expensive and export will reduce as price of the imports is more expensive. Current account deficit will take place.

Objective of the Study

There are mixed results regarding the twin deficit hypothesis. Some found no causal relationship, some found unidirectional causal relationship or bidirectional causal relation. So it is important to empirically examine if the current account deficit is responsible to carry the Indian economy in deficit or if the budget deficit is responsible to keep the economy in deficit. It is also important to find the direction of causality in the Indian economy. This article focuses on Impulse response functions and variance decomposition.

Variables, Data, Stationarity and Cointegration

For the empirical investigation two variables are used. One is current account deficit and another is budget deficit. The study period is 1990-2018 and it is based on secondary data. Current account deficit implies (export – import) and budget deficit implies (tax revenue- government expenditure). Source of the data is the following.

(i) https://databank.worldbank.org/views/reports report widget. aspx? Report_Name=CountryProfile&Id=b450fd57&tbar=y&dd =y&inf=n&zm=n&country=IND

(ii) https://www.rbi.org.in/Scripts/AnnualPublications.aspx?head =Handbook%20of%20Statistics%20on%20Indian%20Economy

(iii) Handbook of Statistics on Indian Economy.

The stationarity of the data sets are verified by applying Unit Root test. ADF, PP-test and Correlogram. Table-3, table-4, figure-5 and figure-

6 respectively represent Unit Root tests. As the data sets are stationary at level they are cointegrated. There is long-run association between the variables concerned. In the next section we will introduce the VAR model for finding out the causality between the two variables.

Table-3: Results of ADF Tests for Unit Root in Budget Deficit (BD_t) and Trade Deficit (TD_t)

					Mackinon Critical Value		
Variable	*Exogenous*	*ADF t Stat*	*P-value*	*Lag*	*1%*	*5%*	*10%*
BDt at level	Constant	-5.109	0.0003	0	-3.699	-2.976	-2.627
BDt at level	Trend	-5.010	0.0021	0	-4.339	-3.587	-3.229
TDt at level	Constant	-7.079	0.0000	0	-3.699	-2.976	-2.627
TDt at level	Trend	-8.058	0.0000	0	-4.339	-3.587	-3.229

Source: Author's Estimation.

Table-4: Results of ADF Tests for Unit Root in Budget Deficit (BD_t) and Trade Deficit (TD_t)

					Mackinon Critical Value		
Variable	*Exogenous*	*PP test Stat*	*P-value*	*Bandwith*	*1%*	*5%*	*10%*
BDt at level	Constant	-5.324	0.0002	5	-3.699	-2.976	-2.627
BDt at level	Trend	-5.209	0.0013	5	-4.339	-3.587	-3.229
TDt at level	Constant	-6.908	0.0000	1	-3.699	-2.976	-2.627
TDt at level	Trend	-8.283	0.0000	4	-4.339	-3.587	-3.229

Source: Author's Estimation

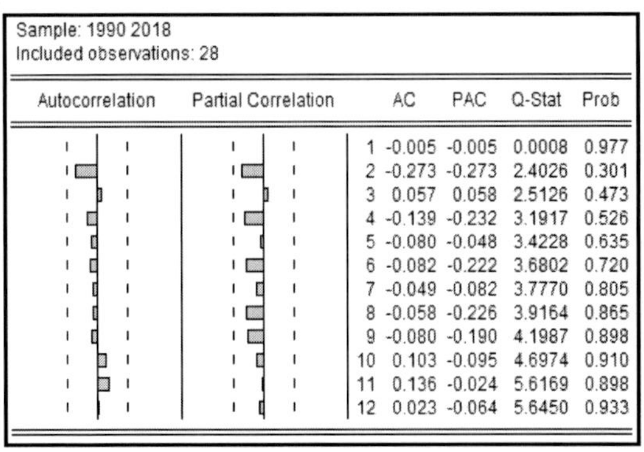

Source: Author's Estimation

Figure-4: Correlogram of BD_t at level

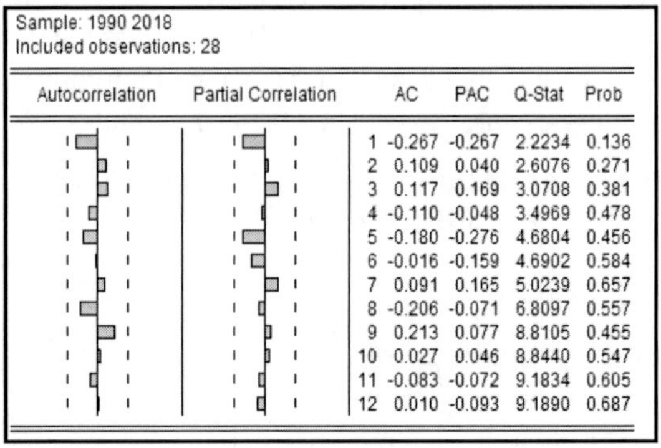

Sample: 1990 2018
Included observations: 28

Autocorrelation	Partial Correlation		AC	PAC	Q-Stat	Prob
		1	-0.267	-0.267	2.2234	0.136
		2	0.109	0.040	2.6076	0.271
		3	0.117	0.169	3.0708	0.381
		4	-0.110	-0.048	3.4969	0.478
		5	-0.180	-0.276	4.6804	0.456
		6	-0.016	-0.159	4.6902	0.584
		7	0.091	0.165	5.0239	0.657
		8	-0.206	-0.071	6.8097	0.557
		9	0.213	0.077	8.8105	0.455
		10	0.027	0.046	8.8440	0.547
		11	-0.083	-0.072	9.1834	0.605
		12	0.010	-0.093	9.1890	0.687

Source: Author's Estimation

Figure-5: Correlogram of TD_t at level

The VAR Model

In order to find out the long-run dynamic relationship between budget deficit and trade deficit in the economy of India. VAR model treats all variables symmetrically without making reference to the issue of dependence versus independence. The model also offers a scope for intervention Analysis through the study of Impulse Response Functions for the endogenous variables in the model. Variance Decomposition allows us to study the Variance Decompositions for these variables and thus help us understand the interrelationships among the variables concerned. VAR model (Appendix table-6) for BD_t and TD_t consists of the equations.

$$BD_{t-1} = \alpha_1 + \sum_{i=1}^{k} \beta_{1i} BD_{t-1} + \sum_{i=1}^{k} \gamma_{1i} TD_{t-1} + u_{1t} \quad ...(1)$$

$$TD_{t-1} = \alpha_2 + \sum_{i=1}^{k} \beta_{1i} TD_{t-1} + \sum_{i=1}^{k} \gamma_{2i} BD_{t-1} + u_{2t} \quad ...(2)$$

Estimated VAR Model:

$BD_t = 208 + (-0.006)BD_t + (-0.281)\ BD_{t-2} + (0.016)TD_{t-1}$

t-state: [2.118] [–0.028] [1.320] [0.136]

$+ (-0.042)\ TD_{t-2}$ ...(3)

[–0.3777]

$TD_t = 0.358 + (-0.293)BD_{t-1} + (-0.080)\ BD_{t-2} + (0.017)TD_{t-1}$

t-state: [2.278] [–0.872] [1.235] [0.539]

$+ (-0.093)\ TD_{t-2}$ ...(4)

[–0.517]

Economic Interpretation

Since no coefficients are found significant in equations (3) and (4) budget deficit failed to granger cause trade deficit and vice versa.

Consequently, the economy of India was marked by the absence of any causal relationship from any direction over the period 1990-2018.

Impulse Response and Variance Decomposition

By using the impulse response functions and variance decomposition the model is examined. The motional feature was tried to catch here. Shocks (one-standard deviation) transmitted from the channel of one variable to other variable's present and future values were traced in this response functions. Figure-6 to figure-9 (figures are given in the appendix) depict the response of one variable by the shocks generated from other variable. The horizontal axis measures the duration of the shocks and vertical axis measures path & intensity of the impulse in the dependent variable away from its base line level.

Figure-6, Increases in the trade deficit has a positive effect on trade deficit itself. The force is less important after four years. The impact of changes of the budget deficit on trade deficit is represented in the figure 7, although TD_t is relatively unaffected by the BD_t shock from period four onward, the TD_t is effected from sixth year onwards with small changes. Figure 8, shows the response of the budget deficit to a one standard deviation shock to the Trade deficit. The graph shows that a positive shock to the trade deficit variable has less significant effect on BD_t. Shock in trade deficit makes a non significant impact on BD_t. The impact of a BD_t shock in trade deficit is decreases from periods 4 onwards. Figure 9, represents the impact of shocks of the budget deficit creates a little impact on budget deficit from period 5.

In order to determine how much of the forecast error variance of each of the variable can be explained by exogenous shocks to the other variables, this section examines the variance decomposition analysis. Variance decomposition shows the amount of information each variable donates to the other variables. Statistical findings are depicted in table 7A and 7B in the appendix. The column gives the percentage of variance in BDF and CAD that are associated with specified variables, with each row adding up to 100.

According to the above empirical results, within four years about 99.5 percentage of the variation in budget deficit is due to variations in its own innovations while 0.5 percentage of the variation in budget deficit are due to its trade deficit innovations. It is also examined, over 96 percent variation in trade deficit is due to its own innovations from second year variations of 4 percentage in trade deficit were due to variation in budget deficit. The variation in trade deficit is largely due to its own innovations.

Conclusion and Policy Implication

This article focused on the applicability of well renowned twin deficit hypothesis in the developing country India. The data observed over the period 1990 to 2018. Sophisticated econometric tools like Unit root test, VAR, Impulse response functions and variance decomposition were used in this article. As the variables Budget deficit and trade deficit were stationary at level they are cointegrated. There are long-run association between the variables as the theory suggested. From the Vector Auto Regression analysis it is found that there is no causal relationship between the variables over the period of study. From impulse response function we came to know that any shocks transmitted from trade deficit will not have any significant effect on budget deficit. On other hand any shocks generated from budget deficit will have less significant effect on trade deficit.

It is observed that shocks transmitted through budget deficit, trade deficit exhibited response by falling below the base level at $t = 2$ and rise above the base level at $t = 4$. Trade deficit following impulse from budget deficit collapsed on the base level at period 5. In case of shocks transmitted through trade deficit, budget deficit followed damped oscillation and budget deficit collapsed on base level at period 4. Variations in budget deficit in $1 \leq t \leq 15$ were mainly due to shocks transmitted through the channel of budget deficit. Contribution trade deficit shocks in budget deficit variations remained almost stable for $t \leq 15$. budget deficit shocks accounted for at most 99.5 percent of total variations in budget deficit. Budget deficit shocks accounted for at most 3 percent of total variations in trade deficit for $t \geq 1$. On the other hand trade deficit shocks accounted for about 96 percent of total variations in trade deficit for $t \geq 1$. These two observations also testify for no causal relationship between budget deficit and trade deficit in the economy of India over the period 1990-2018.

As no apparent causal relation was found this research findings support the Recardian Equivalence Hypothesis which denies any connection between budget deficit and the imbalance in current account. The empirical evidences are in favor of the RE hypothesis and hence suggests that the fiscal policy did not pursue during the study period had not been harmful to generational wellbeing.

Further Scope of research

As there are other variables such as inflation, interest rate and exchange rate that are responsible for twin deficit hypothesis these variables should be included in further research to get better result on the applicability of twin deficit hypothesis in the context of Indian economy.

References

Abell, J. (1990), "Twin Deficits during the 1980s: An Empirical Investigation", *Journal of Macroeconomics*, 12:81-96.

Anoruo, E. and Ramchander, S. (1998) Current Account and Fiscal Deficits: Evidence from Five Developing Economies of Asia. *Journal of Asian Economics*, **9**, 487-501. http://dx.doi.org/10.1016/S1049-0078(99)80099-2

Abell, J. (1990), "Twin Deficits during the 1980s: An Empirical Investigation", *Journal of Macroeconomics*, 12:81-96.

Afonso A, Huart F, Jalles JT, Stanek, PL (2018) Twin deficits revisited: a role for fiscal institutions? REM working paper, 031-2018

Aghevli, B.B, and Sassanpur, C., (1982), Prices, Output and the Balance of Trade in Iran, World Development, Vol. 10, (9): 791-800

Anoruo, E. and Ramchander, S. (1998) Current Account and Fiscal Deficits: Evidence from Five Developing Economies of Asia. *Journal of Asian Economics*, **9**, 487-501. http://dx.doi.org/10.1016/S1049-0078(99)80099-2

Asrafuzzaman, Amit Roy, Amit., & Das Gupta, S. (2013). An Empirical Investigation of Budget and Trade Deficits. International Journal of Economics and Financial Issues Vol. 3, No. 3, 2013, pp.570-579

Badinger H, Fichet de Clairfontaine A, Reuter WH (2017) Fiscal rules and twin deficits: the link between fiscal and external balances. World Econ 40(1):21–35

Baharumshah, A.Z., Lau, E. and Khalid, A.M. (2006). Testing Twin Deficit Hypothesis using VAR and Variance Decomposition, *Journal of Asian Pacific Economy,* Vol. 8. No. 1. pp. 331-354.

Barro, R. (1974), "Are Government Bonds Net Wealth?" *Journal of Political Economy*, 82(6):1095–1117.

Baharumshah, A.Z., Lau, E., (2009), Structural breaks and the twin deficits hypothesis: Evidence from East Asian countries, *Economics Bulletin*, 29, 4, 2517-2524.

Basu, S. and Datta, D. (2005) Does Fiscal Deficit Influence Trade Deficit? An Econometric Enquiry. *Economic and Political Weekly*, 40, 3311-3318.

Bhat JA, Sharma NK (2018) The twin-deficit hypothesis: revisiting Indian economy in a nonlinear framework. J Financ Econ Policy 10(3): 386–405

Bose, S. and Jha, S. (2011). India's Twin Deficits: Some Fresh Empirical Evidence. *ICRA Bulletin, Money and Finance.*

Darrat, A. F. (1988), "Have Large Budget Deficits Caused Rising Trade Deficit?", *Southern*

Economics Journal, 54: 879-887.

Enders, W., & Lee, B. (1990). Current Account and Budget Deficits: Twin or Distant Cousins. *Review of Economics and Statistics,* 72, 374-382.

Feldstein, M. (1992), The budget and the trade deficits aren't really twins. *NN BER, Working Paper 3966*. NBER, Cambridge, MA.

Garg B, Prabheesh KP (2017) Drivers of India's current account deficits, with implications for ameliorating them. J Asian Econ 51:23–32.

Ghatak, A., & Ghatak, S. (1996). Budgetary deficits and Ricardian equivalence: The case of India, 1950–1986. *Journal of Public Economics,* Volume 60, Issue 2, Pages 267-282

Goyal A, Kumar A (2018) The effect of oil shocks and cyclicality in hiding Indian twin deficits. J Econ Stud 45(no. 1):27–45

Gupta, S. and Singh, K. (2016) Fiscal Deficit and its Trends in India. *International Journal of Business and Management Invention www.ijbmi.org || Volume 5 Issue 11 || November. 2016 || PP—63-75.*

Hakro, A.N., (2009), Twin Deficits Causality Link-Evidence from Pakistan, *International Research Journal of Finance and Economics*, 24, 54-70.

Islam, M.F., (1998), Brazil's Twin Deficits: An Empirical Examination, *Atlantic Economic Journal*, 26, 2, 121-128.

Khalid, A.M. and Guan, T.W. (1999) Causality Tests of Budget and Current Account Deficits: Cross Country Comparisons. *Empirical Economics*, **24**, 389-402. http://dx.doi.org/10.1007/s001810050062

Kremers, J. J. M., Ericsson, N. R., & Dolado, J. J. (1992).The Power of Cointegration Tests. *Oxford Bulletin of Economics and Statistics*, *54*(3), 325-348.

Kulkarni, G. and Erickson L. (2006). Twin Deficit Revisited: Evidences from India, Pakistan and Mexico. *The Journal of Applied Business Research,* 17(2), 97-107.

Litsios I, Pilbeam K (2017) An empirical analysis of the nexus between investment, fiscal balances and current account balances in Greece, Portugal and Spain. Econ Model 63:143–152

Magazzino, C. (2012), The Twin Deficits Phenomenon: Evidence from Italy, *Journal of Economic Cooperation and Development*, **33**, 3 (2012), 65-80.

Mansur, A.H, (1989), Effect of a Budget Deficit on the Current Account Balance: The case of the Philippines, in M.I. Blejer and K. Chu (eds) Fiscal Policy, Stabilization and Growth in Developing Countries, Washington DC, IMF, 309-345.

Markin, A. J. and Narayan, P.K. (2013), "Re-examining the Twin Deficits Hypothesis: Evidence for Australia", *Empirical Economics*, 45:817-829.

Nazier, H. and Essam, M. (2014). Empirical investigation of twin deficits hypothesis in Egypt (1992-2010). *Middle Eastern Finance and Economics Journal*, 17, 45-58.

Osoro, K.O., Gor, S.O. and Mbithi, M.O. (2014). The Twin Deficit and the Macroeconomic Variables in Kenya. *International Journal for Innovation Education and Research.* Vol. 2, No. 9. pp. 64-84.

Parikh, A. and Rao, B. (2006) Do Fiscal Deficits Influence Current Accounts? A Case Study of India. *Review of DevelopmentEconomics*, **10**, 492-505. http://dx.doi.org/10.1111/j.1467-9361.2006.00370.x

Ratha, A. (2011). Twin Deficits or Distant Cousins? Evidence from India, *Economics Working Paper.* No. 5. in the *Department of Economics at the Repository at St. Cloud State.*

Islam, N. (1995), Growth empirics: A panel data approach. *Quarterly Journal of Economics* 110: 1127–70.

Rajasekar T, Deo M (2016) The Relationship Between Fiscal Deficit and Trade Deficit in India: An Empirical Enquiry Using Time Series Data. The IUP Journal of Applied 28 Economics 15(1).

Ratha, A. (2012) Twin Deficits or Distant Cousins? Evidence from India. *South Asia Economic Journal*, **13**, 51-68.

Rosenswieg JA, Tallman E.W. (1993), Fiscal policy and trade adjustment: Are the deficits really twins? *Economic Inquiry* 31(4):580–94.

Saeed, S. and Khan A. (2012).Twin Deficit Hypothesis: The Case of Pakistan 1972-2008. *Natural and Applied Sciences*, 3(2),155-162.

Sakyi, D. and Eric Evans Osei Opoku, E. E. O. (2016). The twin deficits hypothesis in developing countries: empirical evidence for Ghana. International Growth Centre, *Working paper* S-33201-GHA-1, p. 1-32.

Suresh, K.G. and Tiwari, A. K. (2014), "A Structural VAR (SVAR) Analysis of Fiscal Shocks on Current Accounts in India", *Macroeconomics and Finance in Emerging Market Economies*, 7(1):140-153.

Vamvoukas, G. A. (1999), The twin deficits phenomenon: Evidence from Greece. *Applied Economics* 31: 1093–1100.

Zaidi, I.M, (1985), Savings, Investment, Fiscal Deficit and the External Indebtedness of Developing Countries, World Development, Vol. 13: 573-588.

CASE STUDY - 3

AN ECONOMETRIC ANALYSIS OF EFFECT OF CHANGES IN MONEY SUPPLY ON INTEREST RATE IN BANGLADESH

Introduction

Central banks routinely state monetary policies in terms of interest rates. For example, in May 2001, Brazil's central bank "increased interest rates" because it was worried about mounting inflationary pressure," according to the New York Times (Rice 2001). And in the first of 2000, the U.S. Federal Open Market Committee increased the federal funds rate target three times in order to head off 'inflationary imbalances' (FR Board 2000).

Despite this common practice, central banks do not control interest rate directly. They can target interest rates, but they can only attempt to hit those targets by adjusting other instruments they do control, such as supply of bank reserves. Changes in these instruments directly affect a country's stock of money, and financial market reactions to money supply changes are what actually change the level of interest rates. Clearly in order to hit interest rate targets, central banks must have a reliable view about the relationship between the money supply changes and interest rate changes.

Economic theory offers two seemingly contradictory views of this relationship. One view, which follows from the interaction of money demand and supply, is that money and interest rates are negatively related: increasing interest rates, for example, requires a decrease in the stock of money. According to this view, money demand is a decreasing function of the nominal interest rate because the interest rate is the opportunity cost of holding cash (liquidity). So a decrease in the supply of money must cause interest rates to increase in order to keep the money market equilibrium. We call this the *liquidity effect view*.

Another view, which follows from the Fisher equation, is that money and interest rates are positively related: in- creasing interest rates requires an increase in the rate of money growth. The Fisher equation states that the nominal interest rate equals the real interest rate plus the expected rate of ination (Fisher 1896).2 If monetary policy does not affect the real interest rate (and errors in ination expectations are ignored), then the Fisher equation implies that higher nominal interest rates are associated with higher rates of ination. Since in the long run, high ination rates are associated with high money growth rates, the Fisher equation suggests that an increase in interest rates requires an increase in the money growth rate. It is called this the *Fisher equation view.*

Various theories of interest rates put together explain variables which determine interest rates; these theories differ because of differences of opinion as to whether interest rates are monetary or real phenomenon. According to the classical theory, the interest rate is determined by the intersection of the investment-demand schedule i.e. schedule disclosing the relationship of investment and savings to the rate of interest. However, no solution is possible because the position of the saving-schedule will vary with the level of real income. In the view of classical economists, level of savings is determined by savings rate of interest (Olusoji, 2003). This view holds that increase in this interest rate will lead to increased savings and hence a positive relationship. It is this view that must have encouraged the Nigerian authorities to abandon administratively fixed interest rates for market determined ones. In the words of Ahmed (2003), deregulated interest rate is believed to be critical for both economic stabilization and development. Hence the Keynesian attack of the classical theory of interest on the ground that it is indeterminate, that is, as income rises, the saving-schedule will shift to the right, hence we cannot know what the rate of interest will be unless we already know the income level. But we cannot know the income level without already knowing the rate of interest, since a lower rate will mean a larger volume of investment and so, via the multiplier, a higher level of real income. Thus the classical theory fails to offer a solution. The implication of Ahmed's position above covers the relationship between interest rate and investment. In this case, it has been established that high lending rates discourage borrowing for investment and vice versa (Lawal, 1982; Anyanwu and Oaikhenan, 1995). Since economists hold that investment plays a fundamental role in capital formation, and hence on economy's growth and developments, it becomes obvious that lending rates through perceived influence on investment plays a developmental role. That is, a decrease in lending rate is theorized to cause investment borrowing to rise which leads to increased capital formation and eventually to economic growth (Onoh, 2007).

The Keynesian liquidity preference theory posits that the rate of interest is determined by the intersection of the supply-schedule of money (perhaps interest inelastic, if rigorously fixed by the monetary authorities) and the demand schedule for money (the liquidity-preference schedule). However, this analysis is also indeterminate because the liquidity preference schedule will shift up or down with changes in the income level, thus money supply and demand-schedules cannot give the rate of interest unless we already know the income level.

hence, the same criticism of indeterminacy Keynes leveled against the classics is applicable to his theory.

According to the loanable funds theory of Dennis H. Robertson, the rate of interest is determined by the intersection of the demand-schedule for loanable funds with the supply-schedule, here the supply-schedule is compounded of savings (in the Robertson sense voluntary savings) plus net additions to loanable funds from new monies (change in money supply) and the discharging of idle balance. However, since the savings portion of the schedule varies with the level of disposable income (i.e. yesterday's income) it follows that the total supply schedule of loanable funds also varies with income, therefore this theory is also indeterminate.

In the Pigouvian parlance, interest rate is determined by the intersection of the demand-schedule for money with supply-schedule of savings. Here the revenant supply-schedule is conceived in terms of saving out of current income i.e. the excess of total income received over income received for services in providing for consumption. This income, consumption and savings, all apply to the same period however, whether or not current income is fed in the past from the injection of new money or from the stand point of the pigouvian or neo-classical definition, that is income whether it springs from the spending of funds borrowed from banks credit played a role in the process of income creation. Thus in the neo-classical or pigouvian theory "savings" is in effect the same thing as loanable funds hence the same criticism applies to them.

The Keynesian and neoclassical propositions, taken together supply us with a theory of the interest rate of J. R. Hicks. From the Keynesian view, we get a family of liquidity preference schedule at various income levels. These together with the supply of money fixed by the monetary authorities, gives us the Hicksian LM curve, which tell us what the various rates of interest will be (given the quantity of money and the family of liquidity preference curves) at different levels of income. On the other hand, the neoclassical formulation provides us family saving-schedules at various income levels. These together with the investment demand schedule give us the Hicksian IS-Curve, meaning that the neoclassical framework tells us what the various levels of income will be given the investment-demand schedule and family of saving-schedule at different rates of interest. Thus the IS-Curve and the LM-C refer to functions relating the two variables.

Income and the rate of interest are determined together at the point of intersection, income and the rate of interest stand in a relation to each other such that:

— Investment and saving are in equilibrium (i.e. actual saving equals desired saving).

— The demand for money is in equilibrium with the supply of money (i.e. the desired amount of money is equal to the actual supply of money).

In the monetarists view of interest rate determination even though they accept that interest rate is a monetary phenomenon, they reject the Keynesian analysis that it is determined by money supply and money demand. They had and in fact emphasize another factor; the price expectations/anticipation factor. To the monetarists led by Milton Friedman, an increase in money stocks has three major effects: Liquidity effect, income effect and price expectation/anticipation effect. To them, an increase in money supply initially (immediate observational impact) the interest rate falls i.e. the Keynesian liquidity preference effect. Due to this increase in liquidity position, people go into the market to increase demand resulting in the expansion of the economy (the income effect). This increase in income will put pressure on goods and services and hence prices will rise. As prices increase (due to expectation effect) people will build up an inflationary psychology, i.e. they expect more inflationary effect in future. Suppliers will expand their investment outlet to supply more and this expansionary investment demand will make price to rise more. Also financial institutions expect price to rise more and therefore increase interest rate on their liabilities. Even among consumers, they want to spend more now because they expect higher prices in future hence for durable materials they would demand for more credit and this leads to an increase in interest rate (price expectations/anticipations effect). Because of these effects and more so because of the price expectations effect, when money supply is increased the ultimate result is an increase in interest rate rather than the Keynesian decrease in interest rate. This what Friedman (1976) linked with the Gibson Paradox since prices and interest rates move together from empirical evidence, to them therefore interest rate is not only determined by money supply and money demand but also by price expectations factors.

Literature Review

Belongia T M. & Peter N. Ireland (2012) showed that the stance of monetary policy can be described with exclusive reference to its effects on interest rates and without consideration of simultaneous movements in the monetary aggregates. Whether by replicating and extending the results of a landmark study or by producing new results from a structural VAR, the message from Divisia monetary aggregates is that money always has had a significant role to play as an intermediate target or indicator variable and that any apparent deterioration in its information content can be traced to the measurement errors inherent in the practice of simple sum aggregation. Their results also highlighted the disconnect between modern New Keynesian models, in which the quantity of money plays no special role once the time path for interest rates is accounted for.

Brown W. W. and G. J. Santoni (1983) revealed a statistically significant but economically anemic liquidity effect that dissipates rapidly. This was to be expected, given efficient financial and capital markets. On the other hand, the results concerning the Fisher effect are fairly strong. They suggest that an increase (decrease) in the monetary growth rate that persists for more than one month will result in an increase (decrease) in interest rates, other things constant. As a change in the monetary growth rate comes to be regarded as permanent, short-term rates willfully adjust within 12 months, The direction and magnitude of the change in short-term rates will mirror the change in monetary growth.

Cyril Monnet & Warren E. Weber (2001).This study describes and reconciles two common, seemingly contradictory views about a key monetary policy relationship: that between money and interest rates. Data since 1960 for about 40 countries support the *Fisher equation view,* that these variables are positively related. But studies taking expectations into account support the *liquidity effect view,* that they are negatively related. A simple model incorporates both views and demonstrates that which view applies at any time depends on when the change in money occurs and how long the public expects it to last. A surprise money change that is not expected to change future money growth moves interest rates in the opposite direction; one that is expected to change future money growth moves interest rates in the same direction. The study also demonstrates that stating monetary policy as a rule for interest rates rather than money does not change the relationship between these variables.

The article estimates the responsiveness of interest rate to monetary changes using alternative specifications that have been used in the literature and alternative monetary variables. The equations are estimated over the same time periods using the same data. Several interesting results emerge from this study. First estimates of the response of the interest rates are relatively sensitive to the specification employed, they are however sensitive to the monetary variable used. A significant negative response of interest rate is most likely obtained if nonborrowed reserve is used as the monetary variables.

Keynes (1936) posited that inflation is caused by a situation of excess aggregate demand over aggregate supply when there is no excess capacity, a situation in which the economy operates at full employment of resources. Furthermore, there are strong arguments that fiscal deficits are major cause of inflation. Abolo (1997) among other researchers contented that evidence points to fiscal deficits as major cause of inflation.

The argument that price inflation is significantly determined by the process mark-up on the costs of firm's production process has been advanced in the models of Goacher (1986) and Gordon (1984) believed that inflation could result from the cost of imported goods rising independently of the demand for them in the domestic economy.

Mohamed Benbouziane & Abdelhak Benamar (2000). The objective of this paper is to test for the liquidity effect in Algeria and Morocco using multivariate threshold autoregressive model (MVTAR) as proposed by Tsay (1998). When using bank deposit assets (BDA), results show that there is a negative relationship between monetary shocks and interest rate, and accordingly accepting the liquidity effect. In the case of Morocco, however, results show an asymmetric response of interest rate to positive and negative shock of monetary policy. The threshold behavior offers an interesting alternative for explaining the relationship between interest rates and monetary policy shocks.

Sarbapriya Ray (2012) showed that the relationship between the nominal interest rates and the expected inflation is of crucial importance in financial markets. The Fisher effect postulated that real interest rate is constant and that nominal interest rate and expected inflation move one-for-one together. The paper examines the existence of International fisher effect for United States and selected Asian countries like-India,Korea and Japan, by regressing interest rates differential on inflation rate differential during the period ,2001:Q1 to2012:Q2. The estimated slope coefficients in regressions of nominal interest rates differential on expected inflation rates differential are significantly different than the theoretical value of unity as is evident in our study. The finding lends support to the existence of partial fisher effect in USA because both interest rates and inflation rate move in positive direction but do not move with one-for-one. But in case of India,

Japan and Korea, there do not exist any signs of International Fisher Effect. When each country is treated interchangeably as home country and foreign country to show the direction of International fisher Effect, the result shows mixed picture. The theory holds when some countries were used as home country but was disproved when they were used as foreign countries. In a nut shell, the study suggests that it finds evidence of a positive long run relationship between interest rate and inflation rate for the countries undertaken in our study but the notion of a full International Fisher Effect is rejected.

There are relatively large literature dealing with relations between monetary indicators and other macroeconomic variables. Doroshenko, (2001), consider relation between both money supply and inflation and between money supply and inflation and found a long-run relationship between between money growth and inflation. Clemens and Alex (2002) empirically estimate the relationship between exchange rate accommodation and the degree of inflation persistence using a non-linear autoregressive inflation equation for ten European countries for the period 1974-1998..Thier results provide supportive evidence for the existence of a positive link between exchange rate accommodation and inflation persistence for most of the smaller and more dependant exchange rate mechanism countries, even when mean level shift in inflation are appropriately accounted for.

In Nigeria, there have been several studies on causes on inflation. For instances Oyejide(1972),

Odusanya and Atanda (2010) analyzed the dynamics and simultaneous inter-relationship between inflation and its determinants in Nigeria between 1970 and 2007 examined using the Augmented Dickey Fuller (ADF) and unit root test. The result reveals that inflation rate, growth rate of real output, money supply and real share of fiscal deficit are stationary at levels, while, other incorporated variables-real share of import, exchange rate and interest rate are stationary at first difference. Adeyeye and Kola also examined the causes and effects of inflation in Nigeria between 1969 and 2009 and what could be done to ameliorate the negative effects on the economy. The time series variables properties on some selected variables were examined using ADF unit root test and co- integration analysis. The result reveals that money supply, growth rates, gross domestic product growth rate and expenditure revenue ratio are not spurious but exchange rate of dollar to Naira was non-stationary. The study also revealed that the GDP growth rate is counter inflationary as against inflationary factors. It is suffice to say that causes of inflation is one of the most highly treated subject in economic researches and literature.

Sources of data

The time series data were derived from various secondary sources such as: Indian Financial Statistics etc. The macroeconomic data (annual) covers between 1976- 2010. Base period is 2000. Log of variables has been used in my research work. The data gathered were subjected to various econometric tests with the aid of E-views.

Methodology

The estimated techniques includes the Augmented Dickey- Fuller (ADF) unit root test, Johansen Co-integration test and Vector Auto Regression Model (VAR).The estimations follow three step modeling procedure.

Employing Augmented Dickey-Fuller Unit root test to make non-stationary variables stationary to overcome spurious results.

After establishing stationary of the data, Johansen Co-integration test is applied to determine whether a long run relationship exist among the variables concerned.

When it is established that the variables are co-integrated, VAR Model is developed.

Organization of The Paper

Section II is devoted to the study of stationarity, Section III represents cointegration test. Section IV deals with the long run relationship of the variables concerned through the estimation of Vector Auto Regression Model. Section V presents Concluding Remarks.

Section - II
Study of Stationarity

Stationarity

Results of the Augmented Dickey-Fuller Tests for the presence of Unit roots in the series for Interest rate (r_t) and Money Supply (M_t) are being presented through the Table-1 in the appendix.

It is observed from the Table-1 that

(i) all the variables at level are not free from unit roots. Consequently, the series are not stationary at levels.

(ii) the variables do not have any deterministic trend .

(iii) Interest rate (r_t) and Money Supply (M_t) are I(1).

Correlogram Analysis For Stationarity:

The stationarity of the variables has further been examined through the study of their correlograms. Figures 1-4 present (in the appendix) the correlograms of the variables concerned.

Findings From The Correlograms:

It is observed from the Figures 1-4 that

(i) the corresponding ACFs are free from any dying out pattern of spikes at 1st difference.

(ii) the corresponding PACFs are marked by the absence of any singularly significant spike at lag one.

Consequently, these correlograms testify for the stationarity of the series Inflation (I_t), Exchange rate (E_t), Government Expenditure (G_t), Interest rate (r_t) and Money Supply (M_t) are stationary at 1st difference.

Section - III
Study of Cointegration

Johansen cointegration test results contain in table 3 (appendix) confirm the existence of long run relationship between inflation and the included variables in Bangladesh as indicated by the TRACE-statistic and Max-Eigen Statistics. The TRACE-statistics results revealed that there is 1 cointegrating equation at 5percent level as indicated by its critical value of 28 which is greater than the TRACE statistics of 25 ; this is further supported by its high probability value of 0.3820. This is also confirmed by the Max-Eigen statistics in table 2. The null of at most two cointegrating equations existed was accepted at 5 percent level as indicated by its critical value of 20 which is greater than the Max-Eigen statistics of 19; this is further supported by its high probability value of 0.46.

Section III

Study Of Long-Run Causal Relation: Vector Autoregression Model

Vector Autoregression Model

In order to find the long-run dynamic relationship between economic growth (Y_t) and govt. expenditure (E_t) in the economy of India, we cannot make any *a priory* assumption of endogenity and exogeneity of variables. For this purpose, *Vector Autoregressive Model* **(VAR)** can be applied. This model treats all variables symmetrically without making reference to the issue of dependence versus independence. A **VAR** model also offers a scope for *Intervention Analysis* through the study of *Impulse Response Functions* for the endogenous variables in the model. *Variance Decomposition* allows us to study the 'Variance Decompositions' for these variables and thus help us understand the interrelationships among the variables concerned. We therefore, seek to develop a **VAR** model for economic growth and govt. spending for the economy of India in this section of the article.

The VAR Model

The Vector Autoregression (VAR) Model for money supply (M_t) and interest rate (r_t) for the economy of Bangladesh consists of the equations (19) and (20)

$$M_t = \alpha_1 + \sum_{i=1}^{k} \beta_{1i} M_{t-i} + \sum_{i=1}^{k} \gamma_{1i} r_{t-i} + u_{1t} \qquad ...(19)$$

$$r_t = \alpha_2 + \sum_{i=1}^{k} \beta_{2i} r_{t-i} + \sum_{i=1}^{k} \gamma_{2i} M_{t-i} + u_{2t} \qquad ...(20)$$

Selection of Lag Length

Before estimating VAR, the decision regarding the selection of maximum lag length (k) is important. The decision of the lag length is important to avoid spurious causality (or spurious absence of causality). ***We, therefore, have followed Enders' Method and started with eight lags.*** We have then reduced the lags by one and carried out the test, given that the estimated t-statistics for the coefficient involved is insignificant. In the 2 lag specification a few parameters have been found statistically significant. **We, therefore, have chosen two (2) lags for each endogenous variables in their Autoregressive and Distributed Lag Structures in the estimable VAR model.**

Features of The VAR Model

The VAR model consisting of equations (19) and (20) requires that

(i) M_t and r_t be stationary, and

(ii) u_{1t} and u_{2t} be white-noise terms such that

$u_{1t} \sim iidN(0,\sigma^2_{u1})$, and $u_{2t} \sim iidN(0,\sigma^2_{u1})$.

In this model both M_t and r_t are stationary at 1st difference such that $M_t \sim I(1)$ and $r_t \sim I(1)$. Consequently, the first requirement is satisfied.

However, the properties of u_{1t} and u_{2t} need to be studied. This will enable us to find if u_{1t} and u_{2t} are really white noise terms.

The Estimable VAR Model

The estimable VAR model, therefore, consists of the following equations.

$$M_t = \alpha_1 + \beta_{11}M_{t-1} + \beta_{12}M_{t-2} + \gamma_{11}r_{t-1} + \gamma_{12}r_{t-2} + u_{1t} \qquad ...(21)$$

$$r_t = \alpha_2 + \beta_{21}r_{t-1} + \beta_{22}r_{t-2} + \gamma_{21}M_{t-1} + \gamma_{22}M_{t-2} + u_{2t} \qquad ...(22)$$

Stability of the VAR model is confirmed by the table figure-5. Absolute value of the roots are less than unity and Figure-5 shows that the inverse roots of **AR Characteristic Polynomials** lie within the unit circle.

Results of Estimation of The VAR Model

The results of estimation of the VAR model consisting of equations (21) and (22) are given by the Table-4 in the appendix.

Stability of the Estimated VAR Model:

The roots of the **Characteristic Polynomials** B(L) and A(L) are given by the Figure-3, in the appendix.

It is observed from the Figure-5, that the inverse roots of AR characteristic polynomials lie within the unit circle.

These observations testify for the stability of the VAR model.

Economic Interpretations Of The Findings:

The economic significance of these findings are as follows.

(i) $\hat{\gamma}_{11}$, $\hat{\gamma}_{12}$ being insignificant (even at 10% level) indicates that r_{t-1}, r_{t-2} did not affect M_t. Consequently, r_t, the interest rate did not *Granger cause* M_t, money supply in the economy of Bangladesh over the period of study.

Economic Interpretations of The Findings

The economic significance of these findings is as follows.

(i) $\hat{\gamma}_{22}$, being insignificant (at 10% level), in the presence of r_{t-i} (i=1,2) in the vector of regressors for r_t, implies that money supply did *Granger cause* interest rate in the economy of Bangladesh over the period of study.

Overview of Findings

The findings in this section indicate that in the economy of Bangladesh over the period of study

(i) Interest rate did not Granger Cause Money supply.

(ii) Money supply did Granger Cause interest rate.

Consequently, the economy of Bangladesh was marked by the presence of 'Uni directional causal relationship' between money supply and interest rate over the period 1976-2010.

Conclusion

Here we have considered how central banks should translate their interest rate targets into changes in the money supply. Economic theory offers two, apparently conicting, views about this. One, the liquidity effect view, is that increasing interest rates requires a decrease in the money supply. The other view, the Fisher equation view, is that increasing interest rates requires an increase in the rate of growth of the money supply. It has been examined the empirical evidence and found that it is consistent with one view. According to the Taylor rule, the central bank raises interest rates when the rate of ination is above its target rate. If this deviation of ination from target were expected to be transitory, as would be true if the deviation were due to a shock to velocity, then the central bank could achieve higher interest rates by temporarily reducing the current money supply (which, equivalently, reduces the current rate of growth of the money supply). This works because there is no reason for people to change their expectations of what money growth will be in the future.

However, if the deviation of ination from target were expected to be permanent, as might be true if the real interest rate decreased, then money and interest rates would move in the same direction. The central bank would have to lower its interest rate target, and to achieve this, it would have to lower the expected future rate of money growth, as the Fisher equation prescribe.

This paper investigates the relationship between money supply and interest rate in Bangladesh. The properties of time series variables were examined through the application of Augmented Dickey-Fuller technique in testing the unit root property of the series. The results of unit root suggest that all the variables in the model are stationary at 1st difference. Money supply and interest rate are stationary at first difference. In order to find out whether there exist a long run relationship between the included variables in order consideration in Bangladesh. The Johansen cointegration result shows that despite no causation between some variables of the study, but there existed one cointegrating equation, implying the existence of long run relationship between money supply and the interest rate. The VAR result also confirmed the existence of long run relationship between the variables of the model The results revealed that interest rate does not granger cause MS but MS does granger cause interest rate. Therefore, there is unidirectional causation between money supply and interest rate.

Since there is positive relationship between money supply and interest rate and money supply positively granger cause interest rate, it supports the Fisher's concept on money supply and interest rate i.e., when money supply is increased the ultimate result is an increase in interest rate rather than Keynesian decrease in interest rate.

References

Adeyeye, E.A. and T.O.Fakiyesi (980) "Productivity price and incomes Board and Anti inflationary policy in Nigeria in the Nigerian economy under the military. Proceedings of the 1980, Annual Conference of Nigerian Economic Society, Ibadan.

Adeyeye and Kola (2012)"Empirical Analysis of the causes and effects of Inflation in Nigeria" Journal of Economic and Sustainable Development, www.iiste.org,Vol.3, no.11.Pp35-40.

Akibobola,T.O(2012) "The dynamics of money supply, exchange rate and inflation in Nigeria" Journal of Finance and banking,vol.2 no.4, pp117-141

Alvarez, Fernando; Atkeson, Andrew; and Kehoe, Patrick J. Forthcoming. Money, interest rates, and exchange rates with endogenously segmented markets. *Journal of Political Economy.*

Alvarez, Fernando; Lucas, Robert E., Jr.; and Weber, Warren E. 2001. Interest rates and inflation. *American Economic Review* 91 (May): 219–25.

Asogu, J. O. (1991) "An econometric Analysis of the nature and causes of Inflation in Nigeria" Economic and Financial Review,Vol. 29, no. 2.

Aris, M. J. (1992) "Wage inflation" in current issues on Macroeconomics, London, Macmillan Education Ltd.

Batini,N. (2004)"Achieving and Maintaining Price Stability in Nigeria, IM working paper, 04-97, Washington DC.

Belongia M.T & Peter N. Ireland (2012). Quantitative Easing: Interest Rates and Money in the Measurement of Monetary Policy. http://www.bc.edu/content/dam/files/schools/cas_sites/economics/pdf/workingpapers/wp801.pdfBenbouziane

M. & Abdelhak BENAMAR (2000). On the liquidity effect in Algeria and Morocco: An empirical investigation. http://www.luc.edu/orgs/meea/volume12/PDFS/2benbouziane_on%20the%20liquidity%20effect%20in%20Algeria%20and%20Morocco.pdf

Brown W. W. and G. J. Santoni (1983). Monetary Growth and the Timing of Interest Rate Movements.https://research.stlouisfed.org/publications/review/83/08/Monetary_Aug_Sep1983.pdf

Edwaikhide et al (1994) "Exchange rate, Money supply and Inflation in Nigeria: An Empirical Investigation "African Journal of Economic Policy, Vol.2 pp57-73.

Eihner, A. S. (1973) "A theory of the determinantion of mark-up under oligopoly" Economic Journal, December 1973.

Fuller, T. M. and Ikhide, (1998)'An Economic Analysis of Nigerian Consumer Price Index" Journal of Economics, \Vol.24(2), pp1-15.

Fisher, Irving. 1896. Appreciation and interest. *American Economic Review Publications* 11 (August): 331–442.

Lucas, Robert E., Jr. 1980. Two illustrations of the quantity theory of money. *American Economic Review* 70 (December): 1005–14.

Goaecher, D. J. (1986) An introduction to Monetary Economic, London Financial Training Publication Ltd.

Jhingan, M. L.(2004) Monetary Economics, 6th ed. Vrinda Publications Ltd.

Keynes, J. M. (1936) The General Theory of Employment, Interest and Money. Published for the Royal Economic Society by Macmillian Press Ltd, London and Basingstoke.

Lucas, Robert E., Jr., and Stokey, Nancy L. 1987. Money and interest rates in a cashin-advance economy. *Econometrica* 55 (May): 491–513.

Mahamadu, B. and Philip, A. (2003) " Monetary Growth, Exchange rates and Inflation in Ghana: An Error Correction Analysis, Working Paper, **WO/BOG-2003/05**

Mc Candless, George T. Jr., and Weber, Warren E. 1995. Some monetary facts. *Federal Reserve Bank of Minneapolis Quarterly Review* 19 (Summer): 2–11. Reprinted in this issue.

Monnet C., Warren E. Weber. 1998. Money and Interest Rates, *Federal Reserve Bank of Minneapolis Quarterly Review* Vol. 25, No,4

Odusunya, I. A. and A. A. Atanda (2010): Analysis of inflation and its determinants in Nigeria ,Pakistan Journal of Social Sciences, Volume7, No. 2 pp97-100.

Okpara and Nwoaha (2010) "Government Expenditure, Money supply, Prices and output Relationship in Nigeria: An Econometric Analysis" International Research Journal of Finance and Economic Issues 54.

Oruba, C. O.(2009) "Inflation in Nigeria: Concept, Measurement and Control, Bullion, Central Bank of Nigeria,Vol.33(1)

Osakwe, J.O. (1983) "Government Expenditure, Money supply and prices,1970-1980, CBN Economic and Financial Review, Vol. 21, no.2.

Oyejide, T. A. (1972) "Deficit Financing, Inflation and capital Formation: The analysis the Nigerian economy, 1957-1970" NJESS, vol.14.

Owoye, O. (2007) "Money Targeting, Money Demand and Real GDP growth in Nigeria: Do rule Apply? Journal of Business and Public Affairs Vol.1 (2) Pp 1-20.

Sarbapriya Ray (2012). Empirical Testing of International Fisher Effect in United States and Selected Asian Economies. *Advances in Information Technology and Management (AITM)* 216 Vol. 2, No. 1, 2012, ISSN 2167-6372

Selialia, F.L. (1995) The Dynamics of Inflation in Lesotho, Unpublished M.A Thesis, University College, Dublin.

Taylor, John B. 1993. Discretion versus policy rules in practice. *Carnegie-Rochester Conference Series on Public Policy* 39 (December): 195–214.

Taiwo, J. K. (2011) "Econometric Analysis of the cuases and effects of Inflation, MSc Thesis, Department of Mathematics, University of Abuja, Nigeria.

Taiwo, J. K. and Adeyeye (2012) "Empirical analysis of the effects and causes of Inflation in Nigeria" Journal of Economics and Sustainable Devlopment, Vol.3, no.11,www.iiste.org

CASE STUDY - 4

AN ECONOMETRIC ENQUIRY TO THE RELATIONSHIP BETWEEN EXPORT AND ECONOMIC GROWTH IN BANGLADESH

I. Introduction

An economy is said to grow when the country's *gross domestic product* (GDP) rises. Economic growth is of fundamental importance for all economies. Since virtually all countries experience growth in population over time, GDP growth is a prerequisite for maintaining current standard of living. In fact, if standards of living are to rise over time, GDP must grow faster than population.

Economic growth is also critical for **economic development.** Economic development is characterized by such things as high levels of consumption, broad-based educational achievement, adequate housing and access to high-quality health care etc. These goals may be achieved only after long periods of sustained high levels of economic growth.

International Trade can affect the level of economic growth of an economy. An increase in export sales may lead to an overall expansion in production and accompanying fall in unemployment rate. International trade also allows for purchase of capital goods from foreign countries and exposes an economy to technological advances achieved round the globe.Conversely, economic growth may affect the types of goods which a country is able to trade. A technological advance in a country's import-competing sector could lead to an overall reduction in the volume of trade of a country. Thus, international trade and economic growth are closely related.

II. Variants of Hypotheses

The relation between export and economic growth is really complex and economists differ among themselves on this issue. There are five schools of thought regarding the relationship between export growth and income growth. These are as follows:

(i) **Export-Led Income Growth Hypothesis:** It is argued that export growth leads to income growth. Consequently, this hypothesis indicates *Uni-directional Granger Causality running from export growth to income growth.*

(ii) **Income-led Export Growth:** This view postulates that income growth is the main source of export growth in any economy. Consequently, *there exists Uni-directional Granger Causality running from income growth to export growth.*

(iii) **Income-Led Export Growth Led Income:** This hypothesis holds that, there exists a '*Two-Way Linkage*' between income growth and export growth. In such relationship the income growth occurs initially and then it leads to export growth. Export growth subsequently leads to further growth in income. Thus there exists a *Bi-directional Granger Causality between income growth and export growth where initial causal impulse comes from income growth.*

(iv) **Export Growth-Led Income Growth-Led Export Growth:** This hypothesis states that there exists a '*Two-Way Linkage*' between export growth and income growth. In such relationship export growth occurs initially and then it leads to income growth. Income growth, in turn, causes further growth in export. Thus, *there exists a 'Bi-directional Granger Causality between export growth and income growth where initial causal impulse comes from export growth.*

(v) **Independence:** This hypothesis holds that *there exists no Granger Causality between export and economic growth.* Consequently, these variables are *independent* of each other.

III. Objective of The Study

Under this controversial theoretical framework, we seek to enquire empirically into the relationship between income growth and export growth in Bangladesh, a member country of the SAARC. Export promotion exercises constitute a noticeable economic program for this country. This perspective of the economy fascinates the imagination of researchers to enquire into the contribution of export growth into its economic growth and vice versa. We, therefore, seek to study the relation between economic growth and export growth in this economy.

IV. Specific Issues Under Study

The present study seeks to enquire into

(i) the existence of long-run equilibrium relationship between income growth and export growth in Bangladesh

(ii) the stability of such long-run relationship

(iii) the nature and direction of causality between income growth and export growth in the economy of Bangladesh.

V. The Data

The relationship between Export growth and Income growth in the economy of Bangladesh is being studied for the period 1983-2008. The study involves the use of annual dataset for GDP and Export in Bangladesh. The data cover the period ranging from 1983-2008. Wholesale Price Index (WPI) is used with 2000 as the base period (2000=100). The data have been taken from various issues of IFS (*International Financial Statistics*). For estimating models, we have converted the dataset into (natural) Logarithmic form where first difference of Log Export and first difference of Log GDP series are represented by X_t and Y_t respectively.

VI. Organization of The Paper

Section II is devoted to the study of stationarity, cointegration, dynamics of short-run shock and the stability of the long-run relationship. Section III deals with dynamic relationship through the estimation of Vector Autoregression Model. Section IV presents Concluding Remarks.

Section - II

Study of Stationarity, Cointegration, Dynamics of Short-Run Shock And The Stability of The Long-Run Relationship

I. Stationarity

Results of the Augmented Dickey-Fuller Tests for the presence of Unit roots in the series for economic growth and export growth are being presented through the Table-1 and the Table-2.

It is observed from the Table-1, that

(i) all the variables at level are free from unit roots. Consequently, the series are stationary at levels

(ii) the variables do not have any deterministic trend

(iii) income growth (Y_t) and export (X_t) series are I(0).

The Table-2 also shows that the null-hypothesis of 'unit root', because of structural shift under PP Test

(i) has been rejected in case of income growth at 1% level

Table - 1
Results of Augmented Dickey-Fuller Tests For Unit Root In Income Growth (Y_t) And Export Growth(X_t)

					Mackinnon Critical Value		
Variable	*Exog-enous*	*ADF Test Statistic*	*Prob.* value*	*Lag length*	*1%*	*5%*	*10%*
Interest rate (r_t) at level	none	-0.13	0.62	0	-2.63	-1.9	-1.61
Interest rate (r_t) at 1st difference	none	-3.65	0.0006	0	-2.63	-1.95	-1.61
Money supply(M_t) at level	Constant, Linear Trend	-2.11	0.518	0	-4.25	-3.54	-3.2
Money supply(M_t) at 1st difference	Constant, Linear Trend	-4.4	0.0072		-4.26	-3.55	-3.2

Source: Author's own

(ii) has also been rejected in case of export growth series at 1% level.

Therefore, it is found that the Augmented Dickey-Fuller Tests and Phillips-Perrron Unit Root Tests for the presence of Unit roots in the series for economic growth (Y_t) and export growth (X_t) indicate that Y_t (income growth) and X_t (export growth) series are stationary at level. Consequently, Y_t and X_t are I(0).

Table - 2
Results of Phillips-Perron Tests For Unit Root in Income Growth (Y_t) And Export Growth(X_t)

					Mackinnon Critical Value		
Variable	*Exoge nous*	*P-P Test statistic*	*Prob.* value*	*Band with*	*1%*	*5%*	*10%*
Income Growth at level	Constant	–5.804443	0.0003	19	–3.68803	–3.210363	–2.646119
Export Growth at level	Constant	–7.928558	0	9	–3.59803	–3.210363	–2.646119

Source: Author's own

IV. Study of Cointegration Between Income Growth and Export Growth

Income growth (Y_t) and export growth (X_t) are stationary variables and both the series are I(0). Consequently, they are cointegrated[1] i.e., a long-run relationship must exist between $\{Y_t\}$ and $\{X_t\}$. This means that Y_t must be in a long-run relation with $X_{t.}$ Similarly, X_t must maintain a long-run relationship with Y_{t}.

V. Dynamics if Short-Run Shock and The Stability of the Long-Run Relationship: The Vector Error Correction Model (VECM).

There exists a long-run relationship between income growth and export growth in the economy of Bangladeh. The stability of such relationship needs to be examined. This is done through the estimation of the Vector Error Correction **(VEC)** Model. The estimated model helps us understand if any short-run shock could destabilize the long-run relationship between these variables.

VI. The VEC Model

In this study the **Vector Error Correction Model** is as follows:

$$\Delta Y_t = \gamma_1 + \rho_1 Z_{t-1} + \alpha_1 \Delta Y_{t-1} + \alpha_2 \Delta Y_{t-2} + \alpha_3 \Delta Y_{t-3} + \alpha_4 \Delta X_{t-1} + \alpha_5 \Delta X_{t-2}$$

$$+ \alpha_6 \Delta X_{t-3} + \varepsilon_{1t} \ldots (1)$$

$$\Delta Y_t = \gamma_2 + \rho_2 Z_{t-1} + \beta_1 \Delta Y_{t-1} + \beta_2 \Delta Y_{t-2} + \beta_3 \Delta Y_{t-3} + \beta_4 \Delta X_{t-1} + \beta_5 \Delta X_{t-2}$$

$$+ \beta_6 \Delta X_{t-3} + \varepsilon_{2t} \ldots (2)$$

where ΔY = first difference of Y (income growth), ΔX = first difference of X (export growth), Z_{t-1}= first lag of error term of the regression equation (serving as the virtual cointegrating equation), ε_{1t}, ε_{1t} are white noise error terms, $\alpha_{1 \ldots} \alpha_4$ are the coefficients of ΔY and ΔX in equation (1,) $\beta_{1 \ldots} \beta_4$ are the coefficients of ΔY and ΔX in equation (2), γ_1 and γ_2 are the intercept of the equations (1) and (2) respectively. In the estimation of VEC model at least one of ρ_1 and ρ_2 should be non-zero.

VII. Results of Estimation

The estimated VEC model consisting of equations 1-2 is given by the Table-3.

VIII. Economic Interpretations of The Findings [EQN 1]

The economic significance of these findings is as follows

(i) $\hat{\rho}$ being significant at 1% level indicates that short-run shocks, transmitted through the channel of income growth, significantly affected the long-run relationship which income growth maintained with export growth.

(ii) The negative value of $\hat{\rho}$ indicates that income growth, following any positive shock transmitted through the channel of income

Table - 3

The Results of the VEC Estimation [of Equations (1) and (2)

Dependent Variable	*Independent Variable*	*Coefficients*	*Standard error*	*'t'Statistics*
ΔY	*Constant* (β_1)	–0.001647	–0.0022	[–0.74689]
	Z_{t-1}	–0.794231	–0.27047	[–2.93648]
	ΔY_{t-1}	0.387597	–0.26985	[1.43632]
	ΔY_{t-2}	–0.4184	–0.20906	[–2.00135]
	ΔY_{t-3}	–0.04854	–0.24678	[–0.19669]
	ΔX_{t-1}	–0.044239	–0.05909	[–0.74863]
	ΔX_{t-2}	–0.026251	–0.07459	[–0.35194]
	ΔX_{t-3}	–0.029378	–0.05094	[–0.57670]
R^2 = 0.769646, F-stat = 4.295762, Log likelihood = 63.38483, AIC = -6.515862				
ΔX	*Constant* (β_2)	–0.000139	–0.01174	[–0.01186]
	z_{t-1}	2.549348	–1.43971	[1.77074]
	ΔX_{t-1}	–1.373874	–0.31455	[–4.36770]
	ΔX_{t-2}	–1.253267	–0.39703	[–3.15658]
	ΔX_{t-3}	–0.498664	–0.27116	[–1.83897]
	ΔY_{t-1}	–0.677413	–1.43642	[–0.47160]
	ΔY_{t-2}	–0.539698	–1.11281	[–0.48499]
	ΔY_{t-3}	0.839531	–1.31361	[0.63910]
	R^2 = 0.793634, F-stat = 4.944560, Log likelihood = 98.43309,			
	AIC = –8.190739			

Source: Author's own

growth, declined. Consequently, income growth deviated from its long-run equilibrium level in the short run.

(iii) $|\hat{\rho}| < 1$ indicates that income growth oscillated around the long-run equilibrium level following short-run income shocks and oscillations were convergent. Thus the long-run relationship which income growth maintained with export growth was stable.

(iv) α_4, α_5, α_6, being insignificant (even at 10% level), in the presence of ΔY_{t-i} (i= 1,..3) in the vector of regressors for ΔY_t, indicates that export growth failed to *Granger Cause* economic growth in the short-run.

IX. Economic Interpretations of the Findings from the Table-3 [EQN 2]

The economic significance of these findings is as follows.

(i) $\hat{\rho}_2$ being insignificant (even at 10% level) indicates that the shocks, transmitted through the export channel, failed to disturb the long-run relationship that export growth maintained with economic growth.

(ii) Consequently, this long –run relationship is stable.

(iii) $\hat{\beta}_4, \hat{\beta}_5$ *and* $\hat{\beta}_6$ the coefficients of ΔY_t (i = 4,5,6) respectively, are insignificant

(even at 10 % level). This indicated that economic growth failed *to Granger cause* export growth in the short run.

X. Summary of Findings

It is, therefore, observed that in the economy of Bangladesh over the period 1983-2008

(i) the long-run relationship, that economic growth maintained with export growth, was stable. The shocks, transmitted through income growth channel, had no significant dis-stabilizing impact on the long-run relationship. Consequently, the short-run dynamics of income growth defined an 'equilibrium' process.

(ii) the long-run relationship, that export growth maintained with income growth, was stable. The shocks, transmitted through export growth channel, failed to exert any appreciable impact on the long-run relationship. Consequently, the short-run dynamics of export growth defined a 'stable equilibrium process'.

(iii) there did exist no short-run causal relation between export and income growths in the economy of Bangladesh. Consequently, export growth and income growth appeared to be ***'exogenous'*** *to each other in that economy in the short-run over the period 1983-2008.*

Section - III
Study of Long-Run Causal Relation: Vector Autoregression Model

I. Vector Autoregression Model

In order to find the long-run dynamic relationship between export and economic growth in the economy of Bangladesh, we cannot make any *a priory* assumption of endogenity and exogeneity of variables. For this purpose, *Vector Autoregressive Model* **(VAR)** can be applied. This model treats all variables symmetrically without making reference to the issue of dependence versus independence. A **VAR** model also offers a scope for *Intervention Analysis* through the study of *Impulse Response Functions* for the endogenous variables in the model. *Variance Decomposition* allows us to study the 'Variance Decompositions' for these variables and thus help us understand the interrelationships among the variables concerned. We therefore, seek to develop a **VAR** model for Export and Economic Growth for the economy of Bangladesh in this chapter.

II. The Var Model

The Vector Autoregression (VAR) Model for Y_t (GDP Growth) and X_t (Export Growth) for the economy of Bangladesh consists of the equations (3) and (4)

$$Y_t = \alpha_1 + \sum_{i=1}^{k} \beta_{1i} Y_{t-i} + \sum_{i=1}^{k} \gamma_{1i} X_{t-i} + u_{1t} \quad ...(3)$$

$$X_t = \alpha_2 + \sum_{i=1}^{k} \beta_{2i} X_{t-i} + \sum_{l=1}^{k} \gamma_{2i} Y_{t-i} + u_{2t} \quad ...(4)$$

III. Selection of Lag Length

The appropriate lag-length needs to be determined before the estimation of a VAR model. The lag-length may be selected through the 'Selection Criteria' like AIC, SIC, HQIC etc. The Table 4 gives forth the statistics corresponding to different criteria for different lags.

It is observed from the table-4 that

(i) LR statistics for lag 4 is significant at 5% level

(ii) SIC statistics for lag 4 is significant at 5% level

(iii) FPE, AIC, HQ statistics for lag 4 are significant at 5% level.

We, therefore, choose four (4) lags for each endogenous variables in their **Autoregressive and Distributed Lag Structures** in the estimable VAR model.

IV. Features of The Var Model

The VAR model consisting of equations (3) and (4) requires that

(i) Y_t and X_t be stationary, and

(ii) u_{1t} and u_{2t} be white-noise terms such that

$u_{1t} \sim \text{iidN}(0,\sigma^2_{u1})$, and $u_{2t} \sim \text{iidN}(0,\sigma^2_{u1})$.

Table-4: Var Lag Order Selection Criteria

VAR Lag Order Selection Criteria						
Endogenous variables: LOGGDPD LOGEXPORTD						
Exogenous variables: C						
Sample: 1983 2008						
Included observations: 16						
Lag	LogL	LR	FPE	AIC	SC	HQ
0	80.16075	NA*	1.96E-07	-9.770094	-9.673521	-9.765149
1	83.6025	5.592847	2.12E-07	-9.700313	-9.410592	-9.685477
2	88.06789	6.139898	2.07E-07	-9.758486	-9.275618	-9.733759
3	93.26441	5.846092	1.94E-07	-9.908051	-9.232036	-9.873434
4	95.99645	2.390537	2.69E-07*	-9.749557*	-8.880394*	-9.705048*
5	110.594	9.12348	9.91E-08*	-11.07425*	-10.01194*	-11.01985*
* indicates lag order selected by the criterion						
LR: sequential modified LR test statistic (each test at 5% level)						
FPE: Final prediction error						
AIC: Akaike information criterion						
SC: Schwarz information criterion						
HQ: Hannan-Quinn information criterion						

Source: Author's own

In this model both Y_t and X_t are stationary at level such that $Y_t \sim I(0)$ and $X_t \sim I(0)$. Consequently, the first requirement is satisfied.

However, the properties of u_{1t} and u_{2t} need to be studied. This will enable us to find if u_{1t} and u_{2t} are really white noise terms.

V. The Estimable Var Model

The estimable VAR model, therefore, consists of the following equations.

$$Y_t = \alpha_1 + \beta_{11}Y_{t-1} + \beta_{12}Y_{t-2} + \beta_{13}Y_{t-3} + \beta_{14}Y_{t-4} + \gamma_{11}X_{t-1}$$

$$+ \gamma_{12}X_{t-2} + \gamma_{13}X_{t-3} + \gamma_{14}X_{t-4} \ldots (5)$$

$$X_t = \alpha_2 + \beta_{21}X_{t-1} + \beta_{22}X_{t-2} + \beta_{23}X_{t-3} + \beta_{24}X_{t-4} + \gamma_{21}Y_{t-1}$$

$$+ \gamma_{22}Y_{t-2} + \gamma_{23}Y_{t-3} + \gamma_{24}Y_{t-4} + u_{2t} \ldots (6)$$

VI. Results of Estimation of The Var Model

The results of estimation of the VAR model consisting of equations (5) and (6) are given by the Table-5.

VII. Stability of The Estimated Var Model

Let us consider the equations (5)

$$Y_t = \alpha_1 + \beta_{11}Y_{t-1} + \beta_{12}Y_{t-2} + \beta_{13}Y_{t-3} + \beta_{14}Y_{t-4} + \gamma_{11}X_{t-1} + \gamma_{12}X_{t-2}$$

$$+\gamma_{13}X_{t-3} + \gamma_{14}X_{t-4} + u_{1t} \ \ldots (6)$$

Table - 5
Stability of The Estimated Var Model

Dependent Variable	*Independent Variable*	*Coefficients*	*Standard errors*	*'t'Statistics*
Yt	Constant (α)	0.03515	-0.01819	[1.93272]
	Y_{t-1}	0.563572	-0.32634	[1.72695]
	Y_{t-2}	-0.808898	-0.33628	[-2.40540]
	Y_{t-3}	0.345826	-0.37491	[0.92242]
	Y_{t-4}	0.062873	-0.2577	[0.24398]
	X_{t-1}	0.022141	-0.0663	[0.33395]
	X_{t-2}	-0.013701	-0.06807	[-0.20129]
	X_{t-3}	-0.043384	-0.08288	[-0.52347]
	X_{t-4}	0.003214	-0.06979	[0.04605]

(*Contd...*)

R^2 = 0.617013, F-stat = 1.611058, Log likelihood = 63.72958, AIC = -6.438774				
X_t	Constant (α')	-0.022017	-0.09423	[-0.23365]
	X_{t-1}	-0.717151	-0.34351	[-2.08769]
	X_{t-2}	-0.133482	-0.35267	[-0.37849]
	X_{t-3}	0.431827	-0.42942	[1.00561]
	X_{t-4}	0.288874	-0.36161	[0.79886]
	Y_{t-1}	1.633047	-1.69087	[0.96581]
	Y_{t-2}	0.11445	-1.74239	[0.06569]
	Y_{t-3}	1.186524	-1.94252	[0.61082]
	Y_{t-4}	-0.724605	-1.33523	[-0.54268]
R^2 = 0.477601, F-stat = 0.914247, Log likelihood = 35.76365, AIC =-3.148665				

Source: Author's own

Equation (5) can be written as

$$Y_t - \beta_{11} Y_{t-1} - \beta_{12} Y_{t-2} - \beta_{13} Y_{t-3} - \beta_{14} \gamma_{t-4}$$

$$= \alpha_1 + \gamma_{11} X_{t-1} + \gamma_{12} X_{t-2} + \gamma_{13} X_{t-3} + \gamma_{14} X_{t-4} + u_{1t}$$

or,

$$Y_t - \beta_{11} Y_{t-1} - \beta_{12} Y_{t-2} - \beta_{13} Y_{t-3} - \beta_{14} Y_{t-4}$$

$$= \alpha_1 + \gamma_{11} X_{t-1} + \gamma_{12} X_{t-2} + \gamma_{13} X_{t-3} + \gamma_{14} X_{t-4} + u_{1t}$$

or,

$$Y_t - \beta_{11} Y_{t-1} - \beta_{12} Y_{t-2} - \beta_{13} Y_{t-3} - \beta_{14} Y_{t-4}$$

$$= \alpha_1 + \gamma_{11} X_{t-1} + \gamma_{12} X_{t-2} + \gamma_{13} X_{t-3} + \gamma_{14} X_{t-4} + u_{1t}$$

or,

$$Y_t - \beta_{11} L Y_t - \beta_{12} L^2 Y_t - \beta_{13} L^3 Y_t - \beta_{14} L^4 Y_t$$

$$= \alpha_1 + \gamma_{11} X_{t-1} + \gamma_{12} X_{t-2} + \gamma_{13} X_{t-3} + \gamma_{14} X_{t-4} + u_{1t}$$

or,

$$(1 - \beta_{11} L - \beta_{12} L^2 - \beta_{13} L^3 + \beta_{14} L^4) Y_t$$

$$= \alpha_1 + \gamma_{11} L X_t + \gamma_{12} L^2 X_t + \gamma_{13} L^3 X_t + \gamma_{14} L^4 X_t + u_{1t}$$

or, $B(L)Y_t = \alpha_1 + (\gamma_{11}L + \gamma_{12}L^2 + \gamma_{13}L^3)X_t + u_{1t}$

or, $B(L)Y_t = \alpha_1 + \gamma_1(L)X_t + u_{1t}$

or, $Y_t = [B(L)]^{-1}[\alpha_1 + \gamma_1(L)X_t + u_{1t}]$

where $\gamma_1(L) = (\gamma_{11}L + \gamma_{12}L^2 + \gamma_{13}L^3 + \gamma_{14}L^4)$

The stability of the equation (6) requires that the roots of the **Characteristic Polynomial** B(L) be less than one.

Similarly, let us consider (6)

$$X_t = \alpha_2 + \beta_{21}X_{t-1} + \beta_{22}X_{t-2} + \beta_{23}X_{t-3} + \beta_{24}X_{t-4} + \gamma_{21}Y_{t-1} +$$

$$\gamma_{22}Y_{t-2} + \gamma_{23}Y_{t-3} + \gamma_{24}Y_{t-4} + u_{2t}$$

Again equation (6) can also be written as

$$X_t = [A(L)]^{-1}[\alpha_2 + \gamma_2(L)Y_t + u_{2t}] \qquad 7$$

where $A(L) = (1 - \beta_{21}L - \beta_{22}L^2 - \beta_{23}L^3 - \beta_{24}L^4)$ and

$$\gamma_2(L) = (\gamma_{21}L + \gamma_{22}L^2 + \gamma_{23}L^3 + \gamma_{24}L^4)$$

Stability of the equation (7) requires that the roots of the **Characteristic Polynomial** A(L) be less than unity.

It, therefore, follows that the estimated VAR model, consisting of equations (5) and (6) will be stable iff

(i) the roots of the **Characteristics Polynomial** B(L) are less than unity, and

(ii) the roots of the **Characteristic Polynomials** A(L) are less than unity.

The roots of the **Characteristic Polynomials** B(L) and A(L) are given by the Table-6.

It is observed from the Table-6 that

(i) there are four characteristic roots (eigen value) for B(L),

(ii) there are four characteristic roots (eigen value) for A(L),

(iii) absolute values of the roots are less than unity,

Table - 6
Var Stability Condition Check

Roots of Characteristic Polynomial	
Endogenous variables: Income Growth Export Growth	
Exogenous variables: C	
Lag specification: 1 4	
Root	***Modulus***
0.060700 - 0.875040i	0.877143
0.060700 + 0.875040i	0.877143
-0.399516 - 0.660255i	0.771719
-0.399516 + 0.660255i	0.771719
0.627992 - 0.032815i	0.628849
0.627992 + 0.032815i	0.628849
-0.510335	0.510335
-0.221595	0.221595
No root lies outside the unit circle.	
VAR satisfies the stability condition.	

Source: Author's own

(iv) three of the roots are positive, and

(v) other three roots have negative values.

All these observations testify for the stability of the VAR model **All these observations testify for the stability of the VAR model**.

VIII. Confirmation of Serial Independence for the VAR Residuals ($\hat{u}_{1t}$ and $\hat{u}_{2t}$)

The results of the **VAR Residual Portmanteau Tests** for Auto-correlations are being presented through the Table-7.

The adjusted statistics for the corresponding Chi-square values in the Table-7, given the degree of freedom, show that

(i) the hypothesis of serial correlations have been rejected for upto the 8th lag at 5% level,

Table-7

VAR Residuals Portmanteau Tests for Autocorrelations

VAR Residual Portmanteau Tests for Autocorrelations					
H0: no residual autocorrelations up to lag h					
Sample: 1983 2008					
Included observations: 17					
Lags	Q-Stat	Prob.	Adj Q-Stat	Prob.	df
1	1.13599	NA*	1.20699	NA*	NA*
2	3.208916	NA*	3.556306	NA*	NA*
3	8.846645	NA*	10.40212	NA*	NA*
4	11.89376	NA*	14.38681	NA*	NA*
5	12.84275	0.0121	15.73122	0.0034	4
6	13.61726	0.0923	16.92818	0.0309	8
7	15.95692	0.1932	20.90561	0.0518	12
8	19.68194	0.2349	27.94175	0.0321	16
9	20.11219	0.4509	28.85604	0.0906	20
10	22.51731	0.5484	34.69702	0.073	24
11	23.82735	0.6906	38.4088	0.0909	28
12	24.72854	0.8169	41.47287	0.1219	32
*The test is valid only for lags larger than the VAR lag order.					
df is degrees of freedom for (approximate) chi-square distribution					

Source: Author's own

(ii) the hypotheses of serial correlation has been rejected at 10% level for the 11th lag.

Consequently, the VAR residuals $\hat{u}_{1t}$ and $\hat{u}_{2t}$ are found to be serially independent.

IX. Economic Interpretations of the Findings[Equation (5)]

The economic significance of these findings is stated below.

(i) significant (at 1% level) $\hat{\beta}_{12}$ indicates that current period economic growth was significantly affected by two period back economic growth.

(ii) $\hat{\beta}_{12} < 0$ and $|\hat{\beta}_{12}| < 1$ indicate that two period back economic growth adversely affected the current period economic growth though the effect was less than proportional.

(iii) $\hat{\gamma}_{1i}(i = 1,2,3,4)$ being insignificant even at 10% level indicates that export growth *failed to 'Granger Cause'* economic growth in the economy of Bangladesh over the period of study (1983-2008).

X. Economic Interpretations of the Findings[Equation (6)]:

The economic significance of these findings is as follows.

(i) $\hat{\beta}_{21} < 0$ and $|\hat{\beta}_{21}| < 1$ being significant (at 1% level) indicate that current period export growth was adversely, though non-proportionately, affected by the previous period export growth

(ii) $\hat{\gamma}_{2i}(i = 1,2,3,4)$ being insignificant (even at 10% level) indicates that economic growth (Y_t) *failed to 'Granger Cause'* export growth (X_t) in the economy of Bangladesh over the period 1983-2008.

XI. Overview of Findings:

The findings indicate that in the economy of Bangladesh over the period of study

(i) **export growth failed to Granger Cause** economic growth, and

(ii) **economic growth failed to Granger Cause** export growth.

All these observations indicate that the economy of Bangladesh was marked by the absence of any causal relation between export growth and economic growth. Consequently, export growth and economic growth appeared to be exogenous to each other over the period of study.

Concluding Remarks

The study confirms the **independence** for income and export growth in the economy of Bangladesh over the period 1983-2008. The shocks transmitted through the channel of any of the endogenous variables failed to produce any significant variations in another endogenous variable.

References

Ahmad, J. and Harnhirun, S. (1995). "Unit Roots and Cointegration in Estimating Causality Between Exports and Economic Growth": Empirical Evidence from the ASEAN Countries. *Economics Letters* 49, 329-34.

Ahmad, J. and Harnhirun, S. and Yang, J. (1997)."Export and Economic Growth in the ASEAN Countries: Cointegration and Causality Tests". *International Review of Economics and Business* 44, 419-30.

A. Koutsoyannis,(1993) Theory of Econometrics: "*An Introductory Exposition of Econometric Methods*", 2nd Edition, ELBS with Mcmillan, (1993), New Delhi.

Amoateng, K. and Amoako-Adu, B. (1996). "Economic Growth, Export and External Debt Causality: The Case of African Countries". *Applied Economics* 28, 21-7.

Bagchi, A. (1982) *The Political Economy of Underdevelopment*. Cambridge: Cambridge University Press.

Bahmani-Oskooee, M. and Alse, J. (1993). 'Export Growth and Economic Growth: An Application of Cointegration and Error Correction Modelings.' *The Journal of Developing Areas* 27, 535-42.

Boswijk, H.P. (1995). "Identifiability of Cointegrated System." *Technical Report*, Tinbergen Institute.

Box, G. E. P., G. M. Jenkins and G.C. Reinsel, *Time Series Analysis. Forecasting and Control*, third edition, Prentice Hall, Upper Saddle River, New Jersey (1994).

Chanda, A. (2000), "The Influence of Capital Controls on Long-Run Growth: Where and How Much?" *Working Paper*, North Carolina State University.

Chandra, R. (2000) "Export Growth and Economic Growth: An Investigation of Causality in India" *The Indian Economic Journal*, Vol.49, No.3.

Chang, R; L. Kaltni and N. Loayza (2005), 'Openness can be Good for Growth: The role of Policy Complementarities,' *World Bank Policy Research Working Paper* No. 3763, The World Bank, Washington, DC.

Damodar N. Gujarati (1995), '*Basic Econometrics*', Mcgraw Hill International Edition, Economics Series, Third Edition 1995.

Dickey, D. and Fuller,W.A.(1981). 'Likelihood Ratio Statistics for Autoregressive Time series with a Unit Root', *Econometrica*, Vol. 49, pp1057-72

Dodaro, S.(1993). 'Exports and Growth: A Reconsideration of Causality'. *Journal of Developing Areas* 27, 227-44.

Dufour, J.M. and Renault, E. (1998). "Short Run and Long Run Causality in Time Series Theory", *Econometrica*, Vol. 66,pp.1099-125.

Dutt, S.D. and Ghosh, D. (1994). 'An Empirical Investigation of The Export-Growth-Economic Growth Relationship'. *Applied Economics Letter* 1, 44-8.

Edwards, S. (1998), "Openness, Productivity and Growth: What Do We Really Know?" *Economic Journal*, 108:383-398.

Egwaikhide, F.O.(1992). 'Oil Export and Economic Growth in Nigeria: A Preliminary Investigation.' *Indian Journal of Economics* 72, 221-32.

Enders, W. (2003). '*Applied Econometric Time Series*', John Wiley & Sons.

Engle, R.F. and Granger, C.W.J. (1987). 'Cointegration and Error Correction: Representation, Estimations and Testing', *Econometrica*, Vol. 55, pp. 251-76.

Feder, Gershon. (1982), "On Exports and Economic Growth" *Journal of Development Econpmics,* 12, pp.59-73.

Granger, C.W.J. (1963). 'Economic Processes Involving Feedback'. *Information and Control* 6, 28-48.

Granger, C.W.J. and Newbold, P. (1974). 'Spurious Regressions in Econometrics'. *Journal of Econometrics* 2, 111-20.

Granger, C.W.J. and Swanson, N.R.(1997). 'Introduction to Stochastic Unit Root Processes. *Journal of Econometrics* 80, 35-62.

Greenaway, D. and Sapsford, D. (1994a). What Does Liberalization Do for Exports and Growth.' *Weltwirtschaftliches Archiv* 130, 152-74.

Greenaway, D. and Sapsford, D. (1994b). 'Exports, Growth, and Liberalization: An Evaluation'. *Journal of Policy Modeling* 16, 165-86.

Gupta, S.(1985). 'Export Growth and Economic Growth Revisited.' *Indian Economic Journal* 32, 52-9.

Hamming, R.W., *Digital Filters,* third edition, Dover Publications, Inc., New York,1998.

Harrison, A. (1996), "Openness and Growth: A Time-series, Cross-country Analysis for Developing Countries," *Journal of Development Economics*, 48:419-447.

H.G. Mannur (2000), *International Economics*, Second Revised Edition, Vikas Publishing House, New Delhi, 2000.

Hutchison, M., Singh, N., (1992). "Exports , Non Exports and Externalities: A Granger Causality Approach". *International Economic Journal* 6,79-94.

Hasza, D.P. and Fuller, W.A. (1979). 'Estimation of Autoregressive Processes with Unit Roots', *Annals of Statistics*, Vol.7, pp.1106-20.

Inacobucci, A. and A. Noullez, "Frequency Filters for Short Length Time Series", Working Paper IDEFI-IDEE 2002, n. 1.

Islam, M.N. (1998), "Export Expansion and Economic Growth: Testing for Cointegration and Causality," *Applied Economics*, 30: 415-425.

Jung, S.W. and Marshall, P.J.(1985). 'Exports, Growth and Causality in Developing Countries.' *Journal of Development Economics* 18, 1-12.

Krueger, A.O.(1978). *Foreign Trade Regimes and Economic Development: Liberalization Attempts and Consequences*. Cambridge (Mass.): Balinger.

Krueger, A.O.(1980). 'Trade Policy as an Impact to Development'. *American Economic Review* 2, 288-92.

Krueger, P.R.(1984). 'Import Protection as Export Promotion'. *In Kierzkowski, H. (ed) Monopolistic Competition in International Trade*. Oxford: University press.

Krueger, P.R.(1987). 'Is free trade passé?'. *Economic Perspectives* 1, 131-44.

Kugler, P. (1991). 'Growth, Export and Cointegration: An Empirical Investigation.' *Weltwirtschaftliches Archiv* 127, 73-82.

Kugler, P. and Dridi, J. (1993).'Growth and Exports in LDCs: A Multivariate Time Series Study.' *International Review of Economics and Business* 40, 759-67.

Kundu A. and C.K. Mukhopadhyay (2008) - "GARCH Error Based ARIMA Forecast for GDP in Sri Lanka"- *Journal of Regional Economic Studies,* Vol 2, March, 2008.

Kundu A. and C.K. Mukhopadhyay (2008), Export and Economic Growth in South Asian Countries North Bengal University, West Bengal, India.

Kundu A. and C.K. Mukhopadhyay (2008) - *ARIMA Forecasting For GDP In South Asian Countries*, Department Of Economics, University of North Bengal.

Kundu A. and C.K. Mukhopadhyay (2008) - *ARIMA Forecasting For Exchange Rates In South Asian Economy*, Department Of Economics, University of North Bengal.

Kunst, R.M. and Cotsomities, J.A.(1989). 'On Exports and Productivity: A Causal Analysis.' *Review of Economics and Statistics* 71, 699-703.

Kwan, R.M. and Marin, D. (1989). 'Economic Growth and the Expanding Export Sector: China 1952-1985.' *International Economic Journal* 5, 105-16.

Kwan, A.C.C. and Cotsomitis, J.A.and Kwok, B. (1996). 'Exports, Economic Growth and Exogeneity: Taiwan 1953-1988.' *Applied Economics* 28, 467-71.

Kwiatkowski, D., Phillips, P.C.B., Schmidt, P. and Shin, Y. (1992). 'Testing the Null Hypothesis of Stationarity against the Alternative of a Unit Root', *Journal of Econometrics*, Vol.54, pp. 159-78.

Lucas, R. E. Jr. (1976) "Econometric Policy Evaluation: A Critique," in *The Phillips Curve and Labour Markets* edited by Karl Brunner and Allan H. Neltzer, Amsterdam: North Holand.

Maddala, G.S. and Kim, I.M. (1998). *Unit Roots, Cointegration, and Structural Change*, Cambridge, University Press Cambridge,

McCarville, M. and Nnadozie, E. (1995). 'Causality Tests of Export-led Growth: The Case of Maxico.' *Atlantic Economic Journal* 23, 140-5.

Mukhopadhya C.K. and S.P. Acharya (2007)- "Export-Led Growth Hypothesis: An Econometric Verification on Nepalese Time Series 1964-2004", *Journal of South Asian Economy*, Vol 1,March, 2007.

Mukhopadhya C.K. and B. Maitra (2007)- "The Relationship Between Export and Economic Growth in the Economy of Bangladesh (1972-2005): An Econometric Study"- *Journal of Regional Economic Studies,* Vol 1,March, 2007.

Nachane, D.M. (2006)- Econometrics: "Theoretical Foundations Empirical Perspective", Oxford University Press.

Nandi, S. and B. Biswas (1991). 'Exports and Economic Growth in India: Empirical Evidence.' *Indian Economic Journal* 38, 53-9.

Oppenheim, A. V. and R. W. Schafer, *Discrete-Time Signal Processing*, second edition, Prentice-Hall, New Jersey, 1999

Oxley, L. (1993). "Cointegration, Causality and Export-led Growth in Portugal, 1865-1985". *Economics Letters* 43, 163-6.

Park, H.J. and Fuller, W.A. (1995). 'Alternative Estimators and Unit Root Tests for Autoregressive Process' *Journal of Time Series Analysis*, Vol. 16, pp. 415-29.

Phillips, P. C. B. and P. Perron (1988), "Testing for a Unit Root in Time Series Regression," *Biometrica,* 75: 335-346.

R.S. Pindyck and D.L. Rubinfeld, *Econometric Models and Econometric Forecasts*, McGraw-Hill, New York, 1981.

Serletis, A. (1992). 'Export Growth and Canadian Economic Development.' *Journal of Development Economics* 38, 133-45.

Sims, C.A. (1980). 'Macroeconomics and Reality'. *Econometrica* 48, 1-48.

Notes

1. According to Engle and Granger (1987), let {Yt} and {Xt} be stationary such that Yt ~I(0) and Xt~I(0). Consequently, d = 0 and there cannot be any b>o so that Yt, Xt~CI (d,b).Under this situation, a long run relationship between Yt and Xt does already exist and the classical regression model is appropriate.

1 According to Engle and Granger (1987), let {Yt } and {Xt} be stationary such that Yt ~I(0) and Xt~ I(0). Consequently, d=0 and there cannot be any b>o so that Yt, Xt~CI (d,b).

Under this situation, a long run relationship between Yt and Xt does already exist and the classical regression model is appropriate.

and $\gamma 2$ are the intercept of the equations (1) and (2) respectively. In the estimation of VEC model at least one of $\rho 1$ and $\rho 2$ should be non-zero.

CASE STUDY - 5

EXPORT AND ECONOMIC GROWTH IN THE ECONOMY OF INDONESIA – AN ECONOMETRIC STUDY (1971-2007)

I. Introduction

An economy is said to grow when the country's *gross domestic product* (GDP) rises. Economic growth is of fundamental importance for all economies. Since virtually all countries experience growth in population over time, GDP growth is a prerequisite for maintaining current standard of living. In fact, if standards of living are to rise over time, GDP must grow faster than population.

Economic growth is also critical for **economic development.** Economic development is characterized by such things as high levels of consumption, broad-based educational achievement, adequate housing and access to high-quality health care etc. These goals may be achieved only after long periods of sustained high levels of economic growth.

International Trade can affect the level of economic growth of an economy. An increase in export sales may lead to an overall expansion in production and accompanying fall in unemployment rate. International trade also allows for purchase of capital goods from foreign countries and exposes an economy to technological advances achieved round the globe.Conversely, economic growth may affect the types of goods which a country is able to trade. A technological advance in a country's import-competing sector could lead to an overall reduction in the volume of trade of a country. Thus, international trade and economic growth are closely related.

II. Variants of Hypotheses

The relation between export and economic growth is really complex and economists differ among themselves on this issue. There are five schools of thought regarding the relationship between export growth and income growth. These are as follows:

- **(i) Export-Led Income Growth Hypothesis:**
- **(ii) Income-led Export Growth:**
- **(iii) Income-Led Export Growth Led Income:**
- **(iv) Export Growth-Led Income Growth-Led Export Growth:**
- **(v) Independence:**

III. Objective of The Study

Under this controversial theoretical framework, we seek to enquire empirically into the relationship between income growth and export growth in Indonesia. Export promotion exercises constitute a noticeable economic program for this country. This perspective of the economy fascinates the imagination of researchers to enquire into the contribution of export growth into its economic growth and vice versa. We, therefore, seek to study the relation between economic growth and export growth in this economy.

IV. Specific Issues Under Study

The present study seeks to enquire into

(i) the existence of long-run equilibrium relationship between income growth and export growth in Indonesia.

(ii) the stability of such long-run relationship

(iii) the nature and direction of causality between income growth and export growth in the economy of Indonesia.

V. The Data

The relationship between Export growth and Income growth in the economy of Indonesia is being studied for the period 1971-2007. The study involves the use of annual dataset for GDP and Export in Indonesia. The data cover the period ranging from 1971-2007. Wholesale Price Index (WPI) is used with 2000 as the base period (2000=100). The data have been taken from various issues of IFS (*International Financial Statistics*). For estimating models, we have converted the dataset into (natural) Logarithmic form where first difference of Log Export and first difference of Log GDP series are represented by X_t and Y_t respectively.

Graphical Presentation of Series

Time plots of income growth (Y_t) and export growth (X_t) series are being presented through the

Time Plots of Income Growth (Y_t) and Export Growth (X_t)

The Figure shows that

(i) both series are free from any stochastic trend.

(ii) both the series are measured by the presence of any deterministic trend.

(iii) both the series exhibit no structural shift.

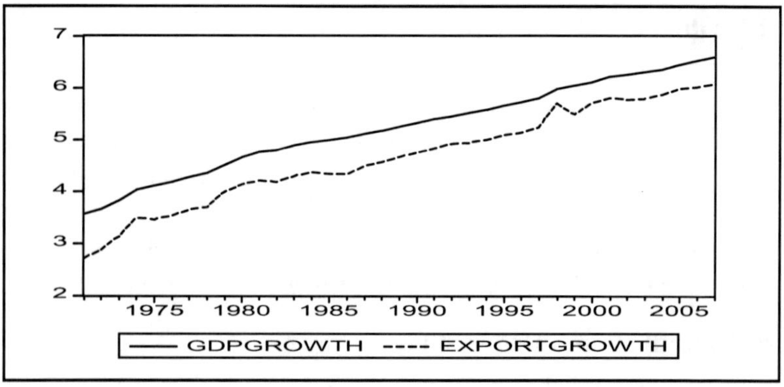

Source: Author's own.

These features of the series are the pointers to their nonstationarity. However, for the confirmation of 'stationarity' in Y_t and X_t, the series are being subject to 'Unit Root Tests'.

Augmented Dickey-Fuller Tests for Unit Roots in Different Series:

Results of the Augmented Dickey-Fuller Tests for the presence of Unit roots in the series for economic growth and export growth are being presented in the Table-1

Table - 1
Results of the Augmented Dickey-Fuller Tests for the Presence of Unit Roots in the Series for Economic Growth and Export Growth

Null hypothesis: GDP growth has a Unit Root.				*Mackinnon Critical Value*		
Exogeneous: Constant, Linear Trend						
Variable	*ADF Test Statistics Statistic*	*Prob.* value*	*Lag length*	*1%*	*5%*	*10%*
GDP growth at level	–3.1112	0.1191	0	–4.2349	–3.5403	–3.2024
GDP growth at 1st difference	–4.6254	0.0038	0	–4.2436	–3.5442	–3.2046
Export growth at level	–3.7428	0.032	0	–4.2349	–3.5403	–3.2024
Export growth at 1st difference	–7.4196	0	0	–4.2436	–3.5442	–3.2046

Source: Author's own

It is observed from the ADF Test results as given in the Table 3.1, that

(i) the null hypothesis of unit root for Y_t series at its 1st difference is rejected at 5 % level

(ii) the null hypothesis of unit root for X_t series at its 1st difference is rejected even at 1 % level.

These results hint at the stationarity of both the Y_t and X_t series.

Phillips-Perron Unit Root Tests

Results of the Augmented Dickey-Fuller Tests for the presence of Unit roots in the series for economic growth and export growth are being presented in the Table-2

Table - 2
Results of The Phillips-Perron Tests For The Presence of Unit Roots In The Series For Economic Growth And Export Growth

Null hypothesis: GDP growth has a Unit Root. Exogeneous: Constant, Linear Trend				*Mackinnon Critical Value*		
Variable	*P-P Test statistic*	*Prob.* value*	*Band with*	*1%*	*5%*	*10%*
GDP growth at level	-3.075476	0.1273	1	-4.234972	-3.54033	-3.202445
GDP growth at 1st difference	-4.656437	0.0035	1	-4.243644	-3.54428	-3.204699
Export growth at level	-3.720215	0.0337	1	-4.234972	-3.54033	-3.202445
Export growth at 1st difference	-7.583916	0	1	-4.243644	-3.54428	-3.204699

Source: Author's own

It is observed from the P-P Test results as given in the Table that

(i) the null hypothesis of Unit Roots in Y_t series at its 1st difference has been rejected at 1% level, and

(ii) the null hypothesis of unit root in X_t series at its 1st difference has been also been rejected at 1% level.

Consequently, both the Y_t and X_t series appear to be stationary.

Correlogram Analysis for Stationarity

The stationarity of the variables has further been examined through the study of their correlograms. Figures 3.2-3.5 present the study of their correlograms of the variables concerned. It is observed from the Figure-3.2 and Figure-3.4 that

(i) the ACF exhibits a dying-out pattern for the spikes,

(ii) there exists only one single spike at lag one.

These observations indicate that the GDP and export series are non-stationary and needs differencing. The ACF and PACF of the first differenced series of GDP and export are being given by the Figure-3 and Figure-.5

The Figure-3 and Figure-5 show that

(i) the ACF is free from the dying-out pattern of spikes, and

(ii) the PACF does not contain any significant spike at lag one.

These observations testify for the stationarity of the first differenced GDP series Export series. Consequently the GDP and Export series are I (1) and d=1.

Sample: 1971 2007
Included observations: 37

Lag	AC	PAC	Q-Stat	Prob
1	0.907	0.907	33.007	0.000
2	0.815	-0.050	60.368	0.000
3	0.728	-0.018	82.842	0.000
4	0.649	-0.004	101.26	0.000
5	0.570	-0.050	115.91	0.000
6	0.490	-0.049	127.10	0.000
7	0.411	-0.052	135.22	0.000
8	0.334	-0.042	140.77	0.000
9	0.263	-0.025	144.33	0.000
10	0.198	-0.021	146.41	0.000
11	0.143	0.004	147.54	0.000
12	0.088	-0.048	147.99	0.000
13	0.037	-0.025	148.07	0.000
14	-0.011	-0.034	148.08	0.000
15	-0.059	-0.051	148.30	0.000
16	-0.105	-0.046	149.05	0.000

Source: Author's own

Figure -2: Correlogram of GDP at Level Data

Sample: 1971 2007
Included observations: 36

Lag	AC	PAC	Q-Stat	Prob
1	0.311	0.311	3.7826	0.052
2	0.021	-0.084	3.8007	0.150
3	0.121	0.156	4.4038	0.221
4	-0.026	-0.130	4.4329	0.351
5	0.006	0.082	4.4346	0.489
6	0.130	0.088	5.2031	0.518
7	0.182	0.152	6.7699	0.453
8	-0.048	-0.187	6.8817	0.549
9	-0.045	0.038	6.9829	0.639
10	0.016	-0.030	6.9970	0.726
11	-0.115	-0.069	7.7149	0.739
12	-0.173	-0.171	9.4212	0.667
13	-0.196	-0.162	11.700	0.552
14	-0.096	0.025	12.279	0.584
15	-0.005	0.082	12.280	0.658
16	-0.132	-0.185	13.474	0.638

Source: Author's own

Figure – 3: Correlogram of GDP at 1st Difference

Sample: 1971 2007
Included observations: 37

Autocorrelation	Partial Correlation		AC	PAC	Q-Stat	Prob
		1	0.897	0.897	32.264	0.000
		2	0.800	-0.027	58.625	0.000
		3	0.711	-0.008	80.080	0.000
		4	0.640	0.041	97.997	0.000
		5	0.564	-0.067	112.33	0.000
		6	0.486	-0.052	123.30	0.000
		7	0.404	-0.064	131.16	0.000
		8	0.321	-0.070	136.31	0.000
		9	0.259	0.044	139.77	0.000
		10	0.191	-0.084	141.72	0.000
		11	0.141	0.044	142.82	0.000
		12	0.087	-0.050	143.26	0.000
		13	0.041	-0.015	143.36	0.000
		14	-0.003	-0.023	143.36	0.000
		15	-0.051	-0.081	143.54	0.000
		16	-0.104	-0.078	144.29	0.000

Source: Author's own

Figure -4: Correlogram of Export at Level Data.

Sample: 1971 2007
Included observations: 36

Autocorrelation	Partial Correlation		AC	PAC	Q-Stat	Prob
		1	-0.208	-0.208	1.6971	0.193
		2	-0.033	-0.080	1.7409	0.419
		3	0.076	0.054	1.9777	0.577
		4	-0.069	-0.045	2.1798	0.703
		5	-0.045	-0.066	2.2685	0.811
		6	0.049	0.016	2.3767	0.882
		7	0.083	0.105	2.7027	0.911
		8	-0.029	0.019	2.7444	0.949
		9	-0.030	-0.039	2.7900	0.972
		10	0.027	0.002	2.8277	0.985
		11	0.043	0.070	2.9309	0.992
		12	-0.220	-0.199	5.7004	0.930
		13	-0.015	-0.130	5.7135	0.956
		14	0.016	-0.048	5.7301	0.973
		15	-0.010	0.022	5.7364	0.984
		16	-0.119	-0.150	6.6992	0.979

Source: Author's own

Figure – 5: Correlogram of Export at 1st Difference

Summary of Findings on Stationarity

(i) Y_t (income growth) and X_t (export growth) series are stationary at 1st difference. Consequently, Y_t and X_t are I(1)

(ii) both the series are free from any deterministic trend

(iii) there exist no structural breaks in the series concerned.

Long-run Relationship Between Income Growth and Export Growth: Cointegration Considered

For testing cointegration we use unit root test on the residuals estimated from the cointegrating regression. Since Income growth (Y_t) and export growth (X_t) are individually nonstationary variables, there is the possibility that the regression between the variables concerned is spurious. If the residuals estimated from the cointegrating regressions are stationary then regressions will not spurious, even though individually the two variables are nonstationary. Therefore, it is imperative to study the unit root test on the residuals.

Augmented Dickey-Fuller Tests for Unit Roots in Residuals

Results of the Augmented Dickey-Fuller Tests for the presence of Unit roots in Residuals are being presented in the Table-3

Table - 3
Results of The Augmented Dickey-Fuller Tests for the Presence of Unit Roots in Residuals

Null hypothesis: Residuals has a Unit Root.				*Mackinnon Critical Value*		
Exogeneous: Constant						
Variable	*ADF Test Statistic*	*Prob.* value*	*Lag length*	*1%*	*5%*	*10%*
Residual 1 (Taking GDP growth as dependent variable)	–4.791074	0.0004	0	–3.626784	–2.94584	–2.611531
Residual 2 (Taking Export growth as dependent variable)	–4.912268	0.0003	0	–3.626784	–2.94584	–2.611531

Source: Author's own

It is observed from the ADF Test results as given in the Table that

(i) the null hypothesis of unit root for residuals at level is rejected at 1 % level

These results hint at the stationarity of residuals.

Phillips-Perron Unit Root Tests

Results of the Phillips-Perron Tests for the presence of Unit roots in the residuals are being presented in the Table - 4

Table - 4
Results of The Phillips-Perron Tests for the Presence of Unit Roots in the Residuals

Null hypothesis: Residuals has a Unit Root. Exogeneous: Constant				*Mackinnon Critical Value*		
Variable	*P-P Test statistic*	*Prob.* value*	*Bandwith*	*1%*	*5%*	*10%*
Residual 1 (Taking GDP growth as dependent variable)	-4.780603	0.0004	2	- 3.626784	- 2.94584	- 2.611531
Residual 2 (Taking Export growth as dependent variable)	-4.89616	0.0003	2	- 3.626784	- 2.94584	- 2.611531

Source: Author's own

It is observed from the P-P Test results as given in the Table 3.4 that

(i) the null hypothesis of Unit Roots in residuals at level has been rejected at 1% level, and

Consequently, both the Residual 1 and Residual 2 appear to be stationary.

Correlogram Analysis for Stationarity of Residuals

The stationarity of the residuals has further been examined through the study of their correlograms. Figures 6-7 present the study of their correlograms of the residuals concerned. It is observed from both the Figure-6and Figure-7 that

(i) the ACF is free from the dying-out pattern of spikes, and
(ii) the PACF does not contain any significant spike at lag one.

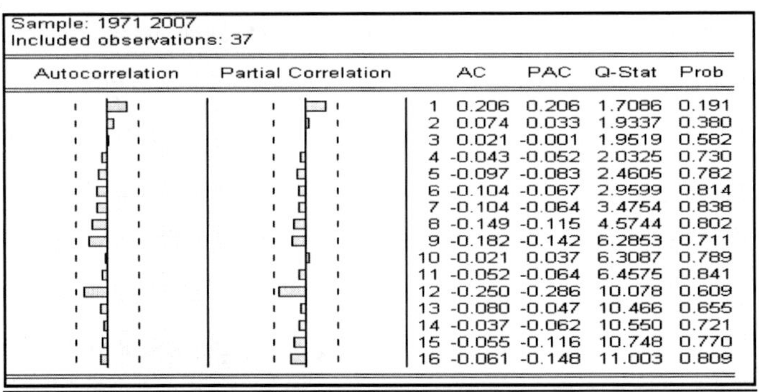

Source: Author's own

Figure -6. Correlogram of Residual 1 at Level Data.

These observations testify for the stationarity of the residuals. Consequently the residuals are I (0) and d = 0.

Sample: 1971 2007
Included observations: 37

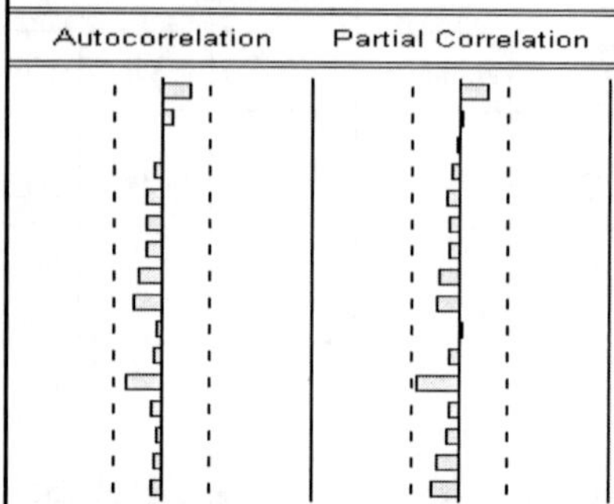

	AC	PAC	Q-Stat	Prob
1	0.196	0.196	1.5430	0.214
2	0.059	0.021	1.6860	0.430
3	0.004	-0.012	1.6867	0.640
4	-0.052	-0.054	1.8043	0.772
5	-0.104	-0.087	2.2879	0.808
6	-0.108	-0.072	2.8351	0.829
7	-0.110	-0.074	3.4192	0.844
8	-0.161	-0.132	4.7099	0.788
9	-0.185	-0.149	6.4811	0.691
10	-0.028	0.018	6.5219	0.770
11	-0.054	-0.076	6.6812	0.824
12	-0.251	-0.300	10.316	0.588
13	-0.076	-0.068	10.662	0.639
14	-0.028	-0.085	10.711	0.709
15	-0.047	-0.148	10.859	0.763
16	-0.061	-0.196	11.112	0.802

Source: Author's own

Figure – 7: Correlogram of Residual 2 at 1st Difference.

Since Income growth (Y_t) and export growth (X_t) are individually nonstationary variables and the residuals are stationary at level. Consequently, a long-run relationship must exist between $\{Y_t\}$ and $\{X_t\}$. This means that Y_t must be in a long-run relation with X_t. Similarly, X_t must maintain a long-run relationship with Y_t.

The existence of long-run relationship between income growth and export growth being assured, it then becomes imperative to enquire into the stability of such relationship. This constitutes the topic of our study in the next chapter.

Stability of the Long-run Income Growth and Export Growth Relationship in Indonesia Vector Error Correction (VEC) Model

There exists a long-run relationship between income growth and export growth in the economy of Indonesia The stability of such relationship needs to be examined. This is done through the estimation of the Vector Error Correction (VEC) Model. The estimated model helps us understand if any short-run shock could destabilize the long-run relationship between these variables.

The VEC Model

In the present study the Vector Error Correction Model is as follows:

$$\Delta Y_t = \gamma_1 + \rho_1 Z_{t-1} + \alpha_1 \Delta Y_{t-1} + \alpha_2 \Delta Y_{t-2} + \alpha_3 \Delta Y_{t-3} + \alpha_4 \Delta X_{t-1}$$

$$+\alpha_5 \Delta X_{t-2} + \alpha_6 \Delta X_{t-3} + \varepsilon_{1t} \qquad 1$$

$$\Delta X_t = \gamma_2 + \rho_2 Z_{t-1} + \beta_1 \Delta Y_{t-1} + \beta_2 \Delta Y_{t-2} + \beta_3 \Delta Y_{t-3} + \beta_4 \Delta X_{t-1}$$

$$+\beta_5 \Delta X_{t-2} + \beta_6 \Delta X_{t-3} + \varepsilon_{2t} \qquad 2$$

where Δ Y = first difference of Y (income growth)

Δ X = first difference of X (export growth)

Z_{t-1}= first lag of error term of the respective regression equation

ε_{1t}, ε_{1t} are white noise error terms

$\alpha_{1 \dots} \alpha_4$ are the coefficients of Δ Y and Δ X in equation (1)

$\beta_{1 \dots} \beta_4$ are the coefficients of Δ Y and Δ X in equation (2)

γ_1 and γ_2 are the intercept of the equations (1) and (2) respectively.

In the estimation of VEC model at least one ρ_1 and ρ_2 should be non-zero.

Results of Estimation: The estimated VEC model consisting of equations 1-2 is given by the Table-5

Results of Estimation

The estimated VEC model consisting of equations 1-2 is given by the Table-5.

Table-5: The Results of the VEC Estimation

Dependent Variable	*Independent Variable*	*Coefficients*	*Standard errors*	*'t'Statistics*
ΔY	Constant(β_1)	0.003253	-0.00688	[0.47309]
	z_{t-1}	0.863777	-0.3578	[2.41417]
	ΔY_{t-1}	-1.308707	-0.44813	[-2.92040]
	ΔY_{t-2}	-0.586156	-0.44491	[-1.31748]
	ΔY_{t-3}	0.131513	-0.28647	[0.45908]
	ΔX_{t-1}	0.731603	-0.27655	[2.64542]
	ΔX_{t-2}	0.426556	-0.20757	[2.05505]
	ΔX_{t-3}	0.115087	-0.1	[1.15088]
ΔX	Constant(β_2)	0.013954	-0.02195	[0.63575]
	z_{t-1}	3.72483	-1.14197	[3.26177]
	ΔY_{t-1}	-2.062624	-1.43027	[-1.44212]
	ΔY_{t-2}	-0.690275	-1.42	[-0.48611]
	ΔY_{t-3}	0.51643	-0.91431	[0.56483]
	ΔX_{t-1}	1.628	-0.88267	[1.84440]
	ΔX_{t-2}	0.775401	-0.66248	[1.17045]
	ΔX_{t-3}	0.16231	-0.31916	[0.50855]

Source: Author's own

Table-6: Relevant Statistics of the VEC Estimation

R-squared	0.423601	0.688343
Adj. R-squared	0.255485	0.597443
Sum sq. resids	0.030337	0.309035
S.E. equation	0.035553	0.113475
F-statistic	2.51969	7.572536
Log likelihood	65.972	28.83454
Akaike AIC	-3.62325	-1.302159
Schwarz SC	-3.256816	-0.935725
Mean dependent	4.97E-05	0.002711
S.D. dependent	0.041204	0.178848
Determinant Residual Covariance		2.29E-06
Log Likelihood		126.2165
Log Likelihood (d.f. adjusted)		117.0106
Akaike Information Criteria		-6.188165
Schwarz Criteria		-5.363688

Source: Author's own

Stability of the VEC Model

The roots of the Characteristic Polynomials corresponding to Autoregressive Structures in equations 1-2 are given by the Table 7.

Table-7: Roots of Characteristic Polynomial

Roots of Characteristic Polynomial	
Endogenous variables: GDPGROWTHD EXPORTGROWTHD	
Exogenous variables:	
Lag specification: 1 3	
Root	**Modulus**
1	1
-0.465072 - 0.523493i	0.70024
-0.465072 + 0.523493i	0.70024
-0.245147 - 0.594093i	0.642684
-0.245147 + 0.594093i	0.642684
-0.593221	0.593221
0.356862 - 0.435511i	0.563045
0.356862 + 0.435511i	0.563045
VEC specification imposes 1 unit root(s).	

Source: Author's own

It is observed from the Table-7 that

(i) the absolute values of the characteristic roots are less than unity

(ii) three of the characteristic roots are positive

(iii) three of the characteristic roots are negative

Again the inverse roots of AR Characteristic Polynomials lie within the unit circle. This is being shown by the Figure-8

All these testify for the stability of the estimated VEC model consisting of equations 1-2

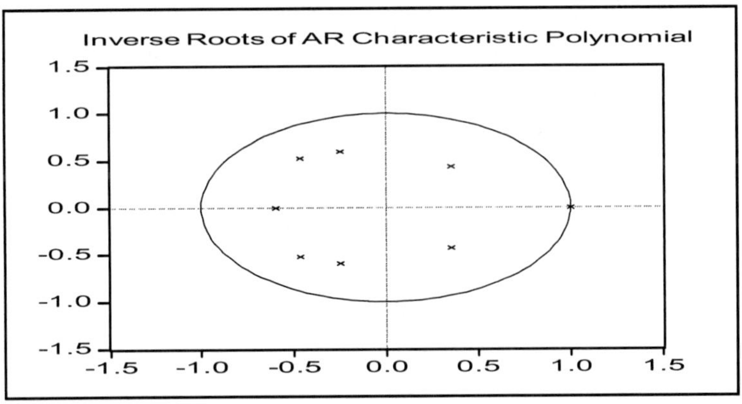

Source: Author's own

Figure-8 Inverse Roots of AR Characteristic Polynomials

Findings From the Table 1 [Eqn 1] in the VEC Model:

In the estimated equation (1)

(a) $\hat{\rho}_1$, the coefficient of Z_{t-1} is significant at 1% level,

(b) $\hat{\rho}_1$, = 0.863777 indicates that $\hat{\rho}_1 < 1$ but positive and $|\hat{\rho}_1| < 1$.

(c) $\hat{\alpha}_4$ *and* $\hat{\alpha}_5$ (i.e, the coefficients of ΔX_{t-1} and ΔX_{t-2} respectively) are significant at 1% level.

Economic Interpretations of the Findings [Eqn 1]:

The economic significance of these findings is as follows

(i) $\hat{\rho}_1$, being significant at 1% level indicates that short-run shocks, transmitted through the channel of income growth, significantly affected the long-run relationship which income growth maintained with export growth.

(ii) The positive value of $\hat{\rho}_1$, indicates that income growth, following any positive shock transmitted through the channel of income growth, pulled up. Consequently, short-run positive income shocks appeared to pull up income growth from its long-run equilibrium level.

(iii) $\left|\hat{\rho}_1\right| < 1$ indicates that income growth oscillated around the long-run equilibrium level following short-run equilibrium level following short-run income shocks and oscillations was not explosive. Thus the long-run relationship which income growth maintained with export growth was not stable.

(iv) $\hat{\alpha}_4$ and $\hat{\alpha}_5$ being significant (at 1% level), even in the presence of ΔY_{t-i} (i= 1,..3) in the vector of regressors for ΔY_t, indicates that export growth *Granger Caused* economic growth in the short-run.

The Findings From the Table-1 [Eqn 2]:

In the estimated equation 4.2 in the VEC model

(a) $\hat{\rho}_2$ is significant even at 1% level.

(b) $\hat{\rho}_2$ = 3.724830 indicates that $\hat{\rho}_1$ >1 but positive and $\left|\hat{\rho}_1\right| > 1$.

(c) $\hat{\beta}_i$ (i=1,4), are significant at 10% and 5% level.

Economic Interpretations of the Findings from the Table 1 [Eqn 2]:

The economic significance of these findings is as follows.

(i) $\hat{\rho}_2$ being significant (at 1 % level) indicates that the shocks, transmitted through the export channel, disturbed the long-run relationship that export growth maintained with economic growth.

(ii) long –run relationship is unstable.

(iii) $\hat{\beta}_1$ is significant (at 10 % level). This indicated that economic growth Granger *caused* export growth in the short run.

Summary of Findings

It is, therefore, observed that in the economy of Indonesia over the period 1971-2007

(i) the long-run relationship, that economic growth maintained with export growth, was stable. The shocks, transmitted through income growth channel, had significant stabilizing impact on the long-run relationship. Consequently, the short-run dynamics of income growth defined an 'equilibrium' process.

(ii) the long-run relationship, that export growth maintained with income growth, was unstable. The shocks, transmitted through export growth channel, exerted any appreciable impact on the long-run relationship. Consequently, the short-run dynamics of export growth defined a 'unstable equilibrium process'.

(iii) there did exist 'Bi-directional' short-run Granger Causality between export growth and income growth .

Chapter - 11

Multiple Choice Questions

(1) If demand for money were perfectly elastic with respect to rate of interest

(a) LM curve will be horizontal
(b) LM curve will be vertical
(c) LM curve will be 45° line
(d) none

Ans. Horizontal

(2) The more interest-inelastic is the demand for money

(a) Steeper the slope of the LM curve
(b) LM curve will be vertical
(c) LM curve will be horizontal
(d) none

Ans. (a)

(3) Equilibrium at full employment has been restored by means of price flexibility in

(a) Neoclassical model
(b) Keynesian model
(c) both models
(d) none of the above

Ans. (a)

(4) In the Keynesian model output and interest rate are:

(a) Endogenous variable
(b) Exogenous variable
(c) Indeterminate

(d) None of the above

Ans. (a)

(5) In the Keynesian model price level is fixed

(a) until full employment is reached

(b) at full employment

(c) beyond full employment

(d) None of the above

Ans. (a)

(6) In the neoclassical model price level and interest rate are

(a) Endogenous variable

(b) Exogenous variable

(c) Indeterminate

(d) None of the above

Ans. (a)

(7) The ISLM model

(a) cannot solve for output, the interest rate and the price level simultaneously.

(b) can solve for output, the interest rate and the price level simultaneously.

(c) Can solve partially for output, the interest rate and the price level.

(d) None

Ans. (a)

(8) The ISLM model is entirely concerned with positions of

(a) Static equilibrium

(b) Dynamic equilibrium

(c) Both

(d) None

Ans. (a)

(9) The fiscal policy multiplier is larger

(a) the more interest-elastic is the demand for money and the less interest-elastic is the demand for investment goods.

(b) the more interest-inelastic is the demand for money and the less interest-inelastic is the demand for investment goods.

(c) both.

(d) none.

Ans. (a)

(10) The size of the money multiplier is larger

(a) the less interest-elastic is the demand for money and the more interest-elastic is the demand for investment goods.

(b) the higher interest-elastic is the demand for money and the less interest-elastic is the demand for investment goods.

(c) the less interest-inelastic is the demand for money and the more interest-inelastic is the demand for investment goods.

(d) none.

Ans. (a)

(11) In rational expectation errors are

(a) random.

(b) systematic.

(c) both.

(d) none.

Ans. (a)

(12) In adaptive expectation hypothesis errors are:

(a) systematic.

(b) random.

(c) both.

(d) none.

Ans. (a)

(13) Keynesian theory of business cycle is

(a) Static fluctuation model.

(b) Dynamic fluctuation model.

(c) Partially static and partially dynamic model.

(d) none of the above.

Ans. (a)

(14) Keynesian theory of trade cycle depends on

(a) Multiplier theory.

(b) Accelerator theory.

(c) Mixture of both.

(d) none.

Ans. (a)

(15) Samuelson's theory of business cycle is

(a) Static fluctuation model.

(b) Dynamic fluctuation model.

(c) Partially static and partially dynamic model.

(d) none of the above.

Ans. (b)

(16) Samuelson's theory of trade cycle depends on

(a) Multiplier theory.

(b) Accelerator theory.

(c) Mixture of both.

(d) none.

Ans. (c)

(17) There is an upper ceiling and a lower ceiling in

(a) Hicks's Model of Trade Cycle.

(b) Samuelson's Model of Trade Cycle.

(c) Keynesian Model of Trade Cycle.

(d) None

Ans. (a)

(18) The concept of upper ceiling in Hicks's trade cycle is based on

(a) Harrod's Natural rate.

(b) Warranted rate.

(c) Both.

(d) None.

Ans. (a)

(19) The concept of equilibrium path in Hicks's trade cycle is based on

(a) Harrod's Natural rate.

(b) Warranted rate.

(c) Both.

(d) None.

Ans. (b)

(20) The concept of equilibrium path in Hicks's trade cycle shows that

(a) Real saving and real investment are equal.

(b) Real saving and real investment are unequal.

(c) Nominal saving and Nominal investment are equal.

(d) Nominal saving and Nominal investment are unequal.

Ans. (a)

(21) Kaldor demonstrates how a cycle could exist in the _________ of growth factor.

(a) absence.

(b) presence.

(c) partially presence.

(d) partially absence.

Ans. (a)

(22) Kaldor in his business cycle theory does not use

(a) acceleration principle.

(b) monetary factors.

(c) both.

(d) none.

Ans. (c)

(23) Kaldor cyclical process is

(a) self generating.

(b) not self generating.

(c) partially self generating.

(d) indeterminate.

Ans. (a)

(24) According to Kaldor saving and investment functions are

(a) non linear.

(b) linear.

(c) partially linear.

(d) partially non linear.

Ans. (a)

(25) If investment is high then marginal efficiency of capital

(a) declines.

(b) increases.

(c) does not change.

(d) none of the above.

Ans. (a)

(26) Consumption function is linear if

(a) mpc is constant

(b) mpc is not constant

(c) mpc is indeterminate

(d) none

Ans. (a)

(27) Consumption function is nonlinear if

(a) mpc is constant.

(b) mpc is not constant.

(c) mpc is indeterminate.

(d) none.

Ans. (b)

(28) Consumption function involving intertemporal choices was developed by

(a) Irving Fisher.

(b) Keynes.

(c) Friedman.

(d) Franco Modigliani.

Ans. (a)

(29) Life cycle hypothesis was developed by

(a) Irving Fisher.

(b) Keynes.

(c) Friedman.

(d) Franco Modigliani.

Ans. (d)

(30) Permanent Income hypothesis was developed by

(a) Irving Fisher.

(b) Keynes.

(c) Friedman.

(d) Franco Modigliani.

Ans. (c)

(31) According to Franco Modigliani average propensity to consume

(a) falls as income increases.

(b) does not fall as income increases.

(c) increases as income increases.

(d) none of the above.

Ans. (b)

(32) In stationary economy

(a) technical progress is absent and capital stock is constant.

(b) only technical progress is absent.

(c) capital stock is not constant.

(d) technical stock and capital stock both are active.

Ans. (a)

(33) If access capacity remains in the economy the

(a) acceleration principle works.

(b) acceleration does not work.

(c) acceleration remains constant.

(d) none of the above.

Ans. (b)

(34) Range of multiplier is

(*a*) $1 < Multiplier < \infty$.

(b) $0 < Multiplier < \infty$.

(c) $0 < Multiplier < 1$.

(d) $0 < Multiplier < 1$.

Ans. (a)

(35) According to Keynes investment is worthwhile if

(a) marginal efficiency of capital is greater than the rate of interest.

(b) marginal efficiency of capital is less than the rate of interest.

(c) marginal efficiency of capital is equal to the rate of interest.

(d) marginal efficiency of capital and rate interest are not interrelated.

Ans. (a)

(36) Marginal efficiency of investment curve is

(a) steeper than marginal efficiency of capital curve.

(b) equal to marginal efficiency of capital curve.

(c) not steeper than marginal efficiency of capital curve.

(d) none

Ans. (a)

(37) The value of multiplier will be higher in an economy

(a) if there is no international trade.

(b) if there is no government activity.

(c) both.

(d) if international trade and government activity are active.

Ans. (c)

(38) Neoclassical theory suggests

(a) Cost of capital services contributes to explaining investment.

(b) Cost of capital services does not contribute to explaining investment.

(c) Cost of capital services is indifferent.

(d) None of the above.

Ans. (a)

(39) Value of Tobin's q is high when

(a) marginal product of capital exceeds the cost of capital.

(b) marginal product of capital is less than the cost of capital.

(c) marginal product of capital equals the cost of capital.

(d) none of the above.

Ans. (a)

(40) Value of Tobin's q is low when

(a) marginal product of capital exceeds the cost of capital.

(b) marginal product of capital is less than the cost of capital.

(c) marginal product of capital equals the cost of capital.

(d) none of the above.

Ans. (b)

(41) Under fixed exchange rate money stock must be

(a) largely endogenous.

(b) largely exogenous.

(c) partially endogenous.

(d) partially exogenous.

Ans. (a)

(42) Under Mundell-Fleming model in case of perfect capital mobility, fiscal policy becomes

(a) effective.

(b) completely effective.

(c) ineffective.

(d) completely ineffective.

Ans. (b)

(43) Identify the model which is concerned with the 'golden age' equilibrium

(a) Kaldor model.

(b) Joan Robinson model.

(c) Keynesian model.

(d) Domar model.

Ans. (b)

(44) Some models focus their attention on the maximum rate of growth at which the economy can grow. Which of the following models is of this type?

(a) Keynesian model.

(b) Hicks model.

(c) Von-Neumann model.

(d) Solow model.

Ans. (c)

(45) Identify the model, which analyses the contribution of technological progress to the overall growth rate

(a) Solow model

(b) Kaldor model

(c) Harrod model

(d) Tobin model

Ans. (a)

(46) Which of the following; is a two-sector model?

(a) Solow model

(b) Harrod-Domar model
(c) Joan Robinson mode
(d) Keynesian model

Ans. (a)

(47) There is a model of inter-industrial relations where technological relations between industries are assumed to remain constant. Which one is it?

(a) Mahalanobis model.
(b) Feldman model.
(c) Leontief model.
(d) Lewis model.

Ans. (c)

(48) India's First Five Year Plan was based on

(a) Mahalanobis model.
(b) Feldman model.
(c) Harrod-Domar model.
(d) Leontief model.

Ans. (c)

(49) Which of the following models uses three distinct concepts of stages of growth?

(a) Ramsey model.
(b) Harrod model.
(c) Domar model.
(d) Lewis model.

Ans. (b)

(50) Marx refers to the concept of organic composition of capital. Which of the following ratios stands for this capital? Constant capital = C; Variable capital = V; Surplus value = S

(a) C/(V+S).
(b) C/V.
(c) C/(C+V).
(d) (C+V)/V.

Ans. (b)

(51) Marx had given a concept of unemployment in the context of the capitalist system which keeps wages down or prevents wages from

rising even as demand for labour increases. What is that concept called?

(a) Surplus labour.

(b) Reserve army of labour.

(c) Under employment.

(d) Disguised unemployment.

Ans. (b)

(52) Marx attributed the capitalist crisis to

(a) High rate of wages.

(b) Falling rate of profit.

(c) Inflationary pressures.

(d) Exploitation of labor.

Ans. (b)

(53) Which *two* of the following statements might be supported?

(a) The natural rate of unemployment is zero.

(b) The natural rate of unemployment is the difference between the amount of labour demanded at the 'market clearing' real wage rate and the labour force.

(c) The natural rate of unemployment is composed of those experiencing frictional unemployment only.

(d) Attempts to push unemployment below the natural rate will result in accelerating inflation.

Ans. (b) & d

(54) Which *two* of the following accurately represents the so-called 'Phillips curve'?

(a) There is a stable and positive relationship between unemployment and inflation.

(b) There is a stable and negative relationship between unemployment and inflation.

(c) There is no relationship between unemployment and inflation.

(d) Statistically a rise in the level of unemployment is associated with a fall in wage and price inflation.

Ans. (b) & d

(55) Which *two* of the following would still be 'costs' of inflation even when inflation rates are perfectly anticipated by markets?

(a) 'Shoe leather' costs.

(b) Losses to borrowers via higher rates of inflation.

(c) Premiums demanded by savers and lenders to cover uncertainty as regards future rates of inflation.

(d) 'Menu' costs.

Ans. (a) & (d)

(56) Which *two* of the following situations are most likely to result in 'demand pull' inflation?

(a) Increases in the rate of savings and the rate of taxation.

(b) A rise in investment of 5% with a rise of productivity of 5%.

(c) A rise in the combined value of investment and government spending of 5% with no change in productivity.

(d) A fall in the rate of savings and the rate of taxation for an economy already operating at full capacity.

Ans. (c) & (d)

(57) In stagflation

(a) Potential output of the economy declines.

(b) the inflation rate is increasing because of rising demand.

(c) the output gap is negative.

(d) none of the above

Ans. (a)

(58) The Phillips curve

(a) is a relationship between unemployment rate and output growth rate.

(b) is a relationship between inflation rate and unemployment rate.

(c) is a relationship between employment rate and inflation rate.

(d) none of the above.

Ans. (b)

(59) Stabilization policies

(a) are discussed in the context of very long run models.

(b) are discussed in the context of business cycles.

(c) were first addressed by the classical macroeconomists.
(d) none of the above

Ans. (b)

(60) Output in long run macroeconomic models

(a) are entirely demand determined.
(b) are both demand and supply determined.
(c) are entirely supply determined.
(d) indeterminate

Ans. (c)

(61) Full employment output

(a) is also the potential output of the economy.
(b) is also the trend output of the economy.
(c) Both (a) and (b) above.
(d) only (a)

Ans. (c)

(62) The inflation rate

(a) is positive during stagflation.
(b) is negative during stagflation.
(c) is always negative during recession.
(d) none

Ans. (a)

(63) The two cornerstones of classical economics are

(a) The Phillips Curve and Say's Law.
(b) Say's Law and the Quantity Theory of Money.
(c) The Quantity Theory of Money and the Liquidity Preference Theory.
(d) Say's Law and the Liquidity Preference Theory.

Ans. (b)

(64) The cornerstone of Classical theory is flexible wages and prices

(a) flexible wages.
(b) flexible prices.
(c) both.
(d) none.

Ans. (c)

(65) Which of the following statements is inconsistent with Say's Law?

(a) The economy has flexible wages and prices.

(b) The economy's level of investment spending depends solely on the level of income.

(c) The economy will produce at the full-employment level of output.

(d) The economy has an environment of "laissez faire."

Ans. (c)

(66) In classical theory, interest rates are determined

(a) by the price level and unemployment.

(b) strictly by the money supply.

(c) by the supply and demand for money.

(d) by saving and investment.

Ans. (d)

(67) In the classical view, the price level is determined by

(a) aggregate supply.

(b) aggregate demand and supply.

(c) supply of money.

(d) aggregate demand.

Ans. (c)

(68) In an economy operating at full employment with constant velocity of 6, an increase in the money supply of 4% will cause

(a) the price level to rise by 24%.

(b) output to rise by 4%.

(c) output to rise by 24%.

(d) the price level to rise by 4%.

Ans. (a)

(69) In the classical model, the aggregate supply curve determines the

(a) money supply.

(b) inflation rate.

(c) level of output.

(d) price level.

Ans. (d)

(70) Which of the following ensures full employment in the classical model?

(a) the equation of exchange.
(b) wage and price flexibility.
(c) a constant velocity.
(d) inventory adjustment.

Ans. (b)

(71) If the inflation rate is 5% and the real rate of interest is 3%, the nominal interest rate is

(a) 15%
(b) 5%
(c) 8%
(d) 3%

Ans. (c)

(72) In the simple Keynesian framework, the price level

(a) varies inversely with wages.
(b) is fixed.
(c) is indeterminate.
(d) varies directly with unemployment.

Ans. (b)

(73) In explaining the level of unemployment, Keynes emphasized

(a) changes in technology.
(b) aggregate demand.
(c) inflationary expectations.
(d) lending my financial institutions.

Ans. (b)

(74) Assume a consumption function of the following form: C = 50 + 8Y. If income is equal to $1,000, then consumption is

(a) $50
(b) $1,050
(c) $1,000
(d) $850

Ans. (d)

(75) In the Keynesian model, an increase in government spending increases

(a) the money supply by an equal amount.

(b) the money supply by a multiple amount.

(c) aggregate demand by a multiple amount.

(d) aggregate demand by an equal amount.

Ans. (c)

(76) In the Keynesian model, liquidity preference refers to the

(a) demand for consumer goods.

(b) demand for capital.

(c) the supply of money.

(d) demand for money.

Ans. (d)

(77) An increase in the money supply in the simple Keynesian model causes interest rates to fall because

(a) demand for capital goods increases.

(b) consumer demand for goods and services increases.

(c) demand for bonds increases.

(d) demand for bonds decreases.

Ans. (d)

(78) In terms of the aggregate demand and supply framework, a decrease in the money supply will shift aggregate

(a) demand to the left.

(b) supply to the right.

(c) supply to the left.

(d) demand to the right.

Ans. (d)

(79) According to which macroeconomic theory is decreasing taxes and increasing government spending a sound policy to recover from a recession?

(a) New Classical.

(b) Keynesian.

(c) Monetarist.

(d) Rational Expectation.

Ans. (b)

(80) Which statement is most consistent with the New Classical Theory?

(a) The velocity of money is unstable.

(b) The Federal Reserve should set interest rate targets.

(c) Government fiscal and monetary policies cause more economic instability than stability.

(d) Fiscal policy works better than monetary policy.

Ans. (c)

(81) Demand Side economics is

(a) a school of economics that believes tax cuts can help an economy by raising supply.

(b) the idea that free markets can regulate themselves.

(c) the idea that government spending and tax cuts help an economy by raising demand.

(d) a form of economics that directs government to eliminate spending and to increase taxes.

Ans. (c)

(82) The maximum output that an economy can produce without large increases in inflation is

(a) productive capacity.

(b) the multiplier effect.

(c) the automatic stabilizer.

(d) the council of economic advisor.

Ans. (a)

(83) Which of the following economic schools of thought is known for viewing the economy "as a whole"?

(a) Council of Economic Advisers.

(b) Keynesian Economics.

(c) Supply side Economics.

(d) Classical Economics.

Ans. (b)

(84) Recessions and depressions can occur because of too little aggregate demand for goods and services.

(a) Council of Economic Advisers.

(b) Keynesian Economics.

(c) Supply side Economics

(d) Classical Economics

Ans. (b)

(85) Monetary policy affects investment spending through interest rates

(a) Council of Economic Advisers.

(b) Keynesian Economics.

(c) Supply side Economics.

(d) Classical Economics.

Ans. (b)

(86) The government's power to influence the macroeconomy is limited and often ineffective.

(a) Council of Economic Advisers.

(b) Keynesian Economics.

(c) Supply side Economics.

(d) New Classical Theory.

Ans. (d)

(87) Rational Expectations theorists emphasize the role of forward-looking expectations in affecting economic growth, inflation and unemployment.

(a) Council of Economic Advisers.

(b) Keynesian Economics.

(c) Supply side Economics.

(d) New Classical Theory.

Ans. (d)

(88) Monetary and fiscal policies affect expectations and have unanticipated secondary effects that make these policies ineffective.

(a) Council of Economic Advisers.

(b) Keynesian Economics.

(c) Supply side Economics.

(d) New Classical Theory.

Ans. (d)

(89) Consumers, business leaders, and investors are intelligent decision makers and take the effects of government policies into account in deciding on their behavior.

(a) Council of Economic Advisers.
(b) Keynesian Economics.
(c) Supply side Economics.
(d) New Classical Theory.

Ans. (d)

(90) A country's central bank is charged by the government with setting interest rates with a view to meeting a given inflation target . What will increase the likelihood that it will decide to raise interest rates?

(a) An appreciation of the country's currency.
(b) a decrease in the household saving ratio.
(c) an increase in the country's long-run trend rate of growth.
(d) an increase in the inflation target.

Ans. (b)

(91) What is the opportunity cost to society of an increase in unemployment

(a) the increase in taxes to pay for unemployment benefits.
(b) the loss in national output.
(c) the reduction in the disposable income of those who lose their jobs.
(d) the resulting increase in the government's fiscal deficit.

Ans. (b)

(92) If the marginal propensity to consume in an economy in a given period becomes greater than unity, this must mean that

(a) consumers will be spending more than they are earning.
(b) demand-pull inflation will be generated in the economy.
(c) the country will suffer a trade deficit.
(d) the marginal propensity to save will be negative.

Ans. (d)

(93) Who is credited with brining the term "the invisible hand" in economics?

(a) Adam Smith.
(b) John Maynard Keynes.

(c) F. Hayek.
(d) Samuelson.

Ans. (a)

(94) Who is called as the 'founding father of modern economics'?

(a) Adam Smith
(b) John Maynard Keynes
(c) F. Hayek
(d) Samuelson

Ans. (a)

(95) Macroeconomics as a separate branch came to be studied after the contributions of which economist?

(a) Adam Smith
(b) John Maynard Keynes
(c) F. Hayek
(d) Samuelson

Ans. (b)

(96) When did the Great Depression hit the United States?

(a) 2007
(b) 1929
(c) 1936
(d) 2001

Ans. (b)

(97) Macroeconomics is a study of economics that deals with which 4 major factors:

(a) households, firms, government, and demand-supply.
(b) households, firms, government and external sector.
(c) firms, government, free-market, and regulations.
(d) none of the above.

Ans. (b)

(98) What does the term Gross investment mean while denoting a nation's economy?

(a) Gross investment = Net investment + Depreciation.
(b) Gross investment = Net investment – Depreciation.

(c) Gross investment = Depreciation – Net investment.
(d) None of the above.

Ans. (a)

(99) Friedrich Hayek was a proponent of

(a) Keynesian economics.
(b) Communism.
(c) Classical Liberalism.
(d) Socialism.

Ans. (c)

(100) What is the correct formula for GDP Deflator

(a) Nominal GDP - (minus) Real GDP.
(b) Nominal GDP + Real GDP.
(c) Nominal GDP/ Real GDP.
(d) Real GDP/ Nominal GDP.

Ans. (c)

(101) In the long run, inflation is caused by

(a) governments that raise taxes so high that it increases the cost of doing business and, hence, raises prices.
(b) banks that have market power and refuse to lend money.
(c) governments that print too much money.
(d) increases in the price of inputs, such as labour and oil.

Ans. (c)

(102) When prices rise at an extraordinarily fast rate, it is called

(a) disinflation.
(b) deflation.
(c) hyperinflation.
(d) inflation.

Ans. (c)

(103) If the price level doubles:

(a) the quantity demanded of money falls by half.
(b) the value of money has been cut by half.
(c) nominal income is unaffected.
(d) the money supply has been cut by half.

Ans. (b)

(104) In the long run, the demand for money is most dependent upon

(a) the level of prices.

(b) the interest rate.

(c) the availability of banking outlets.

(d) the availability of credit cards.

Ans. (a)

(105) The quantity theory of money concludes that an increase in the money supply causes:

(a) a proportional increase in prices.

(b) a proportional increase in real output.

(c) a proportional decrease in velocity.

(d) a proportional increase in velocity.

Ans. (a)

(106) An example of a real variable is

(a) the wage rate in euros.

(b) the price of corn.

(c) the nominal interest rate.

(d) the ratio of the value of wages to the price of soda.

Ans. (d)

(107) The quantity equation states that:

(a) money 3 real output = velocity 3 price level.

(b) money 3 velocity = price level 3 real output.

(c) money 3 price level = velocity 3 real output.

(d) none.

Ans. (b)

(108) If money is neutral,

(a) an increase in the money supply does nothing.

(b) a change in the money supply only affects real variables such as real output.

(c) a change in the money supply reduces velocity proportionately; therefore there is no effect on either prices or real output.

(d) a change in the money supply only affects nominal variables such as prices and wages.

Ans. (d)

(109) If the money supply grows 5 per cent, and real output grows 2 per cent, prices should rise by

(a) 5 per cent.

(b) more than 5 per cent.

(c) less than 5 per cent.

(d) none.

Ans. (c)

(110) The velocity of money is

(a) highly unstable.

(b) impossible to measure.

(c) the rate at which money loses its value.

(d) the rate at which money changes hands.

Ans. (d)

(111) Suppose the nominal interest rate is 7 per cent while the money supply is growing at a rate of 5 per cent per year. If the government increases the growth rate of the money

(a) 9%

(b) 11%

(c) 6%

(d) 7%

Ans. (b)

(112) If the nominal interest rate is 6 per cent and the inflation rate is 3 per cent, the real interest rate is

(a) 6%

(b) 3%

(c) 17%

(d) 8%

Ans. (b)

(113) Suppose that, because of inflation, people in Brazil economize on currency and go to the bank each day to withdraw their daily currency needs. This is an example of

(a) costs due to inflation induced relative price variability which misallocates resources.

(b) shoeleather costs.

(c) costs due to inflation induced tax distortions.

(d) costs due to confusion and inconvenience.

Ans. (b)

(114) Fisher equation represents

(a) Nominal interest rate = Real interest rate + Inflation.

(b) Real interest rate = Nominal interest rate + Inflation.

(c) Real interest rate = Nominal interest rate / Inflation.

(d) None.

Ans. (a)

(115) Seigniorage is

(a) the revenue that the government raises by printing money.

(b) the revenue that the government raises by borrowing money.

(c) both.

(d) none.

Ans. (a)

(116) The Cagan model shows

(a) how the price level is related to current and future money.

(b) how the price level is related to current money only.

(c) how the price level is related to future money.

(d) none.

Ans. (a)

(117) Cost of holding money is

(a) nominal rate of interest.

(b) real interest rate.

(c) inflation.

(d) expected inflation.

Ans. (a)

(118) Functions of money are

(a) a store of value.

(b) a unit of account.

(c) a medium of exchange.

(d) all the above.

Ans. (d)

(119) An economy that interacts with other economies is known as

(a) A balanced trade economy.

(b) An export economy.

(c) A closed economy.

(d) An open economy.

Ans. (d)

(120) If USA exports more than its imports

(a) USA's net capital outflow must be positive.

(b) USA runs trade deficit.

(c) USA net capital outflow must be negative.

(d) None.

Ans. (b)

(121) If the exchange rate changes from 3 Indian rupees per dollar to 4 rupees per dollar,

(a) The dollar has appreciated.

(b) The dollar has depreciated.

(c) Depends on relative prices in both countries.

(d) None.

Ans. (a)

(122) If the nominal exchange rate between Bangladesh taka and Indian rupees is 5 taka per rupee, how many rupees can you get for a Bangladesh taka?

(a) 2 rupees

(b) 1 rupee

(c) 1/5 rupees

(d) None

Ans. (c)

(123) Suppose the inflation rate over the last 15 years has been 12 percent in Great Britain, 9 percent in India, and 5 percent in the Bangladesh. If purchasing-power parity holds, which of the following statements is *true?* Over this period,

(a) The rupee should have risen in the value compared to the taka and fallen compared to the dollar.

(b) The taka should have risen in the value compared to the rupee and fallen compared to the dollar.

(c) The dollar should have risen in the value compared to the taka and fallen compared to the taka.

(d) None.

Ans. (a)

Glossary

Accelerator Coefficient: Net investment to the increase in output times the optimal capital-output ratio. This ratio is called Accelerator Coefficient.

Adaptive Expectation Hypothesis: Only past information is used for the expectation of inflation. Here errors are serially correlated. There is systematic error.

Break-Even Investment: The amount necessary to keep constant the capital stock per worker.

Budget constraint: Under budget constraint consumer can buy limited goods or services with given income and constant price.

Budget deficit: When expenditure of the government is more than revenue of the government then budget deficit exists.

Budget surplus: It is just opposite of the budget deficit. When tax revenue of the government is more than expenditure of the government then budget surplus exists.

Business cycle: It is a cycle where GDP moves upward or downward. It is a general form of an economy. There are boom, peak, recession, depression, trough and recovery.

Cagon Model: It shows how the price level is related to today's and tomorrow's money.

Capital: According to the classical economics capital is one of the four factors of production. It is a financial asset that is required to establish a business.

Central bank: It is an establishment that regulates the economy and controls other banks.

Classical dichotomy: Monetary variables do not have any effects on real variables. If money supply increases price level changes but output will remain unchanged.

Closed economy: When an economy is economically separate from others economies then the economy is called closed economy. In closed economy Y represents C+I+G. Export and import are not considered here.

Consumer price index: It is a weighted average of a basket of goods and services of a consumer.

Consumption: It shows what percentage of disposable income one spends on consumption.

Crowding out: Decrease in private investment because of public debt. It is a neoclassical concept.

Demand for Money: The amount of money which an economic agent wishes to hold on average over a given period of time is called the demand for money.

Demand for labor: Total number of workers employed and number of vacancies in the economy.

Dependent variables: Dependent variables are those assumed to be determined within the system or model. These variables are also known as endogenous variables.

Depreciation: The value of home currency falls in terms of foreign currency.

Durable goods: The length of time over which goods provide services is long for durable goods. Buses/cars are durables goods.

Non-durable goods: The length of time over which goods provide services is short for non-durables goods. Vegetables are non-durable goods.

Economics: It is a science that deals with factors of production, production, consumption and allocation. Mostly how to deal with scarce factors is a matter of Economics.

Efficiency wage: It is a wage that is paid by firms to their workers over the minimum wage to increase their productivity.

Equilibrium: It is a situation where demand is equal to supply and determine values of economic variable.

Ex ante real interest rate: It is nominal interest rate adjusted to expected inflation. That is $(i–\pi^e)$. Here i is nominal interest rate and π^e is the expected inflation.

Ex post real interest rate: It is nominal interest rate adjusted to actual inflation. That is $(i\text{-}\pi)$. Here i is nominal interest rate and π is the actual inflation.

Excess demand for labor: Excess demand for labor exists when demand for labor exceeds supply of labor. It is the difference between vacancies and unemployed workers.

Exports: It plays an important part in a open economy. It represents the amount of goods that produced within the country and is transported to other country for trade.

Exogenous or independent variables: Exogenous variables are those assumed to be determined outside the system or model.

Factors of production: According to the classical economics land, labor, capital and entrepreneur are the factors of production. These factors are used to produce to goods.

Fiat money: Money does not have inherent value and only on the basis of government order that money is used as money

Fiscal Deficit: Revenue and capital expenditure – revenue and capital receipt.

Fisher effect: It names after Irving Fisher. Nominal rate of interest = real rate of interest + inflation.

Flow Variable: A flow variable is one that can only be measured as a rate of flow per period of time.

Frictional Unemployment: It is the time while workers search for a job.

Golden Rule Level of Capital: This occurs at the capital-labor ratio at which the slope of the production function is equal to the slope of the investment requirements line. Marginal product of capital – the rate at which labor force is growing.

Gross Domestic Product: It is the value at current market prices of all final goods and services produced within the economy in the current year.

Gross National Product (GNP): It is the value of final goods and services produced in the current period by domestically-owned factors of production at home or abroad.

GNP=GDP+ net factor earning from abroad.

GDP Deflator: (Current GDP/Real GDP) X 100

Gross Investment: It is the addition of replacement capital and net investment.

Hyperinflation: It is one type of inflation that runs at a speed more than 50% per month.

Induced Investment: Induced investment is a function of national income. [I=b+dY; b is the autonomous investment, dY is the induced investment]

Inflation: Average rate of increase in the level of price is called inflation rate. Persistent increase in the price level is inflation.

Interest rate: Interest rate in one sense is marginal efficiency of capital.

Investment: Additional increase in capital stock is investment.

Labor force: Number of workers including employed, unemployed workers is called labor force.

Liberalism: Free markets and privatization of capital assets.

Life cycle: Individuals savings and consumption pattern over the life.

Liquidity: How speedily an asset can be sold in the market depends on the liquidity of the asset.

Liquidity Trap: It is a situation in which the interest rate is so low that nobody wants to hold bonds. Here LM curve becomes horizontal.

Linear Consumption Function: If *mpc* is constant as income rises then consumption function is linear.

Macroeconomics: It is a branch of knowledge where economic variables like GDP, unemployment, inflation, interest rate, exchange rate etc. are discussed. It takes entire activity of a nation as an individual activity.

Marginal Product of Capital: It shows increase in output if we increase the amount of capital by one unit.

Monetary policy: To have control over economic variables some time central bank takes policy regarding money supply.

Money: Money has functions four- A medium of exchange, a measure of value, store of value and standard of postponed payment.

M_1: The sum of currency, traveler's checks, and checkable deposits – assets that can be used directly in transactions. It is also called narrow money.

M_2: M_1 plus money market mutual fund shares, money market and savings deposits, and time deposits. It is also called broad money.

M_3: M_3 can be thought of as a flock of all the other classifications of money (M_0, M_1 and M_2) plus all of the less liquid components of the money supply. M_0 refers to the currency in circulation, such as coins and cash.

Money illusion: When workers do not fully take inflation into their account in calculating real wages from given nominal wages workers are said to have money illusion

Mundell-Fleming model: A model of simultaneous equilibrium in both goods and money markets for an open economy.

Multiplier Coefficient: Change in Income to the change in investment times inverse of marginal propensity to save or (1 – marginal propensity to consume). [1/1-mpc] is called multiplier coefficient.

National saving: Total amount of saving that a country saves after consumption.

Natural Rate of Unemployment: Economy fluctuates around the rate which is called Natural rate of unemployment.

Negative economics: Statements under negative economics are not verifiable or tested.

Net Export: It is trade balance. It is a difference between export and import.

Net Investment: Change in output multiplied by capital output ratio.

Nonlinear Consumption Function: If *mpc* falls as income rises consumption function is non-linear.

Nonlinear Investment & Saving Functions: Kaldor introduced nonlinear form of investment and saving curve. According to him if income increases investment or saving will not increase proportionately. Erratic changes could be found in saving or investment due to changes in income.

Okun's Law: It is an empirical relationship between the growth of real GDP and the resulting change in the unemployment rate.

Phillips curve: According to Phillips there is anon linear and inverse relationship between nominal wage rate and unemployment.

Positive economics: Statements under positive economics are verifiable or tested.

Price flexibility: Prices are flexible in neoclassical model. Prices are fixed in Keynesian models or are flexible upwards but are sticky downwards.

Primary Deficit: Non-interest expenditure – revenue and capital receipt

Propensity to Save: The effect of an additional euro of disposable income on saving.

Propensity to consume: The effect of an additional euro of disposable income on consumption.

Purchasing Power: Income in terms of product.

Quantity theory of money: According to this theory quantity of money determines price level keeping other things constant.

Real variable: It is a ratio of nominal variable to price level.

Rational Expectation Hypothesis: In rational expectation hypothesis all information is used for the expectation of inflation. Here errors are random.

Reduced-form equations: Reduced-form equations express each endogenous variable in terms of the exogenous variables only.

Revenue Deficit: Revenue expenditure – revenue receipts.

Seigniorage: It is the revenue that government increases by printing money.

Simple Multiplier: At constant price level multiplier is called simple multiplier. The value of simple multiplier is 1/(1-mpc).

Stagflation: Decline in output and persistent increase in price level is called stagflation.

Stationary Economy: A stationary economy is one in which technical progress is absent and the capital stock is constant.

Stock Variable: A stock variable is one that is measured at a moment in time. For example, stock of money.

Stock: The shares in the ownership of corporations.

Stock Market: The market in which shares are traded.

Structural unemployment: Unemployment due to the structure of the economy is structural unemployment.

Supply of labor: Total number of employed and unemployed workers.

The natural rate of growth: The maximum sustainable rate of growth on the supply side is the natural rate of growth which is equal to the sum of the rate of technical progress and the rate of growth in labor force.

The Paradox of Thrift: If the households become more thrifty, the effect on output will be adverse and savings may actually fail to increase. A cutback in consumption is a bad thing, because it reduces aggregate demand.

The warranted rate of growth: It is that rate of growth which allows desired savings to be equal to desired investment while maintaining full capacity output at every point in time.

Velocity of money: When transactions increase the velocity of money increases. Money passes hands. The speed of passing hands is calculated in terms of velocity of money.

Voluntary Unemployment: When voluntary unemployment prevails in an economy it means workers like to work but do not like to accept the job at the given wage rate.

Wage rigidity: Wage is unable to regulate to the point where demand for labor is equal to supply of labor.

Appendices

APPENDIX - 1

Chapter - 6

Keynesian Theory of Involuntary Unemployment

Keynes said that due to rigidity in money wage involuntary unemployment of labor emerges. As supply of labor exceeds demand for labor workers become unemployed at a given wage rate. Keynes supposed that money wage rate would not vary adequately to keep the economy at full employment in the short run. According to classical economists money wages are flexible and bring equilibrium in the labor market at full employment level. It means that demand for labor and supply of labor become same and get equilibrium. Keynes presented three reasons behind the rigidity of money wage rate. Stickiness of money wage rate means that money wage rate does not change quickly towards downward direction to maintain full employment in labor market.

Grounds of Money Wage Stickiness

1. Money Illusion

The first cause why firms be unsuccessful to cut wages despite an excess supply of labor is that workers will oppose any move about for cut in money wages though they might believe fall in real wages accomplished by rise in prices of goods. Keynes characterized this to money illusion on the part of the workforce. By money illusion it is denoted that workers fail to realize that purchasing power of money changes when prices go up. They regard money such as a rupee as something which has a stable value. Therefore, while they would strongly oppose and resist any cut in money wages, they would not resist much if their real wages are reduced through increase in prices of goods with money wages remaining constant. Thus Keynes wrote, "Whilst workers will usually resist a reduction of money wages, it is not their practice to withdraw their labor whenever there is a rise in the price of wage goods".

Reasons for money illusion

(i) Workers of a firm believe that though rise in prices reduce their real wages, but that this increase in prices equally have an effect on workers in other industries so that their relative wages as compared to those employed in other industries remain the same.

Therefore, workers who are more concerned with their relative position with other workers will strongly resist the cut in their money wages, while they will not oppose so strongly their cut in real wages through rise in the general price level.

(ii) The second reason for strong resistance to cut in money wages is that the workers blame their own employers for this, whereas they think that a cut in real wages through rise in prices in general is the outcome of the working of general economic forces over which strikes in an industry would have little effect. However, it does not necessarily mean that trade unions remain silent spectators if they feel that changes in Government policy adversely affect their economic interests.

From the above two reasons given for money illusion it follows that if additional employment can be created by lowering real wages, it is more practical to do so through bringing about rise in general price level rather than by cutting money wages.

2. Wage Fixation through Contracts

In most of the free market economies such as those of USA and Great Britain, wages are fixed by the firms through contracts made with the workers for a year or two. There is little possibility of changing money wages fixed through contracts when the situation of either surplus labor or shortage emerges. For workers organized into trade unions wages are even rigid. Through collective bargaining by trade unions with the employers wage scales are fixed for 3 to 4 years by contract. Money wages cannot be changed when either surplus or shortage of labor emerges during the period of the contract. Trade unions of workers never accept wage cuts even if some of union workers remain unemployed. Thus the sticky or rigid money wages lead to the existence of involuntary unemployment. This means that labor market does not clear in the short run.

3. Minimum Wage Laws

There is another reason for stickiness of nominal wage rate. Governments do intervention in fixing minimum wages below which employers are not permitted to pay wages to the workers.

4. Efficiency Wages

Employers themselves are not interested in lowering wages as high wages make workers more efficient and productive. The unpleasant effect of lower wages on workers' efficiency may explain the unwillingness on the part of employers to cut money wages despite the excess supply of or unemployment of workers at higher money wages. The practical difficulties pointed out by Keynes and his followers which are faced by firms in reducing wages and which therefore explain money wage rigidity or stickiness. The sticky or rigid money wages above the equilibrium level cause unemployment of labor.

Involuntary Unemployment and Keynes

In Keynes' contractual view of labor market, it is assumed that whereas prices are free to vary, the money wage is fixed. It is important to note that Keynesians do not believe that money wage rate is completely fixed or sticky. What they actually mean by sticky wages is that money wages do not fall quickly to bring demand for and supply of labor in equilibrium at full employment. In their view money wages are very slow to adjust sufficiently to ensure full employment of labor when there is a decline in aggregate demand resulting in lowering of prices of products. As a consequence, involuntary unemployment comes into existence. It may be further noted that Keynes was particularly concerned with downward rigidity of money wages at which the demand for labor exceeds the supply of labor and consequently unemployment or excess supply of labor emerges. It is important to note that Keynes accepted the classical theory of labor demand according to which firms demand labor up to the point at which real wage rate (that is, money wage rate divided by the price level or, W/P) is equal to the marginal product of labor. At a higher real wage rate, less amount of labor will be demanded and, at a lower real wage rate, more labor will be demanded or employed. In other words, demand curve of labor is downward sloping. Keynes' theory of involuntary unemployment based on price flexibility and money wage rigidity is depicted in Figure

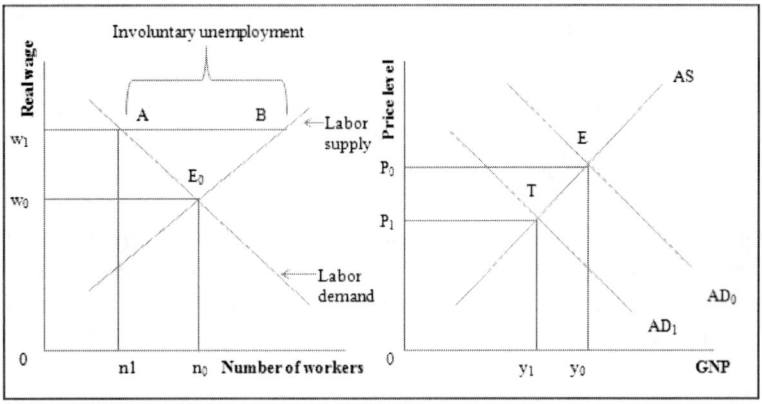

Source: Rosalind, L., & Alexander, R.1982

Figure 6.6 Emergence of Involuntary Unemployment in Keynesian Model

In panel (b) of the figure short-run aggregate supply curve AS and aggregate demand curve AD_0 have been drawn and through their interaction determine price level P_0 and the level of GNP equal to Y_0. It is important to note that short-run aggregate supply curve AS has been drawn with a given fixed money wage rate, say W_0. In panel (a) of the figure the level of labor employment n_0 shows the number of jobs when the economy is producing Y_0 level of national output in panel (b) corresponding to the equilibrium between aggregate supply AS and aggregate demand AD_0 at price level P_0, with a fixed money wage and the level of GNP equal to Y_0. The labor market must be in equilibrium at point E_0 or at real wage rate W_0/P_0 at which n_0 workers are demanded and employed. All those who are willing to get jobs at the real wage rate W_0/P_0 are in fact demanded and employed. Thus, equilibrium at E_0 or at level of employment n_0 represents full-employment equilibrium. Now consider again panel (b) of the figure. Suppose due to fall in marginal efficiency of capital there is reduction in investment demand which along with its multiplier effect causes a leftward shift in the aggregate demand curve AD. Since Keynes believed that with a fixed money wage rate aggregate Supply curve AS is given and remains unchanged, it will be seen from panel (b) of the figure that new aggregate demand curve AD_1 and the fixed aggregate supply curve AS intersect at point T determining new equilibrium lower price P_1 and smaller real GNP equal to Y_1.

Keynes asserted that the economy would remain stuck at point T with less than full-employment level of output Y_1 and lower price level P_1. Now, a glance at panel (a) of the figure shows that with fixed money image W_0

and lower price level P_1 ($P_1 < P_0$), the real wage rate rises to W_0/P_1. It will be seen from panel (a) of the figure that at this higher real wage rate W_0/P_1 the smaller amount of labor n_1 will be demanded and employed by all firms in the economy.

However, at this higher wage rate W_0/P_1 (with money wage rate fixed at W_0), AB number of workers are rendered unemployed. It is in this way that Keynes explained that with money wage rate remaining fixed at the level W_0 and with flexible prices, the fall in aggregate demand results in persistent involuntary unemployment.

Thus, by explaining the emergence of persistent involuntary unemployment Keynes made a fundamental departure from the classical view of a free market economy which denied the existence of involuntary unemployment except for a short time.

APPENDIX - 3

(Case Study-1)

Table: Estimated Model based on equation (2)

Dependent variable: 1st difference inflation(DInflation)				
Variable	***Coefficient***	***Std. Error***	***t-Statistic***	***Prob.***
C	-1.077	5.821	-0.185	0.85
D(INFLATION(-1))	0.309	0.427	0.725	0.47
D(INFLATION(-2))	0.279	0.27	1.032	0.31
D(EXCHANGERATE(-1))	-8.98	6.636	-1.353	0.19
D(EXCHANGERATE(-2))	-7.575	4.93	-1.536	0.14
D(MONEYSUPPLY(-1))	3.445	3.554	0.969	0.34
D(MONEYSUPPLY(-2))	4.165	3.236	1.286	0.21
D(INTERESTRATE(-1))	-1.953	2.087	-0.935	0.36
D(INTERESTRATE(-2))	4.8	1.772	2.708	0.01
D(GOVTEXPENDITURE(-1))	-3.534	2.375	-1.488	0.15
D(GOVTEXPENDITURE(-2))	2.226	1.285	1.731	0.1
INFLATION(-1)	-1.1	0.577	-1.904	0.07
EXCHANGERATE(-1)	8.983	9.88	0.909	0.37
MONEYSUPPLY(-1)	-1.813	1.782	-1.017	0.32
INTERESTRATE(-1)	-0.493	0.966	-0.509	0.61
GOVTEXPENDITURE(-1)	-1.823	2.349	-0.776	0.44
R^2=0.86, Adjusted R^2=0.74, log likelyhood=1.94, F-Stat=6.94, AIC=0.87, SIC=1.61, D.W.=2.47				

Source: Author's own

APPENDIX - 4

(Case Study-2)

Table -5: Lag Selection Criterion

VAR Lag Order Selection Criteria						
Endogenous variables: BUDGETDEFICIT TRADEDEFICIT						
Exogenous variables: C						
Sample: 1990 2018						
Included observations: 26						
Lag	LogL	LR	FPE	AIC	SC	HQ
0	-18.357	NA*	0.0164*	1.565*	1.662*	1.593*
1	-17.633	1.280	0.0211	1.817	2.108	1.901
2	-16.320	2.121	0.0262	2.024	2.508	2.163
* indicates lag order selected by the criterion						

Source: Author's own

Table-6: Results of Estimations of Equations (5) and (6)

Dependent Variable	***Independent Variable***	***Coefficients***	***Standard errors***	***'t' Statistics***
BD_t	Constant (α)	0.2083	(0.0983	[2.118]
	BD_{t-1}	–0.0060	(0.210)	[–0.028]
	Bd_{t-2}	–0.2812	(0.212)	[–1.320]
	TD_{t-1}	–0.0169	(0.124)	[–0.136]
	TD_{t-2}	–0.0426	(0.112)	[–0.377]
R_2 = **0.085**, F-stat = **0.492**, Log likelihood = **–2.059**, AIC = **0.543**				
TD_t	Constant(α′)	0.3583	(0.157)	[2.278]
	TD_{t-1}	0.1072	(0.198)	[–0.539]
	TD_{t-2}	0.0933	(0.180)	[0.517]
	BD_{t-1}	–0.2936	(0.336)	[–0.872]
	BD_{t-2}	–0.0800	(0.340)	[–0.235]
R_2 = **0.064831**, F-stat = **0.363957**, Log likelihood = **–14.26437**, AIC =**1.481875**				

Source: Author's own

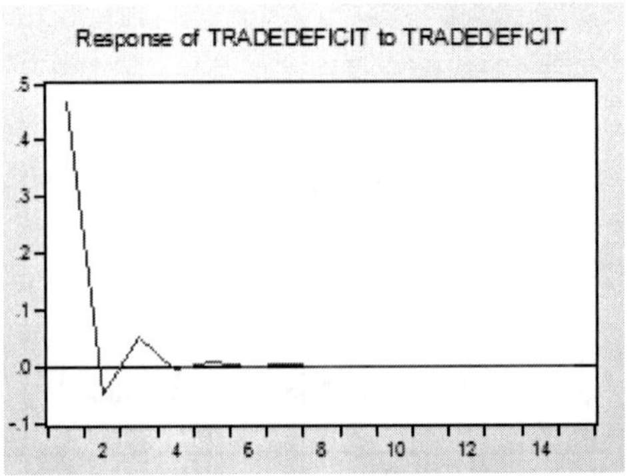

Author's Estimation

Figure-6

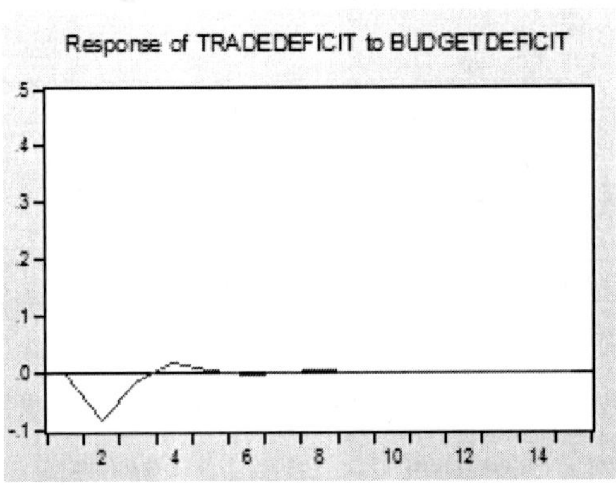

Author's Estimation

Figure-7

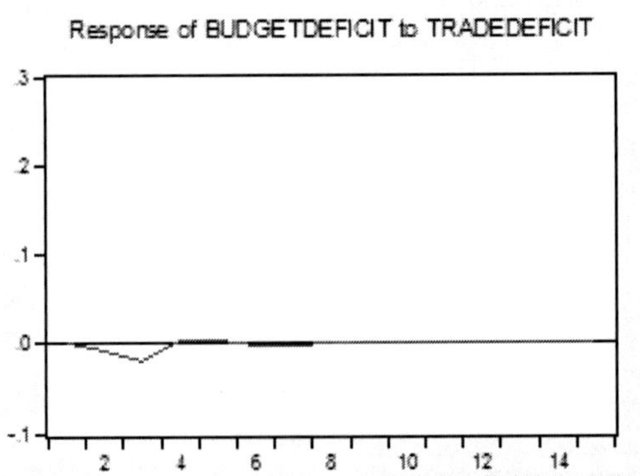

Author's Estimation

Figure-8

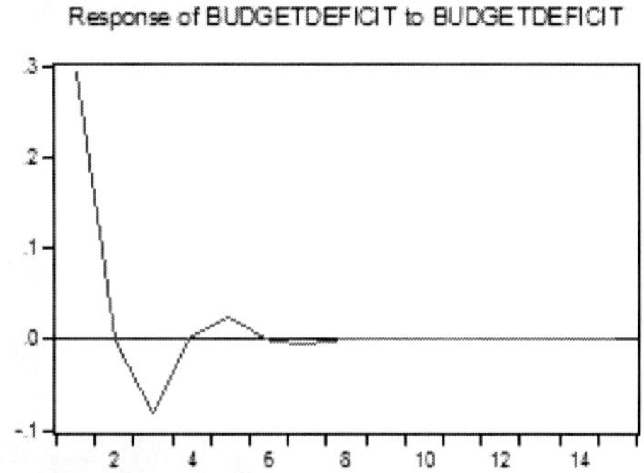

Author's Estimation

Figure-9

Table-7A: Variance Decomposition of BD_t

Variance Decomposition of Budget Deficit			
Period	***S.E.***	***BUDGET DEFICIT***	***TRADE DEFICIT***
1	0.2914	100.00	0.0000
2	0.2915	99.926	0.0737
3	0.3029	99.539	0.4605
4	0.3030	99.525	0.4745
5	0.3039	99.517	0.4828
6	0.3039	99.516	0.4838
7	0.3039	99.515	0.4849
8	0.3039	99.514	0.4850
9	0.3039	99.514	0.4851
10	0.3039	99.514	0.4851
11	0.3039	99.514	0.4851
12	0.3039	99.514	0.4851
13	0.3039	99.514	0.4851
14	0.3039	99.514	0.4851
15	0.3039	99.514	0.4851

Author's Estimation

Table-7B: Variance Decomposition of TD_t

Variance Decomposition of Trade Deficit			
Period	***S.E.***	***BUDGET DEFICIT***	***TRADE DEFICIT***
1	0.4660	0.0233	99.976
2	0.4763	3.1939	96.806
3	0.4792	3.2452	96.754
4	0.4795	3.3712	96.628
5	0.4796	3.3721	96.627
6	0.4796	3.3855	96.614
7	0.4796	3.3856	96.614
8	0.4796	3.3866	96.613
9	0.4796	3.3866	96.613
10	0.4796	3.3867	96.613
11	0.4796	3.3867	96.613
12	0.4796	3.3867	96.613
13	0.4796	3.3867	96.613
14	0.4796	3.3867	96.613
15	0.4796	3.3867	96.613

Author's Estimation

Appendix - 5

(Case Study-3)

Table-1

Results of Augmented Dickey-Fuller Tests For Unit Root of variables concerned

					Mackinnon Critical Value		
Variable	***Exogenous***	***ADF Test Statistic***	***Prob.* value***	***Lag length***	***1%***	***5%***	***10%***
Interest rate (rt) at level	none	-0.13	0.62	0	-2.63	-1.9	-1.61
Interest rate (rt) at 1st difference	none	-3.65	0.0006	0	-2.63	-1.95	-1.61
Money supply(Mt) at level	Constant, Linear Trend	-2.11	0.518	0	-4.25	-3.54	-3.2
Money supply(Mt) at 1st difference	Constant, Linear Trend	-4.4	0.0072		-4.26	-3.55	-3.2

Source: Author's own

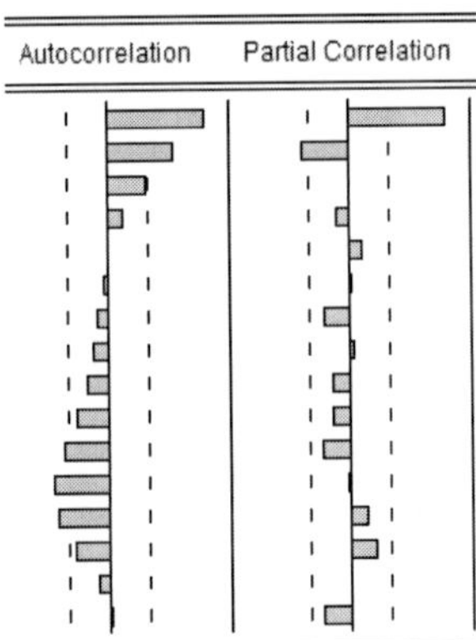

	AC	PAC	Q-Stat	Prob
1	0.829	0.829	26.177	0.000
2	0.562	-0.401	38.559	0.000
3	0.321	0.003	42.718	0.000
4	0.120	-0.106	43.320	0.000
5	0.007	0.105	43.322	0.000
6	-0.031	0.008	43.365	0.000
7	-0.084	-0.209	43.689	0.000
8	-0.128	0.041	44.471	0.000
9	-0.179	-0.149	46.074	0.000
10	-0.266	-0.151	49.753	0.000
11	-0.385	-0.243	57.739	0.000
12	-0.462	-0.010	69.772	0.000
13	-0.442	0.135	81.295	0.000
14	-0.295	0.214	86.644	0.000
15	-0.098	0.005	87.268	0.000
16	0.022	-0.241	87.300	0.000

Source: Author's own

Figure-1: Interest rate at level

Autocorrelation	Partial Correlation		AC	PAC	Q-Stat	Prob
		1	0.461	0.461	7.8815	0.005
		2	-0.018	-0.293	7.8940	0.019
		3	-0.181	-0.050	9.1941	0.027
		4	-0.231	-0.150	11.374	0.023
		5	-0.111	0.052	11.894	0.036
		6	-0.006	-0.042	11.895	0.064
		7	0.017	-0.023	11.908	0.104
		8	0.053	0.037	12.042	0.149
		9	0.156	0.150	13.235	0.152
		10	0.123	-0.026	14.012	0.172
		11	-0.143	-0.242	15.103	0.178
		12	-0.389	-0.244	23.519	0.024
		13	-0.506	-0.308	38.436	0.000
		14	-0.238	0.065	41.902	0.000
		15	0.201	0.191	44.504	0.000
		16	0.286	-0.041	50.083	0.000

Source: Author's own

Figure- 2: Interest rate at 1st difference

Autocorrelation	Partial Correlation		AC	PAC	Q-Stat	Prob
		1	0.909	0.909	31.468	0.000
		2	0.812	-0.079	57.373	0.000
		3	0.720	-0.030	78.348	0.000
		4	0.629	-0.043	94.900	0.000
		5	0.540	-0.048	107.50	0.000
		6	0.453	-0.048	116.66	0.000
		7	0.366	-0.059	122.84	0.000
		8	0.294	0.025	126.97	0.000
		9	0.229	-0.018	129.59	0.000
		10	0.166	-0.045	131.02	0.000
		11	0.106	-0.038	131.63	0.000
		12	0.051	-0.027	131.78	0.000
		13	-0.000	-0.039	131.78	0.000
		14	-0.048	-0.036	131.92	0.000
		15	-0.096	-0.047	132.52	0.000
		16	-0.141	-0.042	133.87	0.000

Source: Author's own

Figure-3: Money supply at level

Autocorrelation	Partial Correlation		AC	PAC	Q-Stat	Prob
		1	0.096	0.096	0.3435	0.558
		2	0.008	-0.001	0.3460	0.841
		3	0.066	0.066	0.5204	0.914
		4	0.061	0.049	0.6710	0.955
		5	0.177	0.169	1.9926	0.850
		6	-0.171	-0.215	3.2670	0.775
		7	-0.032	0.004	3.3130	0.855
		8	-0.051	-0.083	3.4358	0.904
		9	-0.079	-0.058	3.7378	0.928
		10	-0.018	-0.018	3.7535	0.958
		11	-0.044	0.043	3.8543	0.974
		12	-0.074	-0.100	4.1631	0.980
		13	-0.084	-0.041	4.5745	0.983
		14	-0.113	-0.110	5.3587	0.980
		15	0.000	0.014	5.3587	0.989
		16	-0.076	-0.088	5.7506	0.991

Source: Author's own

Figure-4: Money Supply at 1st difference

Table – 2: Johansen cointegration

Sample (adjusted): 1978 2010				
Included observations: 33 after adjustments				
Trend assumption: Linear deterministic trend (restricted)				
Series: MONEYSUPPLY INTERESTRATE				
Lags interval (in first differences): 1 to 1				
Unrestricted Cointegration Rank Test (Trace)				
Hypothesized		***Trace***	***0.05***	
No. of CE(s)	***Eigen value***	***Statistic***	***Critical Value***	***Prob.****
None *	0.461468	28.44282	25.87211	0.0234
At most 1	0.215724	8.018813	12.51798	0.2501
Trace test indicates 1 cointegrating eqn(s) at the 0.05 level				
* denotes rejection of the hypothesis at the 0.05 level				
**MacKinnon-Haug-Michelis (1999) p-values				
Unrestricted Cointegration Rank Test (Maximum Eigenvalue)				
Hypothesized		***Max-Eigen***	***0.05***	
No. of CE(s)	***Eigen value***	***Statistic***	***Critical Value***	***Prob.****
None *	0.461468	20.42400	19.38704	0.0353
At most 1	0.215724	8.018813	12.51798	0.2501
Max-eigenvalue test indicates 1 cointegrating eqn(s) at the 0.05 level				
* denotes rejection of the hypothesis at the 0.05 level				
**MacKinnon-Haug-Michelis (1999) p-values				

Source: Author's own

Table -3: Vector Autoregression Estimates

Vector Autoregression Estimates		
Sample (adjusted): 1979 2010		
Included observations: 32 after adjustments		
Standard errors in ( ) & t-statistics in [ ]		
	MONEY SUPPLYD	INTERESTRATED
MONEYSUPPLYD (-1)	0.131627	-0.112801
	(0.22607)	(0.26356)
	[0.58223]	[-0.42799]
MONEYSUPPLYD (-2)	0.008431	0.468305
	(0.22368)	(0.26077)
	[0.03769]	[1.79586]
INTERESTRATED (-1)	0.141699	1.341481
	(0.13662)	(0.15927)
	[1.03720]	[8.42273]
INTERESTRATED (-2)	-0.127392	-0.547946
	(0.13314)	(0.15522)
	[-0.95682]	[-3.53018]
C	0.041780	0.173125
	(0.06784)	(0.07909)
	[0.61582]	[2.18888]
R-squared	0.047762	0.834387
Adj. R-squared	-0.09331	0.809852
Sum sq. resids	0.034715	0.047182
S.E. equation	0.035857	0.041803
F-statistic	0.338565	34.00763
Log likelihood	63.81504	58.90567
Akaike AIC	-3.67594	-3.369105
Schwarz SC	-3.446919	-3.140083
Mean dependent	0.066040	0.965179
S.D. dependent	0.034293	0.095865
Determinant resid covariance (dof adj.)		2.25E-06
Determinant resid covariance		1.60E-06
Log likelihood		122.7208
Akaike information criterion		-7.045048
Schwarz criterion		-6.587005

Source: Author's own

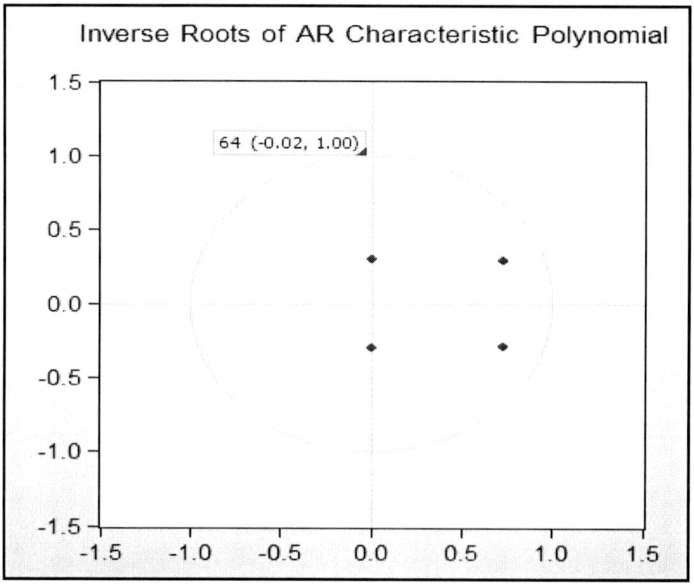

Source: Author's own

Figure-5

References

Amit, K. (2016). *Export and economic growth in Sri Lanka-An econometric study,* Lambert Academic Publishing, Germany.

Amit, K. (2016). *Macro economic theory: An econometric approach,* Lambert Academic Publishing, Germany.

Andrew Abel and Ben Bernanke. (2003). *Macroeconomics,* Pearson, Indian Ed.

Brahmannd P.R. (1980). *Growth less inflation by the means of stockless money.*

Brian Snowdon and Howard R.Vane. *Modern macroeconomics its origins, development and current state.* Edward Elgar Publishing, Inc.

Brian Snowdon and Howard R. Vane. *A Macroeconomics Reader.*

Culbertson, J.M. (1971). *Macroeconomic theory and stabilization policy.* McGraw Hill, London.

David Romer. (2006). *Advanced macroeconomics.* McGrawhill

Errol D'Souza. (2012). *Macroeconomics,* Dorling Kinder, South Asia.

Gupta, S.B. (1982). *Monetary planning in India*, Oxford Publication, New Delhi.

Hallm R. and J.B. Tayl (1986). *Macroeconomics.* W.W. N/ton, New York.

Hamberg, Daniel (1971). *Models of economic growth.* Harper & Row Publishers, New York.

Heijdra, Ben J. and Frederick van der Ploeg. (2004). *Foundations of modern macroeconomics*, OUP, NY

Jhingan, M.L. (1997), *Macro- Economic Theory.* (10th Edition). Vrinda Publications (P) Ltd.

Keynes, J. M. (1936). *The general theory of employment, interest and money.* Macmillan, London.

Mankiw N. Gregory (2010). *Macroeconomics.* (7th Edition). Worth Publishers

N. Gregory M. (2012). *Macroeconomics,* Worth Publishers, New York.

Oliver, B. (2012). *Macroeconomics.* Dorling Kinder, South Asia.

Rosalind, L., & Alexander, R. (1982). *Macroeconomics: An introduction to Keynesian-neoclassical controversies.* Macmillan, China.

Rudiger Dornbusch and Stanley Fischer. (2009). *Macroeconomics*, McGrawhill

Rosalind Levacic and Alexander Rebman. (1982) *Macroeconomics.* McMillan Routledge

Richard T. Froyen. (2003). *Macroeconomics.* Pearson Indian Ed

Jha, R. (1991). *Contemporary macroeconomic theory and policy.* Wiley Eastern Ltd. New Delhi.

Romer, D.L. (1996). *Advanced macroeconomics*. McGraw Hill Company Ltd. New York.

Shapiro, E. (1996). *Macroeconomic analysis*. Golgotha Publications, New Delhi.

Surrey, MJC (Ed). (1976). *Macroeconomic themes*. Oxford University Press, Oxford.

Reddy, Y.V. (2000). A review of monetary and financial sector reforms in India- Central bank's perspectives. UBSPD, New Delhi.

Samuelson, P.A. (1966). *The collected scientific papers of Paul A. Samuelson*. Oxford and IBH Publishing Company, New Delhi.

Index